BABE

Books by John McCabe include:

Mr Laurel and Mr Hardy
The Comedy World of Stan Laurel
Charlie Chaplain
George M Cohan: The Man who Owned Broadway
The Grand Hotel

BABE: The Life of Oliver Hardy

John McCabe

ROBSON BOOKS

This paperback edition published in Great Britain in 2004 by Robson Books,
The Chrysalis Building, Bramley Road, London, W10 6SP

An imprint of Chrysalis Books Group

British Library Cataloguing in Publication Data
A catalogue record for this title is available from the British Library.

ISBN 1 86105 781 4

Printed by Creative Print and Design (Wales), Ebbw Vale

For
OLIVER NORVELL HARDY

O, that I was where I would be!
Then would I be where I am not.
But where I am, I must be –
And where I would be, I cannot.

MOTHER GOOSE

and for Vija: *Manai sirds mīļai sievai*

Contents

Foreword

At last, at long last, Oliver Hardy.

This consummate artist, a shade the surer film performer than his partner, has not yet received – for a variety of reasons – his full meed of critical praise and biographical notice.

Like Stan Laurel, Oliver Hardy did not welcome scrutiny of his personal life. He actively discouraged it. Also, artistically, Hardy deferred to Laurel in virtually every aspect of their professional activity. This was partly due to a kind of genial indolence on Hardy's part but also, and far more substantially, because he regarded his partner as the creative centre of their work. 'Oh, ask Stan about that,' Hardy said to me whenever I inquired about the team's comedic functions. 'That's Stan's business, not mine.'

As it proved to be. In consequence, to understand the team's genesis, one had to go first to Laurel and examine his comedic overview and life influences, the things determining in large measure Laurel and Hardy's personae. It was Stan who primarily guided the team to top form artistically. Stan once evaluated, as he has been, on now to the superb actor who completed the equation that was Laurel and Hardy. The delay in assessing his contribution Hardy would have well understood.

It is to Oliver Hardy that prime thanks go among the following acknowledgements for my source material. He gave me two extended interviews during their 1953–54 tour of Great Britain, one in Birmingham, the other in Aston.

I am also deeply indebted to Stan Laurel who, during our

twelve-year friendship (1953–1965), spoke often of his part ner's personal and professional life. The fact that neither Stan nor I expected a biography of Oliver Hardy to emerge from our chats gives his comments a truth they might never have had were Stan aware he was speaking for posterity. I certainly never envisioned writing more than a single book about this blest pair – my *Mr Laurel and Mr Hardy* (1961). (As it happens, I wrote four.)

For the fullest and most authentic look into the mind and heart of Oliver Hardy, I rejoice in having had the thoughts of the one person who knew him best in all the world, his widow Lucille, the one who first asked me to undertake this project. I am deeply obligated to that charming and forthright lady for the details of her marriage.

I owe a very special obligation to Benjamin J. Shipman, for over two decades Laurel and Hardy's manager and lawyer. He loved his clients in both paternal and fraternal fashion, and on numerous occasions acted as father confessor to them both. Quiet and gentle Ben shared all his Laurel and Hardy memories with me, in that process causing me to understand why Babe and Stan treasured him so.

I received vital information on the teaming of Laurel and Hardy in an interview with joyous Leo McCarey not long before he died.

Much of Hardy's life in Florida was told me by Bert Tracey, a dear little man of cheerful soul whom Babe loved.

Randy Skretvedt purchased Myrtle Lee Hardy's scrapbooks a few years ago, and these were available for my inspection. My full thanks to Randy for them, for other source interviews, and for interviewing Lucille Hardy at a time when I was unable to do so. He was also the source for most of this book's photographs.

I am very much indebted to Leo M. Brooks Jr. for his thorough researches into the genealogies of the Norvell, Hardy and Tante families, Oliver Hardy's forebears. Robert Johnson helped in this respect.

Oliver Hardy's nieces, Margaret and Mary Sage, aided me a great deal by describing some of their uncle's early days and especially that period of his Hollywood history when they were a part of it.

I am also grateful for contributions to this account from the following: Raymond L. Ahern, my uncle, and Lakeside Golf Club's oldest member, who told me stories of Babe at the club antedating by a good decade my own meeting with Babe; Richard W. Bann; Billy and Arlene Bletcher; Charles Barton; James Cagney; Rev Richard Coogan S.J.; Bernard, Lord Delfont; Malcolm Stuart Fellows; Redford C. Fleming; Eddie Gannon; Fred Laurence Guiles; Lois Laurel Hawes and Tony Hawes; Mrs Lowry Hunt; Ida Kitaeva Laurel; William Janney; Al Kilgore; Marshall Korby; Venice Lloyd; Betty Libott; Glenn MacWilliams; A. J. Marriott; Rosina Lawrence McCabe; Vija McCabe; Glenn Mitchell; Jimmy Murphy; Richard Alan Nelson; W. T. Rabe; Hal Roach; Charlie Rogers; Robert Rogers; Charles Silver; Anita Garvin Stanley; George Stevens; Jack Stevenson; Dan Waldron.

A blanket thanks also to those members of The Sons of the Desert who in any measure helped me. If I have missed thanking anyone among them or elsewhere who added to my knowledge of Oliver Hardy, pray forgive a faltering memory. The only one more absent-minded than an absent-minded actor is yours faithfully, an ageing absent-minded actor.

Laurel and Hardy began for me when my oldest friend in the world, John Carroll, insisted at the age of eleven that we go to our neighbourhood theatre to see Stan and Ollie. 'You'll love these guys,' John said. Did I not.

Not to put too fine a point upon it – well, all right, why *not* put a fine point on it: in a pretty long and unsheltered life, I have never met anyone of discernment who either did not love or deeply appreciate Laurel and Hardy. 'I thought they were wonderful,' said James Cagney, speaking of them to me. 'Just simplicity itself. They took all the liberties, pushed them as far as they could, and –' At that point we broke into laughter. 'Look what we're doing now. We're laughing at them. When suddenly the little man starts to cry –' Cagney screwed up his face to imitate Stan. 'This is crying that never happened in the history of the world, and Oliver using people for –', Cagney went on to describe Hardy in a stage appearance I cite in Chapter 9, and we laughed again, finding it hard to stop.

In trying to sum up these enchanting two, the best and last words belong to J. D. Salinger who called them 'two Heaven-sent artists and men', and to Graham Greene speaking in 1940 of *A Chump at Oxford*: 'Laurel and Hardy are together again – this is better news than anything the papers print. *A Chump at Oxford* ranks with their best pictures – which to one heretic are more agreeable than Chaplin's. Their clowning is purer; they aren't out to better an unbetterable world; they've never wanted to play Hamlet.'

J. McC.
Mackinac Island, Michigan.
August 1989

1

Norvell

'Strr-r-r-ike three, and you're *out!*'

The big-boned, chubby boy with the angelic face lifted his right arm theatrically, and there was a loud crash of applause from the stands. The crowd cheered umpire Norvell Hardy every bit as much as they did their favourite players in Milledgeville, Georgia.

In response to the applause, Norvell bowed profoundly, one arm splendidly askew, and this got the response he desired – another wave of applause mixed with laughter. The long-standing saying in Milledgeville was that they'd close the banks to see the Hardy boy empire. This was almost the truth. Fifteen-year-old Norvell, like many other small-town fat boys, had early learned the profit of turning clown both to soften the sting of taunts like 'Fat-ty, fat-ty!' and to win approbation. He knew laughter brought balm and pleasure, and to cause it was a source of pride. He saw that if they laughed with you, they could not laugh *at* you.

On this day in June 1907, Milledgeville was playing an intra-mural game, Town vs Town, and Norvell was studiedly neutral. And imposing. 'He was always,' the school principal said, 'a sight to see.' While umpiring, Norvell affected some of the mannerisms of the travelling actors who stayed at his widowed mother's hotel. Emily Hardy enjoyed the company of show people, and her son – the youngest of her five children – had developed a talent for declaiming poems and singing songs in what he fondly thought was the leading theatrical style.

As the Milledgeville ball game progressed, there came to

plate a burly and vigorous man, name lost to history, whom we shall call Dell, the town's leading player. But not this day. In his previous turns at bat he had walked, popped out and struck out. This innings Dell was determined to sock one far down the outfield and redeem himself with a home run. Dell was a mite theatrical, too. With some flourish, he advanced to three balls and two strikes, all manifestly what Norvell had called them.

The moment of truth. Dell leaned in toward the pitcher, but at a killer's angle, all set to tear the hide off the ball. It sailed in to him at middle level where, as Norvell saw, he could have struck it for a good double. Dell let the ball go by.

'Sttttrr-r-r-ike three!' Norvell shouted.

There was no joy in Milledgeville at that decision. Dell turned, in anger, to protest. The crowd, backing him up, howled in resentment. Norvell knew what he had seen, and what he had seen was a strike. He was not about to lie to preserve the reputation of a town hero.

Now, instead of affectionate applause from the Milledge-ville fans, Norvell heard the sound – the dreaded, the hated sound – of the word that was to afflict him all his life.

'Fat-ty, fat-ty, FAT-TEE!' The chant began from the crowd. Affronted, Norvell threw his umpire's mask on the ground and stamped off the field, that accursed word echoing in his ears and consciousness.

Norvell Hardy, one day to be a prince of comedy, was experiencing the worst life was ever to offer him – the affirmation that he was fat. That his size would one day become part of his stock-in-trade, a *sine qua non* of his profession as a great comedian, he came in time to realize. But it would never alter his detestation of the word 'fat', or of his being so.

Norvell was born January 18, 1892 in Harlem, Georgia, to Emily 'Emmie' Norvell Hardy and Oliver Hardy. The latter was a Civil War veteran of some distinction. He had been mentioned in despatches and was seriously wounded at Fredericksburg. The Hardy family was English, with a long history of loyal service as men-of-arms to the British crown.

A tradition in the Hardy family holds that a direct ancestor of Oliver was Sir Thomas Hardy, Nelson's flag captain at Trafalgar.

Oliver's wife, Emily, was of a distinguished Scottish family, the Norvells, who came to the United States in the eighteenth century. Both she and Oliver had been married previously, she to T. Sam Tant (later Tante) in a union that produced two boys and two girls. Oliver Hardy, twice married before Emily became his wife, was the father of a son and two daughters by the second of those marriages. He had spent his early years as overseer on his father's plantation, thence going into duration service in the War Between the States. Following the war and into the later 1880s, Oliver Hardy worked as line foreman for the Georgia Southern Railroad, among other duties helping put down new track between Augusta and Madison. He was very well regarded by his crews.

Almost certainly one of the crew members was T. Sam Tant, of whom little more is known than that he is listed at age 18 in the 1880 census as unable to read or write. He was most likely a railroad worker laying track at the time he met Emily. Sam must have had a powerful personality to attract strong-willed Emily who, in addition to being very attractive, was quite literate, having been a school teacher in her youth. Oliver Hardy, like Emily, was of a superior social rank to Sam Tant, being a railroad supervisor and probably Sam's boss. In the latter capacity he would have known Emily Tant, and when Sam Tant died, or otherwise disappeared, before 1890, widower Hardy with children of his own would have found the widowed Emily, mother of four, attractive in several ways.

Hardy and Emily were married in Columbia County, Georgia, on March 12, 1890. At this time Hardy was 48, and not in good health. When he married Emily he had left the railroad and became manager of the Turnell Butler Hotel in Madison, Georgia. That he had business difficulties in verified by the existence of a writ from the City of Madison against him for $143.25, the sum of an unpaid electricity bill. It was paid in time, but clearly things were not easy for him.

In later years, his illustrious son — who took his father's name as a tribute to him — always referred to Oliver Hardy as a Georgia lawyer, and said that for a time he followed in his father's footsteps by briefly attending the University of Georgia's Law School. The latter was certainly a fiction, but Norvell believed the former to be true because it was a family tradition. There is no record of Oliver Hardy on any legal rolls in the Georgia of his day, which did not at all mean that Oliver could not have pursued legal work much in the way para-legals do at the present time. Those who apprenticed long enough with lawyers were allowed to do the general work of a lawyer, particularly in the rural districts.

As to Norvell's attending the University of Georgia Law School, this was a statement first made by the publicity department of Hal Roach Studios. Typically, most film companies of the Twenties and Thirties touched up the biographies of their leading players with little amendments intended to glamorize them or elevate them socially. During the years of his majority as a film star, Oliver Hardy remained loyal to his studio's standardized history of him. It was, he believed, the least he could do for his employer. But more. He easily fell in with the studio biography because he always felt keenly his lack of education.

His father, the Civil war hero, died when Norvell Hardy was eleven months old.

Oliver Hardy Sr., a handsome man of more than average height, much resembled his son. The senior Hardy died on November 22, 1892 of unstated causes, and unexpectedly. In one record of his demise, the Mortuary Committee of the Confederate Survivors Association reported:

Oliver Hardy of the 16th Georgia Regiment, found always faithful at the drumbeat. This man followed the flag and fought the battles of his brave regiment on the historic fields of Virginia. He was a man of great endurance, and having survived the war for more than twenty-five years, died suddenly in the twinkling of an eye.

At her husband's death, Mrs Hardy applied to the county for a year's support out of his estate on the grounds that she had an infant child, Norvell. For reasons not clear, Oliver Hardy had named the court in Madison, Georgia, to handle his estate on behalf of his children. The county court set aside $600 for her, specifying she could take it all in goods if she liked – which she did. She took the amount in tools of the hotelier's trade: bedding, crockery, silverware, lamps, a handcart, fowls and – surely for her travelling salesmen clientele, or drummers as they were then called – cigars, and a show case for them. Norvell was left $1000 in insurance money from his father's death for 'maintenance'.

Emily's other children were Elizabeth, Emily, Sam and Henry Tant, all issue of T. Sam Tant. In the later years some of the Tant children added a distinctive 'e' to their names.

Following the senior Hardy's death, the owners of Turnell Butler Hotel, quite unfeelingly, let his widow go. Emily Hardy had been a vigorous helpmeet to her husband in hotel duties. Undaunted after being fired, she at once took over management of another hotel, The White House, a large white 'drummers' hotel' near to Georgia and Central Railroad depot in Madison, and here she entered again into the hotel trade with all her considerable energy. One of her most valuable employees was Sam, a wiry, small black man. Sam was hot-tempered. He worked as a 'runner', a factotum who not only did errands for Mrs Hardy but solicited potential guests at train arrivals.

Emily's successor as manager at the Turnell Butler was J. W. Bearden, a very tall, burly and aggressive man. Bearden also believed in going out to drum up trade in person. One day he went to the depot to cull some guests and found Sam there before him. Sam had just convinced a newly-arrived salesman to go to the White House when Bearden approached, tried to get the man for the Turnell Butler, and did so. Little Sam, hot with anger, rushed the hefty Bearden and attacked him. Bystanders tried to break up the fight but Sam persisted, going back to strike Bearden each time the men were separated. It was not an even match, and one of Bearden's blows killed Sam.

This was another great loss to Emily Hardy but she persevered, running The White House unaided for a time, then going to nearby Covington to manage the Delancey Hotel. Thirty-two at the time of her husband's death, a recent mother, tall, vigorously beautiful, she was prepared to make her own way in the world. With five children to support, she had little other choice.

Raised very much in the Southern tradition, young Norvell had a black 'mammy', or 'mama', the name by which he called her, encountering his own mother rarely. Also very much in the Southern tradition, he called his mother 'Miss Emmie'. When he came to recognize the difference between the two women, he also had cause to see that 'Miss Emmie' was – as she had to be – a worker of prodigious energies and abilities.

These were bitter, hardscrabble times for Emily. For a while she moved to Atlanta with her children in the belief there were greater opportunities for her there. It did not seem so at first. One unhappy Christmas she was unable to buy her children a single Christmas present. But good fortune eventually did come Emily's way in the big city. While there, her oldest daughter, Elizabeth, was married in 1901 to a prominent and wealthy Atlantan, Ira Yale Sage Jr. Ira's father was a man of some influence, and not long after the wedding Emily moved to Milledgeville, Georgia, to operate the best hotel in town, The Baldwin.

Emily ran the hotel with unbounded thoroughness. She soon gained a reputation in town for her extremely hard work, and her children always appreciated her devotion to their welfare. One day little Norvell came up to her, threw his arms around her skirt, looked up and said, 'Miss Emmie, some day I'm going to make a lot of money, and you'll never have to work any more, ever.' When she was an old woman and it had all come true, 'Miss Emmie' would remind her son proudly of that well-kept promise.

Emily's children were all fascinated by the hotel's guests. Young Norvell particularly watched the 'theatricals', as show business guests at the hotel were called, and of their number he felt a special interest in the singers. Music was strongly encouraged in the Hardy family. It soon became apparent that Norvell had a strikingly good boy's soprano. He learned to entertain family and visitors with two songs that became his standard repertoire, 'Silver Threads Among the Gold', and 'When You and I Were Young, Maggie'. This last, as sung by an eight-year-old, commanded respectful hilarity from Norvell's listeners, among them at one time a brace of troupers staying at The Baldwin. These were members of Coburn's Minstrels, a typical company of its kind, headed by a Charles Coburn, third cousin of the film actor of that name. Their applause and Norvell's intense admiration of the group made him do something that became rather a pattern in his early life. He ran away.

When Coburn arrived in the next town, he found that the Sweet Singer of Milledgeville was a volunteer member of the troupe. Loving show business himself, Coburn admired the boy for his action, and thought there might be a satisfactory solution. Knowing Mrs Hardy well and having her faith and trust, he wrote and explained where Norvell was. He said the best way to handle the problem was not to make it one. Do not force the boy home post-haste. Rather, Coburn suggested, let him stay with the company until he got show business out of his system. Coburn would guarantee the boy's safety.

Mrs Hardy agreed, and it worked. Norvell came home in a few weeks to get more of Miss Emmie's good cooking. He was happy at home but there was one aspect of life at Baldwin Hotel young Norvell disliked. His mother, knowing the practical values of advertising for any enterprising hostelry, took an idea then current in large cities – the sandwich-man. The man chosen was Norvell, and he did not relish walking Milledgeville streets with boards fore and aft proclaiming the virtues of Baldwin Hotel's blue plate special that evening.

Norvell did not get show business out of his system. But he grew increasingly aware of how much his mother needed him, both emotionally and practically. As in the case of the sandwich-boards, all the children were put to helpful chores around the hotel. Even taking ashes out of the stoves was a real contribution to the hotel's life, the boy learned. He gritted his teeth, thinking what joy it would be travelling with a troupe, a musical troupe, as his hands grew daily more and more soot-ingrained.

His mother, sensing his unhappiness, saved pennies until, from time to time, she could give him the fare to Atlanta, seventy-five miles away, to see an occasional stage show – usually the musicals or operettas he adored. Norvell, too, saved whatever pennies came his way in tips as the Baldwin's porter to help pay for the Atlanta jaunts. So important were these trips to him that he would go despite heavy obstacles. One time, in order to see *The Bohemian Girl*, a film version of which he was to make years later, Norvell had saved enough money to reach Atlanta, buy the cheapest ticket in the house – but with nothing left for return. He went anyway, and walked most of the way back to Milledgeville, riding the last six miles on a friendly farmer's hay wagon.

It was on a later trip to Atlanta that Norvell's utter devotion to music was sealed forever. He knew the greatest tenor of the day was Enrico Caruso, but the hollow, tinny sounds purporting to be that magnificent voice coming from recordings did not satisfy Norvell. He had to hear the great man and discover that voice for himself. As he sat in the top gallery of the Atlanta theatre where Caruso was appearing in concert, the boy waited apprehensively, hoping that the singer would not cancel the performance as he had been known to do when not at top form. Caruso appeared, and was in full voice.

It was, Hardy said later, the single greatest musical event of his entire life, bar none – virtually a religious experience. Norvell determined to give his life over to music, if music would have him.

As the years went on in Milledgeville, his constant dream of appearing on stage as a singer – a dream he was never really to lose – obsessed him continually. He began to neglect school, and his forthright mother embodied that adjective more and more. She tried to find ways to help him. He had great confidence in her because she was a woman who faced life straight on.

One time Norvell and two young pals heard that a tattoo artist had just opened his parlour in town. Inquisitive, as boys are, they went down to the shop and marvelled at the illustrated board of available tattoos in the man's window. Each decided what he wanted and they went in for the trifling ordeal they considered one of the necessary rites of passage to manhood. Norvell selected a fancy maple leaf pattern which he elected to have inscribed on his inner right forearm. He then proudly went home, secure in his manliness, even though the arm was smarting considerably. He did not show the tattoo to Miss Emmie.

A few days later he did not have to. His arm had swollen, and he could no longer hide the pain – or the truth – from his mother. That redoubtable lady took a large horsewhip down from the wall of the hotel, marched over to the skin parlour and publicly whipped the offending tattooer. Miss Emmie never believed in doing things by halves or even nine-tenths. As the years went by, Hardy came to regret his tattoo. (It can be seen fleetingly in several of the films.)

Realizing that Norvell was not paying proper attention to his studies as the months rolled on, his mother sent him to a boarding school north of Atlanta, and for a time he concentrated on his books. For a time. Again he decided to run away, on this occasion to Atlanta. He was fourteen.

He chose to run away on April 17, 1906, the day a great race riot broke out in the city. This was frightening enough, but as the ugly sounds of hatred began to sweep through Atlanta, it started to rain. Norvell found himself trudging along a forgotten road, in red mud a foot deep. Ultimately he followed a railroad track to the Atlanta depot where a kindly stationmaster helped him get cleaned up and alerted Mrs Hardy. Norvell insisted on walking all the way to Milledgeville with the rain sluicing down. 'I was,' he remembered, 'quite a remarkable sight.'

He flatly refused to go back to boarding school, and

pleaded with his mother to let him study music. Strong-minded Miss Emmie pondered this, and determined that if Norvell was to study music and singing, he would do it all the way. She sent him back to Atlanta with enough money for lessons with Professor Adolph Dahm Patterson, one of the best musicians in the South. Norvell was greatly pleased. For a while.

Vocal work is unrelentingly hard, and it was especially hard at the Atlanta Conservatory of Music where Patterson taught. Norvell knew that he just wanted to sing to audiences, and he soon discovered the means to do just that. Near the Conservatory he found a movie house, where he got a job singing to illustrated slides several times a day for $3.50 a week. To do this he had to cut most, then finally all, of Professor Patterson's classes.

Miss Emmie, on a routine check of her boy's progress, went up to Atlanta and inquired of Patterson how Norvell was doing. Not doing well at all, the professor replied grimly. He had not seen the boy for weeks, he said. 'The young man has a beautiful voice,' said the teacher, concluding with an emphatic slang phrase of the day, 'but – no *damned ambish*!'

Norvell in fact had plenty of ambish, but not for the kind of singing offered by the Conservatory. He was looking for popular audiences, to regale with popular songs, that would make *him* popular. He went back to Patterson for a time, Mrs Hardy allowing Norvell to sing at the film house, but only on Saturdays and Sundays. This did not long continue.

When he again threatened to become something of a discipline problem by evading his studies, his mother was prompt in action. She sent him to military school, Georgia Military College, in Milledgeville, directly across the street from the Baldwin Hotel. Norvell quickly became popular there among all the students and faculty – he was a powerhouse on the College's football team – but his old nemesis, weight, continued to haunt him. He was accustomed to being the neighbourhood fat boy, and even the class fat boy – but to be the fat boy in a military school, where trimness was necessarily prized, was quite a different thing.

He cared not one little bit for the rigid discipline of the school – an integral part of its structure – and he particularly despised drilling, which not surprisingly caused some problems. Once, exhausted to the point of no return while drilling, Norvell dropped heavily to the ground, and would not move when ordered to his feet. Several cadets were ordered to carry him off the parade ground. This proving an impossibility, Norvell lay there until sufficiently refreshed. Then he went to his room, and his drill instructor was happy to see him go.

This and similar episodes caused him to run away again – not very far – across the street to his home. His principal cause for complaint was simple: the chow line at the military academy was inadequate. He said in response to his mother's plea to return, that he would go only if she prepared some of his favourite baking powder biscuits. She baked several batches, and he ate twenty big biscuits before he was content.

He had reason to be fat. He ate too much. He ate voraciously because he loved food and (said his oldest sister) because he missed the father he never met. Norvell at this time experienced another telling loss, that of his brother, Sam Tant. The two boys had been close, and when Sam was drowned in the wild Oconee River at the age of twelve, it left its mark on Norvell. He and another boy had tried to pull Sam out of the water but failed. Eating, it seemed, was Norvell's one solace when faced with trauma. By the age of fifteen he weighed 250 pounds.

To please his mother, Norvell tried to do his best at the military academy. The headmaster of the school was a good friend of Mrs Hardy, and he gave the boy every support he could. Like everyone on the staff, he liked Norvell, whose talent for making people laugh had grown with the years. The headmaster encouraged this both because it was a psychological prop for Norvell and because it delighted the other students.

At Commencement, 1907, Norvell joined with some fellow undergraduates to stage a 'Who killed Cock Robin?' skit that was climaxed by most of the cast coming out to sing the title song in chorus. When the query as to who *did* kill Cock Robin sounded, Norvell appeared in the bulky costume of a bull to confess his guilt. He looked every inch the role, but his voice was in vivid contrast to his appearance. He sang out in high, lyric tenor:

> *I killed Cock Robin!*
> *I tolled the bell because*
> *I could pull the rope.*
> *I am the bull!!*

hitting high C on the final word. At this the audience exploded into wild laughter, the headmaster telling Norvell later that he was 'the funniest boy in the world'.

But triumphs such as these were not good enough to maintain Norvell's interest in the academy. He asked his mother to send him away to 'any other place'. Fortunately a friend of Mrs Hardy was on the staff of a progressive mountain school in the high hills of northern Georgia. Young Harris College, at Young Harris, Georgia, was then principally a high school and college offering ample outdoor activity in addition to academic work. Today authorities at the College cite a tradition still extant there that (in their words) 'Hardy's mother sent him to school at Young Harris to get him away from the influence of travelling salesmen staying at her hotel. It seems Hardy had begun to play cards, started smoking cigars, etc, and Mrs Hardy decided he needed a more wholesome environment in which to grow.'

Young Harris was singularly broad-minded about smoking on its premises. Although cigarettes and cigars were generally forbidden for the younger students, pipe smoking was not anathematized, and a photograph survives in Young Harris files of Norvell and several of his classmates posed with pipes in their mouths. This was a pipe smokers' club, and Norvell was one of its officers.

As at his previous schools, Norvell was much loved at Young Harris, both by faculty and students, although a Professor Adams is on record for having 'paddled' Norvell for misbehaviour. The good professor must have had quite an arm. In one of the regular camping expeditions through the Georgian hills required of all students, Norvell was inspired on behalf of laughter to imitate a rural mountaineer being chased by a bear. Pantomiming a rustic walk, Norvell approached a big tree, and turned around in simulated horror to 'see' an approaching bear. Conveying perfectly the fear one would feel in such circumstances, Norvell quickly climbed the tree. At the top he leaned down to observe the non-existent animal scratching at the tree's base, and in flawless Georgia mountain-man accent, shouted, 'Lawd, if you don't help me, don't help that bear!' Howls of appreciative laughter came from his fellow students, and Norvell was satisfied. Again, for a time.

He asked his mother if he could come home. She sent money for his train ticket from Young Harris, advising him to take a side trip to visit relatives in Augusta on his way home.

On the train to Augusta, Norvell had one of his great life experiences. Not a very able baseball player because of his size, he nevertheless knew and loved the game. On the Augusta train he fell in conversation with a sharp-eyed young man with a trenchant manner of speaking who seemed vaguely connected with sports. The conversation came around to baseball, and the young man spoke knowingly of various people on the Augusta team, spoke indeed as if he had been in the team's dug-out during the games.

'Are you the bat boy?' Norvell asked him. Let Grantland Rice continue the story:

> 'Bat boy?' blurted Ty Cobb. 'You come to the game today. I'll show you!' Hardy took in the game. 'It was something at that,' reflected Hardy one day forty years later on the Hal Roach lot. Cobb hammered a single, two doubles, a triple, a home run, and stole two bases.

When Norvell arrived home after his pleasant stay at Young Harris College, he realized that education was by and large an unsatisfactory substitute for show business. He could only think of one exception, his father's supposed profession, that distinguished branch of show business, the law. Briefly he considered law school and mentioned it to his family. Elizabeth, his oldest sister, talked him out of it. She treasured him as the baby of the family and knew his limitations. 'Norvell honey,' she said, 'you're just a big, fat baby. How'd you ever win a lawsuit?'

He was determined to win at least one thing – applause – and as much of it as he could get. Applause, he knew, was the best anodyne for all his troubles, and in Milledgeville he increasingly became the town character, not only for flashes of comic brilliance as baseball umpire, but as the star of ama- teur theatricals where he could sing popular vaudeville hits.

As a teenager, he also worked at Milledgeville Opera House. The Opera House, despite its designation, was basically a vaudeville theatre on a standard Southern circuit featuring Lillian Russell and other popular artists of the day. When one of the acts got sick or cancelled, Norvell was called on as substitute, his two or three songs always winning great acclaim. There were two reasons for this: he was a local boy making good over and over, and he *was* good. The climax of his act was always 'You Are the Ideal of My Dreams', a song he was to revive humorously in his 1931 film, *Beau Hunks*. It was at Milledgeville Opera House that Norvell was to meet his first wife, a top-act vaudeville pianist.

It was in his eighteenth year, after years of working in his mother's hotel with periodic appearances at the Opera House, that Norvell found satisfactory employment, if only peripherally, in the movie business. In 1910 a local business- man opened the first movie house in Milledgeville, the Electric Theatre (later the Palace) across the street from the Opera House, and it became instantly popular. Norvell went to the owner for a job and got at least five of them.

In Milledgeville's census list for 1910, Norvell Hardy is shown to be the 'electrician' of the theatre, a word then mostly used in film circles for 'projectionist'. But he did far more than that. He took tickets, he swept out the theatre, he sang to illustrated slides as he had in Atlanta, he acted as manager when the boss was gone. Norvell was a great asset to the Electric Theatre because Milledgeville knew and loved him. When people came to see a movie, they enjoyed his jokes and friendly chaffing as he took their tickets, and his warming farewell, 'Come back now, hear?'

Norvell's interest in the movies playing at the Electric was profound. He empathized with hero, heroine and villain. The comedies, Norvell thought, were very much a mixed bag. Many of them he thought plain silly; running the gamut from fair to good to the occasional work of genius, the last a film or two of Max Linder. Norvell was sure he was no Linder, but as for the rest he had no doubt.

'I knew,' he said years later. 'I *knew*. I thought to myself that I could be as good – or maybe as bad – as some of those boys.' He certainly wanted to try, and he did.

2

Babe

Norvell's prime interest as an entertainer continued to be music.

Just prior to finding his job at the Electric Theatre, he had gone briefly on tour with a minstrel show, modelling his speaking and singing style on the exuberant minstrel man, Lew Dockstader. He had seen Dockstader several times in Atlanta, and liked the man's hearty flair for a comic line. But Norvell felt that life in a minstrel show was necessarily restrictive with its formula approach to song and dance.

The movie house at Milledgeville was in a real sense a school for Norvell as he learned what to do and especially what not to do as a performer. This schooling was thorough. He saw films daily for three years, and they never bored him. Indeed, the worse they were, the more he learned. Early in 1913 a Milledgeville friend who had been vacationing in Florida returned with stories of a growing film-making colony in Jacksonville. Since this was only two hundred miles away, Norvell decided to visit.

He quit his job, went to Jacksonville and quickly found work as a singer in local vaudeville and cabaret. Realizing that his size made him something either less or more than a leading man and operatic hero, he decided to capitalize on his bulk and bill himself accordingly. He chose his act description as 'The Ton of Jollity', and one of his first jobs under that billing was at Cutie Pearce's roadhouse in Jacksonville. He alternated work there with stints at the Orpheum Theatre in town, primarily a vaudeville house.

Playing in the pit orchestra at the Orpheum was a girl he

had met backstage at Milledgeville Opera House, intelligent, dark-haired Madelyn Saloshin. Attracted by her sparkling eyes but especially by her virtuoso ability at the piano, Norvell began to court her. He felt slightly intimidated in this because she was, if not exactly a vaudeville headliner, at least a featured performer as a pianist, with a wide and favourable reputation through the South.

He was making $40 a week as a vaudeville singer; she was in the $300 bracket. Other than her eyes, Madelyn, a middle-class Jewish girl, was rather plain. However, she was very personable. 'A very sweet person,' a friend of Hardy's described her years later. On his first dates with Madelyn, Norvell learned she came from a prominent song publishing family, then doing extensive business at their offices in Tin Pan Alley. He was intrigued.

Madelyn, attracted to the portly but quite handsome young man, got him a job with a touring vaudeville unit she starred in, and while on the road short months after they met, the two were married in Macon, Georgia, on November 17, 1913. Norvell was twenty-one. Madelyn was always shy about giving her age, but friends guessed she was close to a decade older than her husband. The groom's mother, friends reported, was 'in a rage for days' when she heard of the elopement.

The newly-weds returned to Jacksonville, and Norvell, working almost exclusively at night, continued a practice he had begun on first coming to Jacksonville. He haunted the film studios by day to see how they operated. He particularly enjoyed watching the Lubin Film Company because its performers all seemed to have such fun as they worked. The Lubin people had leased the defunct Jacksonville Yacht Club's building in the posh Riverside district of the city. There they fitted up a good interior shooting stage but most of their filming was done outdoors in the marvellous Florida sunshine.

Lubin's large exterior stage was openly accessible to tourists in those pre-sound days, and Norvell, standing among them, delighted in watching the antics of the comedy players. He felt an instant and instinctive kinship with them. He even volunteered to be company water boy, simply to be near the actors.

One day a Lubin director, who had become used to seeing the big youth carrying water and standing nearby during shooting, remembered that their next comedy called for the services of a fat boy. He asked Norvell if he was available, and finding the lad mightily available, put him in the film, *Outwitting Dad*. Norvell proved so adept at the new work that Lubin hired him at five dollars a day with a contract for three days' work each week.

Outwitting Dad is no longer extant but a Lubin advertisement in a 1914 trade paper gives us the plot. Norvell, under the billing 'O. N. Hardy', played Reggie.

> Lena Gross's sweetheart, Bob Kemp, is thrown into a sand pile by her father for daring to propose to his daughter. Bound that he will marry Lena, Bob dresses up his brother, Reggie, as a bad-man. Father is chased into a stable. The boys shoot blanks through the door until father, believing his life is in danger, gives his consent to the marriage. Reggie is left on guard at the stable door while Bob dashes to the minister and marries Lena. Reggie, exhausted, falls asleep. Father discovers how he has been fooled, jumps on the sleeping Reggie and gives him a thrashing, then starts off looking for Bob. The young couple return. Father at first wants to kill Bob, but Lena's pleadings finally win him over and the two children receive his blessings.

In the single still photograph sent out with the film at its release date, April 14, 1914, one can see why a man of heft was needed for the role of Reggie. Wearing Mexican hat, drooping moustache, and bullet belt over the chest, Hardy looks the very spit if not the image of Pancho Villa.

In billing himself 'O. N. Hardy' he was taking his father's name as tribute to the parent he could not remember, but shortly after this first film, Norvell acquired a new and permanent name. Near the Lubin studio was a barber shop run by a genial little Italian named Enzo. Enzo loved almost everyone of the male persuasion but he look a particular fancy to Norvell. Every time he finished shaving the handsome young fat man, Enzo would rub talc into the rubicund cheeks and say, 'Nice-a babe-e-e. Nice-a babe-e-e!' The Lubin actors picked it up, first calling Norvell 'Baby', then shortening it to 'Babe'. That name was to be his for the rest of his life, although he never cared for it, regarding it as slightly demeaning. It was the nickname used thereafter by all his intimates. To his family in Georgia, however, it was and would always be Norvell.

His mother deeply regretted the 'Babe', and pointedly called him Norvell when she was around his friends. Her family pride, much like Pooh Bah's in *The Mikado*, was splendidly inordinate. She loved her son deeply, and when her little boy was given such a frivolous nickname, she resented it profoundly. She even mildly disliked Babe's taking his father's Christian name, but there she had herself to fault. To compensate for his father's loss, Mrs Hardy told Babe in enthralling detail all his father's virtues as a Southern gentleman. She succeeded in impressing him to the point that Norvell made up his mind before he reached Florida that he would assume his father's name, in that way coming closer to him. This was utterly typical of Babe, whose quotient of sentimentality was to remain high all his life.

The Lubin company issued its comedies in what were called 'split-reels', two comedies of varying length on the same reel, adding up to a thousand feet. *Outwitting Dad*, for instance, was four hundred feet long, accompanied by a six-hundred-foot comedy, *The Rube's Duck*. But on occasion the entire reel would be given over to a single story, as in the Lubin release of August 18, 1914, *Back to the Farm*. In this, the co-star is billed as 'Babe' Hardy, the name he was mostly to use in his Florida film-making days. Babe rose from the extra ranks to star billing in just over four months.

Back to the Farm well illustrates how these early comedies could cram a plethora of action into a very short period. Babe's co-star in the picture was Bert Tracey, a feisty little Australian actor and former jockey, who had become Babe's best friend at Lubin, and who years later was to be wardrobe man for Laurel and Hardy's music hall tours of Britain.

In *Back to the Farm*, Babe and Bert portray respectively Tom and Bob, well-mannered bumpkins who plan to visit their aunt in the city. Auntie writes them she will be gone when they arrive, but they will find the key to her place under the doormat. The boys arrive as scheduled but mistakenly search for the key under the doormat of the apartment a floor beneath Auntie's. They find a key there and open the door, not realizing it is the key of a Mr and Mrs Cassett who, like Auntie, are briefly away.

Babe and Bert cheerfully enter the Cassett apartment, and are most pleased to see dinner on the table. Loving Auntie for her thoughtfulness, they eat the meal and retire. Babe, in proprietary fashion, kicks Bert out of bed, and Bert, too sleepy to climb back in again, rolls under the bed and falls asleep. Mr Cassett comes home and is astounded to find a man in his bed. He draws his revolver and chases Babe out of the house.

This caterwauling momentarily arouses Bert, who crawls into bed. Enter Mrs Cassett who, horrified to find a stranger where her husband should be, takes a gun from the bureau, and shoots at the intruder a number of times. Mr and Mrs Cassett are arrested for their liberality with firearms. The boys, seeking Auntie, re-enter the house and once again encounter a hail of bullets from the arms-obsessed Cassetts, despite the presence of police, and this time Bert and Babe are arrested for breaking and entering. Auntie comes back just in the nick, and explains all. The boys decide city living is too complicated for them, and retire to the safety of the farm.

Forty years after the making of this and other Lubin films featuring Babe and himself, Bert Tracey was interviewed about his old friend. His memories were warm:

Babe was one of the funniest and most charming human beings I have ever met in my pretty long life. At Lubin he was everywhere regarded as the life of the party, and a terrific tease and gagster. He became very popular with Jacksonville citizens. He was certainly great fun for all of us at Lubin, a joy to work with. I remember in one film I had escaped from prison and was swimming down a river. Babe was working a big crane on the banks, supposedly cleaning the river bed, swinging the big claw-like dipper over the water. I was directed to climb into it, and Babe was to hoist it up over the bank, lower it and let me out. All went well when he swung the dipper up in the air, but – always the great kidder – he pulled the wrong lever on purpose, the claws opened under me, and down I went. These things happened all the time. He knew I loved the water anyway.

Movie-making at Lubin was not without its perils. Tracey goes on to say:

One of our movies was a Foreign Legion story. I was a lousy little colonel, he was the handsome private, and we were both in love with the same gal. To get rid of him in battle, I placed him by a tree where the enemy couldn't miss him. We had a number of real-looking fake cannons, fashioned of wood and metal strips, made so they could fire a charge of smoky powder. These all looked good but couldn't hurt anyone. Well, this day we had a new property man who had been used to nice quiet parlour films. He knew nothing of firearms, and even less of cannon – although he didn't say so. Instead of just placing a handful of powder and a small wad in this dummy cannon, I swear he must have poured in half a can of powder and, what was more terrible, wadded it in with a ramrod.

The scene started, yells, rifles shooting, and Babe is waiting for this cannon to go off. It sure did, a really terrific explosion, and a piece of iron was blown into the tree where Babe was, a lethal piece of iron, only two inches from Babe's head. Like all of us, I was terribly upset, but all Babe said was, 'After all this, I think we'd better have a cup of tea.' What a guy.

In all his Florida-made films, 'Babe' is an appropriate designation for Hardy. One sees why his co-workers persisted in calling him that. Without the brush moustache he later used to confer age on himself, he owns the classic baby face with apple-round cheeks, innocent eyes, a face well given over to enormous poutings. In many ways it was the face he would retain all his working life – that of an overwrought cherub. His nickname well suited.

Babe essayed all kinds of roles for Lubin – many comic villains and loathsome 'heavies', roles mostly played by literally heavy men who could convey either menace or laughter, or both together. For such roles Babe seemed predestined. A born actor, he used his body in full function. His frenetic reactions or 'takes' were, from his earliest films, his prime comic stock-in-trade. He was an utterly natural actor-comic with equal ability at both. Bert Tracey recalls:

> Now mind you, any fairly good actor or comic can do a take well enough. A take is just a very big reaction to something. It is an over-reaction, really, and I think outside of Edward Everett Horton, Babe could do takes better than anyone in the history of motion pictures. The average comic does the take mostly with his face, and it can be quite funny, serving its purpose of helping build up the laugh. But Babe did takes with his whole body, not just his face or shoulders the way most comics do it.

Babe first saw comics do takes at the Electric Theatre at Milledgeville, and at Lubin he not only learned how to do them but how to do them surpassingly well. 'When I started to do takes,' he said years later, 'I just naturally put everything I had into them.' The Hardy takes, even from his earliest films, literally start from the toes. With the supreme grace of the great comic athlete, he swings his entire body into an arc of shocked surprise. He becomes a living question mark in blend with the exclamation point.

After the 1914–15 winter season at Jacksonville, in response to a long-felt desire to visit New York City, Babe persuaded fellow player Ray McKee to go with him. McKee, who knew the city well, promised to show Babe all the sights with the hope that they also might find film work there. The two took a steamer for New York, and Babe, who knew naught of the sea, suffered *mal de mer* in its worst forms. He spent much time on deck away from his tossing bunk, and was dreadfully sunburned, mainly on the lips, which puffed up in horrid caricature of a pout. His worst agony was the inability to eat.

On arrival in New York, not knowing how long they might be out of a job, they opted for a very inexpensive hotel, the Mills, near the corner of 35th and Seventh Avenue. The Mills was more a flophouse than a hotel, and when they got there after midnight, the elevator had stopped running. They walked up twenty storeys to a very seedy room.

New York, especially its tearing, noisome traffic, made Babe very nervous. Finally he could take no more, and three days later returned to Jacksonville. By train.

He resumed films at Lubin in the spring of 1915 and stayed with them until the company ceased production in August of that year, going out of business, and selling its assets to Vitagraph. Bert Tracey approached Babe about going north again, this time to try his fortunes as a vaudeville singer in addition to film acting. During World War I there were many movies being shot in New York City, out on Long Island and across the Hudson at Fort Lee, New Jersey. Babe thought it over carefully, felt that he had not given the big city a fair try, and agreed to return.

This time he had a modicum of success, but in pictures, not in singing, where his heart was. He and Bert were able to get jobs in a number of mostly small film studios – Casino, Novelty, Star Light, Gaumont, Edison, and even the larger Pathé studio. He was featured in the Wharton Brothers Inc. 'Get-Rich-Quick Wallingford' series. These scattered appearances were made in September and October, 1915.

But he was desperately looking for vaudeville booking as a singer. No one seemed interested in an outsize young man with a beautiful voice. The two did not seem to make sense to bookers; they didn't fit, one agent told Babe. Babe knew where he could always get work as a singer. Besides, autumn or any other season in New York, in his view, paled beside winter in Florida.

In returning to Jacksonville cabaret, Babe found himself in friendly, cosy surroundings once again. He resumed singing at his old hideout, Cutie Pearce's roadhouse. Meanwhile, the Vim Comedy Company, a new group of film-makers with headquarters in New York, had taken over the old Lubin studios in Jacksonville on lease, and had settled in to make their speciality. Vim began its work in November 1915.

Vim was the property of two aggressive – some said aggressively tricky – motion picture pioneers, Mark Dintenfass and Louis Burstein. Dintenfass ran the home office in New York and Burstein moved to Florida to supervise and produce the films. Burstein placed under contract an old Lubin friend of Babe's, Bobby Burns, and teamed him with another comic, Walter Stull, in Vim's first films, a series called 'Pokes and Jabbs'. As headliners for the company, Burns and Stull turned out most of Vim's product through the span of the studio's existence.

Burstein also placed under contract a marvellously versatile comedian, Billy Bletcher, later a Laurel and Hardy supporting player and now immortal as the voice of the Big Bad Wolf in Disney's *Three Little Pigs*. In the early Vim days, Bletcher, his actress wife Arline, and Burstein went to Cutie Pearce's roadhouse and heard Babe sing. They were particularly impressed by his style of singing. He not only had a true and affecting tenor but he moved easily about the stage, with a graceful control of gesture. Seeing him, and having heard from Bobby Burns about the young man's worth as a Lubin comic, Burstein asked Babe to join Vim.

Babe was elated. Like almost all film companies of the time, Vim worked only in daylight hours. Madelyn Hardy was director of the ragtime orchestra playing at the Burbidge Hotel Cabaret in Jacksonville. Babe was able to join her there in the evenings under his own billing, 'The Ton of Jollity'. He quickly became a favourite of the largely theatrical and movie player crowd that patronized the Burbidge Cabaret. He treasured his work there because he loved singing more than anything in the world, and it effectively augmented his Vim salary.

His total income increased dramatically, and he did not hesitate to spend it. His liberality became well-known in the Vim company, and at times people, even casual acquaintances, would take advantage of him, promising to repay a loan by a certain date, then conveniently forgetting the obligation. Babe was too soft-hearted to remind the delinquent debtor, and in this way (said Bert Tracey), 'he spent more money on more damned deadbeats than anyone you ever heard of. He was the original Mr Soft Touch.'

Babe was charitable by instinct. As a result of his boyhood years, when he saw how every penny of income could matter, he had a natural sympathy for people in financial trouble.

Babe and most of the Vim company stayed at the Atlantic Hotel in Jacksonville, a clean and comparatively inexpensive apartment complex. At the Burbidge Hotel, working at dishwashing and other thankless jobs, was a young man close to poverty level, hoping to break into show business as a singer. Newly married, the boy and his bride, also a singer, had been travelling through the South on a battered motorcycle, looking for work. The young people were so poor they frequently had to sleep on benches in public parks.

Hearing of this, Babe was deeply shocked. He found it incredible that anyone could be reduced to such primitive living. He insisted the young people move into an apartment at the Atlantic Hotel, paid their rent for three months, found the young man a better job, then gave him fifty dollars – and instructions not to repay it.

'But I must repay it, Mr Hardy,' the young man said.

'There is only one way in the world you can repay me,' Babe said. 'When, some day, as most likely you will, you find someone who is worse off than you, just help *him* out. That will be ample repayment for me.' The young man wept and Babe left the room hastily.

Babe and Madelyn were happy at this time, pleased with their own special little family – Babe Jr, a small, fluffy white dog, and Babe III, a controllable but mischievous Capuchin monkey. To further his career at the Burbidge, Babe organized a quartet, the Twentieth Century Four, singing with them every evening, and also in duet with good friend, Margaret Arata. Patronage increased and Babe was placed in charge of all entertainment at the Burbidge. The Burbidge Cabaret became the place to go among the fashionable in Jacksonville.

Cabaret entertainment then always ended at midnight, at which time Babe, Madelyn and their friends at Vim would frequently go six miles out of town up the St John River to the Panama Club. Here was another cabaret, open only to members. Margaret Arata was the featured singer at the Panama. Babe loved to sing with her, his silver tenor blending beautifully with her lustrous contralto. He would not accept payment for his work at the Panama so she reciprocated in kind by coming, unpaid, to the Burbidge to sing with him there. The two became the best-known and most admired singers in Jacksonville during World War I.

Babe's initial film at Vim was *A Special Delivery*, produced early in 1916. It was the first of a lively series called 'Plump and Runt'. Babe, inevitably, was Plump, and an acrobatic actor named Bill Ruge played Runt. This was something of a Laurel and Hardy foreshadowing in that physical contrast was an essential of the series. Ruge was actually a thin man of average size but he looked slight compared with Babe, who was not only heavy but big-boned and tall – 6 feet 2 inches.

The physical difference between Babe and Billy Ruge was fully as strong as in the Laurel and Hardy films, albeit shown with less subtlety. Ruge was an ex-circus comic and aerialist, and Babe as Plump would typically pick him up and toss him around like a medicine ball. Ruge and Hardy starred in thirty-five of these diverting one-reelers, all of them marked by a charming, even elegant, crudity.

Single-reel films, about ten minutes in length, hardly allow for subtlety of characterization, or any characterization at all for that matter. Action had to be swift-paced, story line quintessential, but it is amazing how much action these early films carried. *One Too Many*, an early film of the Plump and Runt series, illustrates this.

One Too Many's first shot reveals Babe in sad condition, on a bed of pain, deep in the throes of a shuddering hangover. Needing relief, he vigorously squirts a seltzer water on his head. It helps only a little. In his agony of reaction to the water, he falls off the bed – but exquisitely. No mere simple roll-off this, but a complete end-over-end somersault – compact rotundity in full circle.

His malaise is intensified by news that his rich uncle is coming to visit him – not only him, but his wife and baby as well. Uncle adores families. But Babe has no wife or baby, not even of any kind, and he now regrets having tried to curry Uncle's favour by telling him this bountiful lie.

Nothing for it but to scurry about his rooming house to find an interim family to palm off as his own. The custodian of the rooming house is Billy Ruge (whose sharp-chinned countenance was not unlike Stan Laurel's), now deputized by Babe to find at least a baby for him to pass off as his own during Uncle's visit.

One Too Many consists mainly of the ringing of changes in the wife-and-baby search, Billy renting a variety of them for Babe, only to have them disappear for different reasons until Billy himself is forced to become the baby, thus satisfying near-sighted Uncle John.

All these events, as usual in the early comedy film, are consummated frantically, with much push, shove and wild running about – everywhere punctuated with body-shaking takes. What is so captivating about Babe's art – and this is the hallmark of all his later film work – is his beatific grace under fire, and his abilities to shift comedic gears instantly. Amid this frenzy in *One Too Many*, much of which he generates, he gets most of his laughs by frequent changes from intense agitation to a low key, smarmy sangfroid.

For instance, when carrying a purloined baby back to his room, he encounters someone in the hall. His trenchant anxiety in look and posture dissolves instantly and utterly to greasy amiability as he hides the baby from view. He slips the baby coolly behind himself as one would a stolen pot roast.

Babe's triumph is that we know the little one is quite safe in his care.

At times in the film Babe's physical dexterity astounds. Trying to quiet his nerves, he prepares to drink off a quick shot of liquor. Holding the glass a foot and a half in front of him, he jerks it up slightly, forcing the liquor to leave the glass in an extended high-arc parabola into his mouth. The liquor does no such thing, of course – there is none there – but the dexterity of his motion tells us it does, his pantomime convincing us we see what we do not. Chaplin could not have done it as well.

So much a part of Jacksonville life had Babe become that he even joined a lodge, the local branch of the Masons, Solomon Order Lodge No 20, FAM. In time Babe became a Master Mason, taking all the degrees up to and including the thirty-second. Thirty years later, Solomon Order Lodge of Jacksonville made him a Life Member, an honour of which Babe was intensely proud. Not a formally religious man, he was, all his life, devoted to Masonic ideals and to his very last days read the Bible a great deal.

He almost did not become a Master Mason, almost, in fact, got thrown out of the Order. One morning the studio took literally to the streets, placing a camera artfully hidden from the public on a slow moving truck. The scene of action was a parade of members of a fictitious social group not unlike the Masons. Babe's part in all this was to play a noisy, drunken merry-maker who actually holds up the parade and succeeds in making himself obnoxious to spectators and paraders alike.

The shot began very well and continued beautifully. Babe was directed not only to crash into paraders but also into anything of interest he found along the route of march. He did so, improvising as he went along, bouncing into cars, garbage cans and lamp-posts. He waved, roared, cooed, hiccuped, weaved, stumbled, fell, got up, fell again – and at some length was a superbly disgusting, troublesome drunken bum.

Next day he was summoned to an extraordinary meeting of Solomon Order Lodge where he was asked grimly to explain his incredible behaviour of the day before. Gasping, Babe realized that the Vim camera had been only too well hidden. He explained in patient detail what his roistering had been about. The brothers were relieved because this was a man they were extremely reluctant to lose.

Both private and occasional public practical jokes were interwoven into Babe's working life. The actors enjoyed vying with each other in this way. Babe planned an extended one on a dear friend. He worked occasionally as an assistant director, and in one film where an audience listens to a female singer and applauds her warmly, Babe became the catalyst for a practical joke he wanted to play on old chum Margaret Arata. Still the singing sensations of Jacksonville, their friendship had progressed to the teasing phase.

In engaging Margaret for the role of the singer before the appreciative audience, Babe coached her for the scene by saying that she had to be 'terribly real'. He explained she had to sing with deep, deep pathos to move the audience, to display genuine emotion during her melancholy song. Margaret agreed to sing her heart out.

Babe's gag was that the scene called for the singer to render a lively, wake-'em-up tune, 'The Sunshine of Your Smile'. The audience of extras, prepared to hear the light-hearted tune, would be totally flummoxed by hearing Margaret sing the pathos-soaked 'My Gal Sal', as Babe had instructed her to do.

Margaret arrived on the set early, was made up, and led before the audience of extras. Babe explained to her again that she must wring everyone's hearts with her song. She agreed, and did, almost choking herself with emotion over the dolorous lyrics. At the end, she bowed and the extras applauded energetically, if a little bewilderedly.

Margaret looked at Babe for his approval. At the moment when he should have been savouring every nuance of his elaborate practical joke, he could not. He was crying, crying from the heart, struck to the soul by 'My Gal Sal'. As he explained to Margaret later, hearing her sing this song forced his thoughts back to two dear old people he had known and loved in Milledgeville, and he could not forbear weeping for them.

Babe felt occasional urges to be a director, and in time these feelings would grow stronger. But the success of starring in the Plump and Runt series was very gratifying. All thirty-five of the Plump and Runt films were made in 1916 and despite some falling off in quality, there might have been more had not a new player arrived at Vim. Kate Price, a popular film comedienne, had been featured at Vitagraph where she earned a wide following. Vim teamed her with Babe, and they made fourteen films together extending into 1917.

Then Babe found himself the unwitting star of an off-camera conspiracy that led to the death of the Vim Comedy Company.

Vim's co-founders, New York executive Mark Dintenfass, and lawyer Louis Burstein, had made the company into a paying enterprise. Dintenfass, in supervising Vim's New York headquarters, held the company's purse strings. Or so it seemed. Burstein told Dintenfass weekly how much money to send for Jacksonville production needs. Then rumours began to sweep the film industry that Vim's affairs were not all in order. As early as November 1916 the Florida *Times Union* had run stories saying there were certain problems surfacing at Vim, that there 'was a large shortage of company money, which is being traced by company auditors now working on the books'.

Many years later, Vim comic Billy Bletcher said Vim's trouble came about because either Dintenfass or Burstein was stealing company funds. Said Bletcher:

A little hanky-panky was going on as to payroll. Babe Hardy was the one who discovered it. The New York partner and the Florida partner were cheating each other, and the actors were suffering for it ... Our salaries were pretty secret and so you just didn't ask the other guy 'What are you getting?' The money was in cash in an envelope every Saturday and actors were told, 'That's for you.' Well, Babe discovered the salary list which showed how much we were all being credited with. But the amount the New York office was sending down was more than the actors were really getting. Babe was furious and said, 'Hey, you dirty bastards – you're only paying me so much, but you're charging the guy in New York to pay a lot more.' When that got out, boom. It wrecked the company.

Burstein and Dintenfass started to hurl law suits at each other, and Vim was then subsumed by another group, Amber Star Film Corporation. Burstein quickly formed a new group, King Bee Film Corporation, and with the persuasive power of much hard cash persuaded Babe and several other Vim players to support King Bee's star, Billy West, in a series of two-reel comedies.

West (Roy B. Weissberg), a Russian-born comic, entered at this time into direct competition with Chaplin whom he imitated down to the last tattered coat button. This was distressing to Chaplin because West was actually quite competent in his mimicry, and at the time King Bee signed West, Chaplin was in his Lone Star/Mutual phase producing onbzly four short films a year. There was room for competition.

Burstein signed Babe to play the comic heavy opposite Billy West à la Chaplin's Eric Campbell. Babe was even directed to wear the same eyebrow-heavy makeup of Campbell's in some of the films.

The King Bee company produced its Billy West pictures in Jacksonville, then went to the Frohman studio, Flushing, Long Island; from there to the former Vim Studios in Bayonne, New Jersey, in the spring of 1917.

It was while working in Bayonne that Babe decided to enlist in the army. An instinctively patriotic man, he wanted to serve actively in the Great War. His widow, Lucille Hardy Price, tells the story:

Babe had never been enchanted with New York. The final blow came when we entered the war in 1917. Babe was working in one of the studios on the New Jersey side since the day war came, and he headed for the nearest recruiting office, fired with enthusiasm and genuine patriotic feeling. He walked in and announced his intention to enlist. The officer in charge didn't even answer. He gaped at Babe for a moment, looked him up and down, and yelled into another office, 'Hey, Sarge, come and look at what wants to enlist.' The sergeant came out, looked, and the two doubled up with laughter. This was followed by a number of remarks intended to be funny, but they were anything but funny to Babe. He was terribly hurt and embarrassed – and this finished him with New York.

At this time stories about the comforts and job opportunities in California had been reaching Babe. 'They really need good comics and heavies out here,' one friend wrote him, 'and you're both. Come on!' It was also clear to Babe that Florida's importance as a film capital was diminishing. He decided to move west. The King Bee Company had already gone there. Everyone seemed to be going there.

Babe and Madelyn went to California late in 1917, full of a sense of adventure. A number of Jacksonville cronies followed the Hardys, among them Kate Price, Bert Tracey, Ray McKee, Billy and Arline Fletcher. This group of jolly Vimites formed their own little colony. Bert Tracey recalled:

It was a whole new way of life for us. Each one, I suppose, thought he or she would do well enough in his or her own way in Hollywood. We couldn't forsee Babe's great success, of course, but I'll tell you this. Of all our bunch, if success was to come *anyone's* way, its coming to Babe would have pleased us most, and for a very good reason. Surely the best should only happen to the nicest.

3

Hollywood

In Hollywood, Babe had a new world to conquer, and he was ready for it.

The Los Angeles area was congenial to one of his background. The weather was Southern; the constant blue skies seemed specifically Floridian. Babe was released from his contract with King Bee when the company went out of business, having over-extended themselves. He looked about for what so long had been his staple form of employment – playing heavies in one- or two-reel comedies. He was out of work for a few weeks but he had the chance to do free-lance work here and there. It was during one of these catch-as-catch-can opportunities that Babe met the man who was to be his other half.

Arthur Stanley Jefferson was born in Ulverston, north-west England, on June 16, 1890, the son of a prominent North Country showman, Arthur 'AJ' Jefferson, comedian, playwright, director, producer, who had hoped young Stanley would follow him into the most secure branch of show business, stage management. Stan (from a very early age he refused to use 'Stanley' in full except for comedy purposes) would have none of it. He grew to love the comics who played at his dad's theatres, and shortly after his fifteenth birthday decided to become a boy comedian, a type of performer then fairly common in British music halls. (In later years Stan always referred to himself – and others like him – as a 'comic', one who said things funny, in contrast to a 'comedian', one who said funny things.)

Expecting disapproval from his father for this career choice, Stan put together a comic act in secret, approached an old friend of his dad's who owned a rudimentary Glasgow music hall (the Jeffersons being then resident in Scotland), and begged for a chance to put on his act. His ten minute routine – mostly borrowed gags and 'funny sayings' – was offered one afternoon without his father's knowledge. Or so he thought. When he faced his audience that day, there, leaning against a post at the hall entrance was A J. Stan, now doubly nervous, had strength enough to begin his act with the following, which he remembered all his life and which was very typical of his borrowed gag:

> Did you hear about the two butterflies? Mmm? The first butterfly was terribly upset. He said to his friend, 'Ohh, I am bothered. I *am* bothered.' 'Why?' asked his chum. The first one said, 'I couldn't go to the dance last week.' 'You couldn't?' said the other butterfly. 'Why ever not?' 'Well,' said the first butterfly, 'I couldn't go because it was a *moth* ball.'

Despite this and other less-than-sturdy witticisms, AJ decided the boy was worth helping, and through a friend got him a job with a juvenile pantomime company. Stan pursued his profession doggedly, and despite a pronounced lisp that he conquered in time and periodic bouts of joblessness, took a giant step in his career when he joined Fred Karno's pantomime company, or more properly, companies. Karno at the turn of the century in Britain popularized the wordless play or extended story pantomime. Mime was the heart of all these comedies, and Stan learned his craft in this extraordinary school. Karno's star was a glib young cockney, Charles Spencer Chaplin, and Stan was to become his understudy and best friend, even on one occasion loaning Chaplin money for an abortion his current doxy needed. For several years Stan and Charlie roomed together during the Karno tours of Britain and the United States.

On the second American tour in 1912, Chaplin was seen by Mack Sennett, left Karno and walked into film immortality.

Stan decided to try his luck in American vaudeville and after a series of different partners and acts (in one of which he imitated Chaplin, by 1914 the world's leading comic) found himself in a two-act, Stan and Mae Laurel. The latter, his perky, combative, common-law wife, knowing he found the thirteen letters in 'Stan Jefferson' faintly ominous, suggested 'Laurel' as a surname. In time Stan had his name changed legally to ten letters, Stan Laurel. He tried occasionally to join the growing comedy film world. In 1915 he made *The Evolution of Fashion*, a 'shadowgraph' presentation in a vaudeville theatre, actually not a film but the projection of actors' shadows by a powerful lamp on a large white screen. Because its entire story sequence was done visually in mime and without sound, Stan always regarded *The Evolution of Fashion* as his first 'film'. Between subsequent vaudeville engagements he appeared sporadically for Rolin, L-KO, Nestor and Vitagraph Pictures from 1916 through 1918.

It was during one of his vaudeville appearances the latter year that film producer and one-time cowboy star, G M 'Broncho Billy' Anderson saw Stan, and was greatly taken with him. Anderson, realizing the great market open to comedy film, was looking for potential Chaplins, and here, displaying the same remarkable talent, was Chaplin's understudy. Anderson resolved to make a pilot film to show backers in New York. As director, he hired a former Chaplin associate, Jess Robbins, a Vitagraph director, who had produced some of Chaplin's best early films for Essanay. Robbins and Anderson collaborated on a story, and most likely in the summer or September of 1918, *The Lucky Dog*, the first film in which Stan Laurel and Oliver Hardy appear together, was made.*

*In an extant taped radio interview with UCLA's Arthur Friedman, Stan says *The Lucky Dog* was made '. . . I imagine around 1916 or 17, around there.' But he goes on to state that *The Lucky Dog*'s director, Jess Robbins, was 'at this time' directing films of Larry Semon of Vitagraph. Stan was in these films, and records show they were made in July–September of 1918. There was grounds for thinking *The Lucky Dog* was made late in 1919 because of a topical reference on one of the dialogue titles to Bolshevik bombings, then current in the US. However this could have been added well after 1918 because the film was not released in its extant form until 1922.

It is a slight film but a pleasant one. Stan, who was starred, understandably gets most of the footage. It is the story of a stray dog Stan picks up. He enters it in a dog show; the dog's owners appear to accuse him of dognapping, and he is forgiven. The Laurel and Hardy sequences are two. In the first, running after his satchel as it patters down the street – the dog is inside – Stan picks it up at the place where comic-villain Babe is holding his gun on a robbery victim. Accidentally stuffing his newly acquired loot behind him into Stan's pocket, Babe releases his frightened victim and spins around to confront the astonished Stan. Enraged, Babe assaults Stan, and at this moment comes the first 'spoken' communication between them. Babe says, via title card, 'Put 'em both up, insect, before I comb your hair with lead.' He grabs the money from Stan who, dreadfully annoyed, kicks his burly assailant away and runs off down the sidewalk.

Stan scampers through a hole in the fence, and Babe attempts to follow, getting stuck in the process. Delighting in the villain's predicament, Stan climbs back over the fence and plants a hearty kick on Babe's expansive rear before running down the street to freedom.

The second encounter between Stan and Babe in *The Lucky Dog* occurs later when Stan gives the dog to its rightful owner, a charming young lady, whose resentful boy-friend tries to dislodge Stan from the girl's favour and presence through force. The suitor finds yegg Babe on a mean street, bribes him to join the plot, and has him outfitted in full formal morning attire. Babe, disguised, appears at the girl's house, where Stan is visiting, an honoured guest. In Babe's arsenal of oppression he has – as he reveals when he pulls aside his coat – two large horse pistols stuffed into his belt, and to make assurance doubly sure, a stick of dynamite which he lovingly calls his 'Bolshevik candy'. Babe is introduced into the girl's household as the eminent Count de Chease (sic) from Switzerland, and he shortly corners Stan privately and announces, 'You and the world are going to separate.' Babe brings the gun to Stan's head, Stan putting his fingers in his ears to spare himself the impending noise. The gun will not go off. After three more tries, it still will not fire, and Stan asks Babe if he has rubber bullets. 'I'll fix it,' Stan says. 'I used to open shells in an oyster house.' Babe hands the gun over.

Out in the hall, the suitor is being obnoxious to the heroine. Stan, in fixing the gun, fires it accidentally and it singes the boy-friend's rear, sending him into flying splits of fright. Babe goes out to calm him, and the gun in Stan's hand goes off again accidentally, this time creasing Babe's fundament. The suitor lights the stick of dynamite to blow Stan away but the dog picks it up and chases the suitor about the house.

Babe meanwhile has abducted the girl, Stan tries to shoot him with the gun, which now perversely will not operate – so Babe and Stan engage in furious fisticuffs. The dog, still with sizzling dynamite in mouth, chases Babe and the suitor outside on the broad, heavy-hedged lawn. Stan and the girl come out and see the dog resting, the lethal stick on the ground before him. They call him over. There follows a great explosion, and the last shot of the film is of Babe and the suitor, tattered and begrimed, rolling about in a tangled ball of denuded hedge branches.

In *The Lucky Dog*, Stan and Babe are at polar opposites of their later screen selves. Stan is a natty juvenile (he was actually twenty-nine, looking younger), quick – one might say too quick – of movement. He is assertive, glib. Babe is playing his standard comic heavy – menacing, glowering perpetually and, like Stan, very quick of movement, and much given to elaborate, athletic takes. Stan said, years later:

That was my first meeting with Babe Hardy. We were just two working comics; there was nothing remarkable about our getting together, and I really saw little of Babe at that time of course because he had a smaller role in the picture. The scenes between us were shot very quickly, and we certainly had no idea in the world that we'd even see each other again, let alone become partners. It was among my first movies and Babe had done well over a hundred by that time. I didn't think then there was much future in pictures for me.

The Lucky Dog went mostly a dead end journey in New York
film exchanges, but it gave Stan a boost he needed to attain
respect as a comic among producers of screen comedy then.

After *The Lucky Dog*, Babe was again out of work for a
few weeks until an old Vim friend recommended he try his
luck at L-KO. This was December 1918, the fifth year of the
company's existence, and Lehrman-Knock Out, its full name,
was just about to receive one. The company was the child
of Henry 'Pathé' Lehrman, now best remembered as Charlie
Chaplin's first director and early rival at the Sennett Studio.

A breezy Viennese-born entrepreneur who began professional life as a street car conductor, Lehrman got his nickname
by passing himself off as a Pathé man, a representative of
Pathé Frères, the world's first big movie producer. He was a
phoney with a certain amount of talent and Babe found him
amusing. Fascinated by the man's granitic cheekiness, Babe
was grateful to him as a source of employment. Lehrman
signed Babe for a number of two-reelers, *Freckled Fish, Lions
and Ladies* and *Hop the Bellhop*, among others, some made
with Earle Williams, a kind of Clark Gable of his day. When
L-KO was finally KO'd, Babe had only a short distance to go
for work. L-KO had released the films through Vitagraph, a
pioneering studio in Hollywood's history, one that in time
would be taken over by Warner Brothers. Vitagraph made
every kind of film but it had an excellent record of comedy
shorts going all the way back to John Bunny and Flora Finch
in 1910.

Not long before Babe came, Vitagraph had received hearty
comedy talent from England in the persons, first, of Jimmy
Aubrey, a member of the Fred Karno pantomime act, *A Night
at an English Music Hall*, that had toured American vaudeville in 1910 and 1912; and second, of Stan Laurel, also in
that act. Jimmy Aubrey had played a variety of roles in the
company. Aubrey had joined Vitagraph as early as 1917 but,
temperamentally a dissenter, left the studio after a few weeks.
He returned eagerly enough in 1919, realizing that Vitagraph
was a consistent source of work, not at all afraid of backing
its stars with good production values.

Babe worked in over a score of Aubrey films from early 1919 to 1921, mostly in two-reelers that, following a custom of many film comedies then, bore alliterative titles: *Bungs and Bungles, Flips and Flops, Mules and Mortgages, Tootsies and Tamales, Squeaks and Squawks, Dames and Dentists*, and so forth. Aubrey, very conscious of his star status, did not want clever comics working in his films, no matter what good support they provided. He hoped Babe would work elsewhere. But Jess Robbins, Aubrey's director, insisted he stay. Aubrey, sucking up to Robbins, thereafter made a great show of his regard for Babe. Who was not fooled. Babe was too polite to show disaffection for Aubrey. Aubrey was notoriously unkind to supporting actors, and thoroughly mean-spirited. Among other perquisites, he insisted he be paid in gold pieces. He demanded that he be the centre of every shot, and the other actors learned to accommodate to this. Babe saw the situation at once and in self-concern quietly tried to play as close to Aubrey as he could in every scene.

Babe was soon developing a reputation as a consistent performer who always brought something memorable to his comic heavies, for which he now seemed destined. This was considerable accomplishment when one considers the leap-bounding pace of these films. Babe, athletic by temperament, enjoyed the tempo and took all the work he could get. 'Some of those guys I worked with,' he said, 'would get pretty winded. But I took it all in stride because I looked on it as a kind of game, just as if I were out on the football field. I loved my work and I like to think that showed up on the screen.'

It was at this time that Babe began to feel his affection for Madelyn lessen. He had much to be grateful to her for. She had introduced him to the world of vaudeville, and at that time was making more money than he, assuring a lifestyle he found very comfortable. They seemed to be a perfectly natural team.

But Hollywood – and Vitagraph particularly – was aswarm with pretty girls and beautiful girls. Babe was not proof against them. Too, Madelyn's age was beginning to show, and the discrepancy in their years was increasingly notice-able. He did not like to see other women behind her back but at Vitagraph this was very easy to do. Inevitably Madelyn discovered his quiet infidelities, and late in 1919 filed suit against her husband for separate maintenance. The case was to be tried a few weeks later but before the trial date his lawyer and Madelyn's agreed on a settlement. Babe was to pay her $30 a week, not a small part of his Vitagraph salary.

Babe, who was never in his life to be provident until forced to by the steadiest of his wives, was highly irregular in making the payments to Madelyn, and soon neglected them utterly, insisting to friends that he could not subsist on his divided salary. He made an application to the court stating this, an action countered by Madelyn's vigorous legal denial.

It is unclear what happened next, but Madelyn's divorce suit in the summer of 1920 asserted that when she told her husband of her father's illness in Atlanta earlier that year, Babe, dis-playing great sympathy, urged her to go home at once, and that 'they would forget all this nonsense' of the divorce suit. Shortly after reaching Atlanta, Madelyn said she received a telegram from Babe saying, 'I will not receive you as my wife. There is no use returning to Los Angeles.' This brought her back at once, and the divorce suit was implemented, Madelyn consider-ately not asking for alimony. Instead the $30 a week agreement was confirmed, and in November 1920, Madelyn received her interlocutory decree, and vanished from Babe's life for a time.

In 1936 Madelyn Hardy, living in New York and a hundred pounds heavier than when Babe last saw her, sued him for alimony on the grounds that he had allowed their $30 a week agreement to lapse. She could not show the written agreement – it had burned, she said – but she had witnesses to its signing. Babe settled with her out of court for an undisclosed sum.

Newly a bachelor in 1920, Babe rented a hillside house with an old Lubin friend, Ray McKee, at the top of Cahuenga Pass in Hollywood Park. Babe was just then beginning his strong interest in gourmet cooking, and one day he invited Ray, Billy and Arline Bletcher, Bert Tracey and a few other Jacksonville chums to share a dinner of stuffed fish broiled in Babe's own special sauce. There were ten in all at the table. As dinner progressed, it became obvious that the fish was 'off', and Babe's delicious dressing had done little to ameliorate it. The house was small, with only one bathroom. Instant ptomaine poisoning was the order of the hour for everyone at the table. 'There was,' said Ray McKee, 'a mad scramble to the bathroom. Very few made it.'

This odious episode had one positive effect. In later life when Babe had indeed become a superlative cook, he never trusted anyone's word about the quality of meat or fish. He went to market himself and selected his own 'viands', as he liked to call them.

Babe did not maintain bachelor quarters for long. Appearing in his life after Madelyn was yet another Southern girl, almost pretty enough to be called a belle, one of the Vitagraph girls attracted to him when he was ranging about romantically. Myrtle Reeves was born in Atlanta, and her pleasant drawl was the first thing that attracted Babe to her. 'Home folks' he called her, and a more than enterprising Vitagraph publicist stretched this into a publicity story at the time of Babe and Myrtle's marriage, saying that

> The romance is of some standing, since the bride and groom knew each other in Atlanta where they went to school together. The first valentine the bride ever received, she says, was a comic one from her youthful admirer when she was ten years old. She thought he was making fun of her, and wouldn't speak to him for a week. Then he managed to waylay her and explain, 'Why, I thought you'd lots rather have a nice funny valentine than one of those silly things.'

Thus early on Babe learned the conventional Hollywood public relations formula: one must try to spritz up a news release with a 'human interest' anecdote, no matter how untrue. The fictitious valentine story was printed three days after Babe and Myrtle were married, Thanksgiving Day, 1921, in the Church of Christ, Hollywood.

*

In a move considerably strengthening his career, Babe in 1921 moved up in the Vitagraph organization to become chief foil and heavy for the wildly popular Larry Semon. Semon, almost forgotten today, was then close to Chaplin in popularity. A newspaper cartoonist turned performer, Semon felt a natural affinity for the rapid-fire punch of the two-reel comedy film. A wiry, undersized man with the nose of a giant, ascetic hawk, he emphasized his comic credentials in films by wearing a heavy base of clown white, his mouth and eyebrows slashed jet black. Viewing the Semon films today one can see that he is not likely to become a cult figure among comedy film buffs. Semon's gags are excellent, beautifully crafted and executed, but his personality is evanescent. Semon was gag-bound. He is simply the spark and guiding instrument of his elaborate gags, not their true human source. The humour does not come from him as a person; there is no personality there to evoke. Had there been, Semon and Hardy might have become a greao'zt comedy team. For it is Babe alone, seen in thebzse films today, who lends them what little humanity they possess. In later years Babe called Semon:

> . . . a good comedian, a very good acrobatic comedian [a number of whose stunts were performed by Bill Hauber], and he always knew a good gag when he saw one. He used to have a little black book that he'd keep in his back trouser pocket. That little black book was worth thousands and thousands of dollars because he always kept all his comedy ideas in it. I never saw anyone work harder at making a gag work, except maybe Stan.

Semon saw in Babe not only a sterling support player but a worthwhile production assistant as well. He asked Babe's opinion on the structuring of gags on occasion and encouraged his tentative ventures behind the camera already begun in the Aubrey film, *Tootsies and Tamales*, which bears a credit, 'Story by 'Babe' Hardy'. Semon, a man not prone to share credit, went so far as to bill Babe as assistant director in a few of his films. The little man had taken an instant liking to Babe when they met, and a few weeks later introduced him to golf, a Semon passion. It soon became Babe's. 'Golf – that was my game, the thing beside my wife I cared for most in the world,' said Babe.

'I loved it right from my first day on the links. I loved everything about it. I was more or less too big for team games although I'd say I was pretty good on our football team in the Lubin days. But golf was truly my game. I love it because it's social, for one thing – nothing is quite like a good foursome of nice guys enjoying each other's company. And it's challenging. You've got to get that little white pill in the right place without a whole lot of fuss.'

Eventually Babe reached professional skill as a golfer, and became the best known player in the film industry outside of Bob Hope and Bing Crosby.

If Semon treasured Babe as co-worker and friend, he felt quite the opposite about Stan Laurel. In the years following his arrival in the States with the Karno troupe, Stan regarded his peripatetic life with considerable ambivalence. Of movies and the stage, he much preferred the close encounter of live theatre. There was no pleasure for him quite as deep as hearing the loud surge of laughter from an alert audience. But as the experience of his old friend, Chaplin, showed, movies could be mightily remunerative. Moreover, Stan was heartily sick of the endless road that was vaudeville. He hated the thousands of miles travelled every year, the same scenery, the same dingy boarding houses. So, periodically, Stan essayed the movies.

After an unsuccessful film, *Just Nuts*, in 1917, he made five one-reelers in 1918 for Rolin Film Company, three of which were directed by an up-and-coming director/producer, Hal Roach. In October 1918 Stan signed to do a few two-reelers with Semon, and creatively was stopped dead in his tracks. Semon saw the threat at once. Stan was too good a comic to support anyone, so Semon kept him at a distance. Or tried to. Stan remembered Semon as:

entitled to be the star of his movies, of course. But I think in the long run he hurt himself. In one of the few pictures we made together he was my fellow convict and we escaped from prison. The plot was mostly to be about our troubles after escaping. We had shot some footage and Semon and I with some production people watched the rushes next day. It was all pretty good stuff, I thought, and so did a visitor, Antonio Moreno, then a big movie star. In fact at one point, Moreno laughed like crazy at something I did in the picture, and said, 'This guy's funnier than Semon.' You can imagine how Larry appreciated that. So when we went back to shooting, Larry simply wrote me out of the action by having me tied to a tree with handcuffs while he went on with the picture.

Three years later Stan was financially strapped enough to consider working for Semon again, and Semon, needing good support in that film, *The Rent Collector*, wanted Stan back. But it was the mixture as before, Semon utilizing him ineffectively, diluting Stan's strengths.

After *The Lucky Dog* in 1918, Stan had to wait three years before working again for 'Broncho Billy' Anderson. Then Billy produced a series of marvellous parodies – represented at peak by Stan's Rhubarb Vaselino in *Mud and Sand*, perfectly sending up the dramatic excesses of Valentino's *Blood and Sand*. These parodies were filmed in 1922 but were unappreciated for their satiric genius. Stan once more went back to vaudeville.

By 1922 Babe was Semon's irreplaceable chief support, and he was able to steal scene after scene from his boss with impunity. He did so by *not* trying to steal the scene, and by staying as close to Semon as he could in the shots. Unlike Stan, whose credo at the time was to do anything for a laugh, Babe scaled his performances to the prescribed needs at hand, and was never tempted to exceed them. When, as the crooked hotel manager in Semon's *The Bellhop* (1921), he has to project a quality persuasively genial and nasty in equal measure, one sees a fine actor in action.

The title card describing his character as 'A manager with one hand for everyone and the other for himself' finds perfect illustration in Babe's journeys in the film from good to evil and in between. This is a complete performer, and instead of the instant change from virtue to perfidy typical of most silent film comic villains, one sees in Babe a mind at work. Literally. 'If the camera's on you, and you're called on to change your mind about something,' said Babe, 'you don't have to do a thing but *think* that change, and the camera gets it without your moving a muscle. It gets it especially when you *don't* move a muscle. It's all right there. In the eyes.' Babe learned this early on in his career.

In *The Bellhop* a conniver comes to Babe and openly solicits his aid in supplying vital papers from the hotel safe. Mr Nasty, after gently waving a wad of money at Babe to remind him that this and more is his if he will only cooperate, walks off. Left alone, Babe thunders imprecations of outraged virtue at Mr Nasty's retreating figure, and shakes his finger angrily at this bold, bad man. Then, as cupidity dawns, Babe's censorious, scolding finger becomes an instrument of self-counsel, and we watch the finger and his changing expression say quite clearly, 'Slow-w-ww. Take it easy. This is a lot of money. A lot of money *you* can use, dear boy.'

Babe's instinctive physical grace as a performer is seen essentialized in two other quick moments of many such in *The Bellhop*. The first comes when he must placate an irate guest on whom a wash of ink has been spilled. In highest dudgeon the man spouts invective, and Babe – one can almost hear his cooing in this silent film, so effective is the pantomime – lifts his right hand eloquently to soften the loud indignation. His hand is mesmeric as he waves it undulatingly, decrescendo, to soothe. Toscanini would have been proud of it.

The other moment comes all too briefly when he throttles Semon splenetically, shaking the little fellow in volcanic rage. He rocks Semon back and forth like a stubborn root holding ground, and Babe ends the action with a new one, becoming centre post of a human carousel, swinging his victim in a circle around himself several times in precise arc. This entire engagement takes not more than a minute, and it is pure, full-line choreography.

Despite his early training and experience in the frenetic outdoor farce with Lubin and Vim, Babe Hardy was inherently an actor born for the film; Stan Laurel was of the stage – and these two conditioning factors were to shade their performances all their working lives.

It is instructive to see Stan Laurel films of this period, and compare them with Babe's work. Mime was their mutual base, and granted that Babe played heavies and Stan mostly excitable ditherheads, they were both basically working to get as much comedy into twenty minutes as possible. The difference between the two in the early 1920s is made signal by comparing Babe's moment of dawning greed in *The Bellhop* with most of Stan's moments in his early Roach or Broncho Billy comedies, when a shocked leap into the air or contorted-face single takes were his principal devices of reactions. Stan had not found his comic self.

George Stevens, who in his earliest Hollywood days was cameraman for some of the best Laurel and Hardy silents, said:

> Sometime before beginning with Roach, I had seen Stan work, and I thought he was one of the unfunniest comedians around. He wore his hair in a high pompadour and usually played a congenital dude or slicker. He laughed and smiled too much as a comedian. He needed and wanted laughs so much that he made a habit of laughing at himself as a player, which is extremely poor technique. How he changed! In those very early days he was obviously searching for a workable form and formula.

What Stan was also looking for was a profession, a permanent way of life. Babe, although seriously interested in directing as a possible calling, thought of himself at base as an actor. Stan, on the other hand, considered himself at heart a gag man, a craftsman of humour. Indeed, he created gags even when he knew they would not likely be used. It was his hobby as well as his profession.

In the early 1920s Stan's itinerant vaudeville life, plus the burden of a common-law wife who was developing into a shrew, made him think increasingly of Hollywood as a haven. A non-performing haven, where he could work for the comedy studios as writer and director. He began to yearn for that life.

Babe, on the contrary, felt well settled in. As early as 1920 the *Los Angeles Times* referred to him as 'the well-known comedian'. His position as leading heavy in Hollywood seemed assured, and Larry Semon's popularity appeared unassailable.

But change was in the air. Babe began to sense Vitagraph's growing disenchantment with Semon over the matter of budget, and after several years of feeling at home, Babe began to experience the insecurity that clutches most actors' hearts during their careers. He got a good inkling of his profession's instability by seeing it in his boss. Semon's Vitagraph films were initially big money-makers but gradually the profits declined. Semon had only himself to blame. He refused to cut down on budget when it became apparent that he was overspending. For *The Sawmill* (1922), a two-reeler, he built almost an entire village in the California mountains and spent three months on the film with a large crew and cast. Vitagraph found *The Sawmill* an entirely worthwhile film from every aspect save the financial. Semon was told it constituted a classic case of outgo stoutly defeating income, and that this had to stop. Henceforth he would have to finance his own productions, and Vitagraph would be willing to release them. In what can best be described as a fearful snit, Semon went his usual well-measured way and produced three more films on his own in 1922, *The Show, Golf* and *The Counter Jumpers*, all released through Vitagraph.

Then Vitagraph balked. Early in 1923 the studio told Semon that they would not even release his films, let alone finance them. Now considerably upset, Semon pondered his future and took several long months to do so. It was during this fallow period for Semon – most of 1923 – that Babe entered into the only protracted period of unemployment in his life. While Semon ruminated about his future, Babe wondered about his own.

Charles Barton, later a well-known director for Abbott and Costello, was beginning a Hollywood career in 1923, the year he met Babe. Finding temporary work in a drug store, Barton laboured behind the soda counter. Babe would wander in to pass the time with his new friend. Barton felt sure Babe was hungry so he gave him free meals on these occasions, and Babe, taking half home to Myrtle, never forgot that. Years later when he and Barton were both elected to Lakeside Golf Club, and had not met in the interim years, Babe saw Barton's name on the new member roster. Barton, opening his locker a few days later, found a beautiful set of matched golf clubs and a note: 'I don't know if you are the same Charlie Barton who years ago was a soda jerk. But I wanted to repay you for your kindness back then. Babe Hardy.'

In 1923 Babe made another friend who was to reappear in his life many years later. Glen MacWilliams, the cameraman who would be Oscar-nominated for his work on Hitchcock's *Lifeboat*, was beginning his career in 1923 with several other talented neophytes who went on to fame – Howard Hawks, Hawks's brother Kenneth, and Jack Conway. Howard had written and was about to produce a film called *Quicksand*, Kenneth was co-producer, and Conway was set to direct. The film was to be shot at Fort Huachuca, Arizona, using government troops, the well-known 10th Colored Cavalry, the pride of US Army black troops. MacWilliams knew the location area well.

On the company train going to Arizona, he made instant friends with Babe, his strong Southern accent attracting MacWilliams, whose mother had been born in Atlanta. Knowing nothing of Babe's background, he learned the husky, fat young man was not a performer in the picture but part of the production crew. Eager to take any kind of work he could get, Babe had offered himself to Hawks as an assistant director and gag man, and was accepted – probably for expenses only, MacWilliams guessed.

Babe and MacWilliams had much the same sense of humour, and it was possible in those innocent days to offer blackface humour even to blacks and find it appreciated, if – as Babe and his friend did it – it was offered without condescension as a two-man minstrel show. They did it with great success several times before the men of the 10th Regiment after the day's shooting.

There was no question of Babe's appearing in *Quicksand*. He was, as MacWilliams recalls it, a person hired to think of '. . . comedy gags, bits of business. Babe's ambition was to be a producer.' He proved to be a vital part of the film's production team, very much respected for his opinions during story and shooting conferences. It was one of the rare times Babe openly expressed a desire to become a director, and it remained mostly a hidden ambition all his working life.

MacWilliams and Babe were to be reunited eighteen years after *Quicksand* when the former did the camera work for Stan and Babe on a 20th Century-Fox film, a job that would make an enduring difference in MacWilliams' life, a job Babe made sure he got.

By mid-1924 Babe's career slump not only ended but was tellingly reversed. From that time he never really would be out of work again. It was almost inevitable he would find work with Hal Roach, whose studio was basically comedy-oriented. Roach, born in Elmira, New York, the same year as Babe, had as a young man-of-all-work, gone full across the country doing odd jobs as far away as Alaska. As a construction worker, he came to Los Angeles and on a fluke found himself a movie extra. This seemed well-paying work so in turn he became actor, director, and finally a producer when he took a small inheritance and in 1914 made several one-reel comedies with the then unknown Harold Lloyd. Other films with a variety of comics followed.

By 1919 Roach had enough capital to build a new studio on seventeen acres in Culver City, a Los Angeles suburb, and in these quarters were shot a wide variety of comedies and

Westerns. Oddly, one of the latter was Babe's first Roach film, *The King of Wild Horses*, made early in 1924. Cast as a nasty heavy, he wore a patch and a scar of disturbing vividness. This straight drama went wildly comic at one point when Babe, astride a horse, sank with his steed into a sand morass because of their weight. 'The boys behind the camera couldn't go on,' said Babe, 'because they were howling so much.'

Babe did a number of Roach comedies, and other studios beckoned as well. His old boss, Semon, had decided after considerable thought to enter the feature-length field, and he wanted Babe at the same old stand.

In the two-year span of 1924–26, Semon, under the aegis of his own company, Chadwick Pictures Corporation, made six films with Babe: *The Girl in the Limousine, The Wizard of Oz, The Perfect Clown, Stop, Look and Listen*, all feature length; and a pair of two-reelers, *Her Boy Friend* and *Kid Speed*. Of these, *The Wizard of Oz* holds special interest for modern audiences, if only to compare it with the celebrated 1939 MGM version.

Semon's *Wizard of Oz* (1925) is a far distance from that classic story but it does have its moments, some of them a little bizarre. Dorothy was played by Mrs Semon, Dorothy Dwan, an attractive young lady who looked a bit riper than the eighteen years she is supposed to be in the film. The action begins in Oz where handsome Prince Kynd (Bryant Washburn), the country's regent, and the common folk together lament the long absence (since her childhood) of Dorothy, their queen. They demand that Prime Minister Kruel (Joe Swickard) find her. That rogue promptly tries to divert them with the trite buffooneries of Oz's Wizard, well played by old Mack Sennett comic Charlie Murray, he of the droop-down mouth. But the Ozites want Dorothy badly.

We do too by this time, and so we go to Kansas to find her, a toothsome country lass, with her aunt Em and Em's consort, a dyspeptic Uncle Henry. The family farm-hands are Larry Semon, for a change not in white make-up; Dorothy's most persistent suitor, Babe Hardy (and so billed in the credits); and Snowball (Howe Black), an able black actor who must have been galled beyond measure to play the conventional watermelon-eater right down to giving a variation on 'feets-do-your-duty!' in a fright reaction.

Liberally interspersed through the action are the reasons Semon made the film in the first place, his gags. Some of these are bucolic: fighting off a bee and then an entire swarm of them, chasing a duck that in reprisal squirts a stream of milk in Semon's face, falling off a giant silo into a well-placed haystack. The cyclone eventually carries the farmhands *and* Uncle Henry (also a comic) and Dorothy to Oz where she is crowned by her adoring subjects. And where the other Kansans assume various disguises to evade the beastly prime minister Kruel: Semon taking the garments of a field scarecrow, at last giving him the chance to whiten his face and become the film's hero, Babe finding the lineaments of the Tin Woodman on a junk pile, and Snowball obtaining an animal skin to become a cowardly pseudo-lion.

His ambition to succeed at court turns Babe into what he has been in so many Semon films, the little man's nemesis heavy, and they squabble as of old. Babe typically explodes into rage – now a staple of his comic heavies – and in battle with Semon does a fast, rolling somersault with ease. But it all seems rather mandatory. Also mandatory in Semon films is climax in the form of an elaborate chase highlighted by the hero catching a rope ladder floating down from a speeding biplane. Dorothy marries the prince regent, the bad guys come to naught, and Semon has a moment of contrived pathos when Dorothy kisses him and rejects him lovingly.

It is a mildly enjoyable film. Some critics thought rather more of L. Frank Baum's artful story should have been retained but since Baum's son was one of the film's scenarists, presumably dad might have approved. Audiences recognized it for what it is, another trip through Semon's gag book, and as such it did and does entertain. But there is little in it for Babe outside of his formulaic by-play with Semon as of yore.

Semon's new policy of producing feature films failed. He was still spending too much money, not enough money was coming in. It seemed to him that finally his day as a popular

comedian was over. As indeed it was. Semon then made an
unusual decision. In order to stay in Hollywood, he would
leave comedy and become a character actor. He was cast for
a serious role in Josef von Sternberg's thriller, *Underworld*,
and did well enough. But no more offers came. Like many
fading celebrities before him, he went into vaudeville. On
tour in March 1928 he was forced to declare bankruptcy,
this bringing on partial mental collapse. Larry Semon died in
October of that year.

Babe was greatly moved. He said:

> Larry was second only to Stan and Chaplin when it
> came to creating gags. The thing that kept him from
> staying at the top was that at heart he was never really
> an actor. I felt very bad about his end because when I
> worked for him, he gave me every opportunity to shine,
> and that wsn't usually Larry's way with other comics and
> supporting people. He wanted the action to concentrate
> on him, and why shouldn't he? I lost a good friend and
> a very kindly boss.

While working in the last of the Semon films, Babe also
free-lanced actively. In addition to work at Roach, he got
jobs at Fox (in a Buck Jones feature, *Gentle Cyclone*, directed
by W. S. 'Woody' Van Dyke); at Arrow Film Corporation,
teamed with another comic, Bobby Ray; at the fount of all
screen comedy, Mack Sennett's in *A Sea Dog's Tale* with
Andy Clyde, and in another Sennett film, one starring himself,
Crazy To Act. It was also at this time that he was rejected as a
comic sidekick by – of all people – Stan Laurel.

Stan, in one of his periodic swings between Hollywood
and vaudeville, had returned to California in 1923 for a
series of Hal Roach one-reelers on a five-year contract.
These, although filled with marvellously diverting gags, were
basically substandard and Roach was forced to terminate
their agreement after two years. It was at this juncture, late
1924, that Stan met Joe Rock, a robust, charming comedian-
producer, who had come to California earlier to be Semon's
leading juvenile. Later Rock took on a partner named Earl

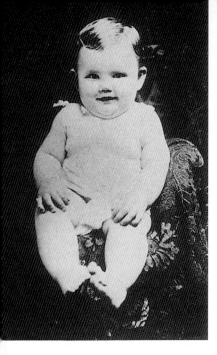

(above left) Babe as a babe, 1892.

(above right) Boyhood, 1897.

(opposite) Babe as a sly servant girl, next to a Vim camera, 1916.

With handlebar moustache, standing behind the bench. In front,
Ethel Burton, Bobby Burns and Walter Stull. Vim Comedies.

On Pablo Beach, Jacksonville, with a bevy of Vim ladies and friend.
January 1917.

Babe and his first wife, Madelyn Saloshin. They called the pup Babe Jr.

Babe and co-star Kate Price outside the Vim Comedies office, Riverside Drive, Jacksonville.

The second Mrs Hardy, Myrtle Lee Reeves, in her days as a film actress, around 1920.

Larry Semon, in stripes, being hustled away in the film *The Perfect Clown,* 1925. Babe is wearing a derby and spit-curl bangs, prefiguring Ollie.

(bottom left) Babe, on his way to golf, kisses Myrtle goodbye in front of their home, 1719 Talmadge, Hollywood, 1924.

(bottom right) He could be very handsome, too. 1925.

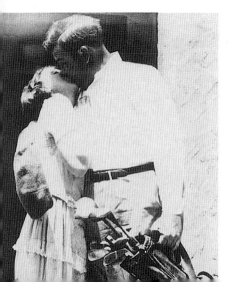

Looking mighty villainous in *No Man's Law,* a 1927 Roach western shot in Moapa, Nevada.

Life at its best – on the golf course. Babe, Our Gang's Bob McGowan, Jim Findlayson and Leo McCarey.

Herbert Rawlinson tells the butler to throw the rogue out. *Slipping Wives,* 1927. The fourth Laurel and Hardy film.

James Findlayson, 'Tiny' Sandford, Stan and Ollie in their classic, *Big Business,* 1929.

STAN LAUREL,
1111 FRANKLIN ST,
SANTA MONICA, CALIF.
U.S.A.

March 20th.'56.

Dear Jack:-

Thanks yours 15th.inst.
I was astounded to hear re Cohan's demands,just can't get over it.I
certainly do'nt blame you for getting burned up,I feel plenty sore
about it too,he sure has a lot of gall.Am sorry I suggested contacting
him now,but of course I was under the impression he was a great friend
of Babe's for many years,& would be happy to give us a couple of
incidents etc.However,we can get along without his information & am
sure he knows what to do with his stills.

I think you misunderstood my suggestion re renting a 16mm camera,I
said that I have a 16mm sound projector & we could probably rent some
of the old films & run them at home here - anyway,we can discuss it
when you arrive.

Frankly,I do'nt know if there are any prints around of the films
you mention "Putting Pants On Philip" & "Battle Of The Century"but am
sure I can give you all details on them you will need,I remember them
quite well as they were our first two pictures,I recall the stories,
most of the caste & directors etc.incidently,Leo McCarey directed
"Pants"& Clyde Bruckman "Battle" - poor Clyde committed suicide a couple
of years ago (shot himself in a cafe in Santa Monica)he might have
come across an old print of "Battle" & had just run it again! poor guy,
he came to see me a few months before this,he was directing Buster
Keaton in some TV shorts at the time & was trying to get us to make
a series to alternate with Buster.

Well,all for now Jack.We are very much looking forward to seeing you
again, imagine you will be flying out to save travel time.
Eda joins in kindest regards & good wishes - trust your Mother
is feeling much better again & allswell with you.

As ever:-

Stan Laurel's letter to John McCabe that identifies *Putting Pants
on Phillip* as Laurel and Hardy's first film as a team. (In 1956, Joe
Cohan, co-worker of Babe's at Vim, refused to talk to anyone about
Babe unless well paid to do so.)

Montgomery, and they were a successful comedy team for Vitagraph until Larry Semon's popularity eclipsed theirs.

After his 1924 stint with Roach, Stan was hard up for money, even to the desperate extent of using cardboard to cover the holes in his shoes, an incident he was to use twice in films of his later years. Rock regarded Stan as the brightest young comic around, and he offered him a five-year contract at a good salary, plus fifteen per cent of the profit from the twelve films they initially planned. Stan was delighted.

He was not so delighted at the nagging of his partner, Mae, who insisted she be given roles in the Rock films on the grounds that she and Stan had been a two-act since 1916. Rock disliked Mae for two reasons: he found her unfunny, he found her vulgar as a performer. He came to Stan's rescue. Sensing that Mae would not be adverse to seeing her native Australia again, he bought her a one-way steamship ticket and gave her a thousand dollars as heart balm. The day Mae sailed, Rock arranged for Stan to meet an attractive Vitagraph actress, Lois Neilson, who became Stan's first wife a year and a half later.

Stan worked enthusiastically on the Rock comedies. The films were greatly advantaged by Rock's being allowed, for a reasonable fee, to use all the sets at Universal when they were not occupied. Rock, a man much concerned with quality at almost any price, had worked previously with Babe, and it seemed to him in planning the new series – to be called the Stan Laurel Comedies – that Babe would be the perfect foil for Stan, as he had been for Semon.

Stan would have none of it.

He not only knew Babe's abilities from their work together in *The Lucky Dog*, but he had seen him in a few Semon films. Stan recognized Babe's natural propensity for inadvertent scene-stealing, and this he regarded as threatening. Rock pointed out quite accurately to Stan that laughs were laughs, and that they could only help buttress the films overall. Stan wasn't much interested in overall, and he told Rock that Babe, a heavy, was not a heavy when he started to get laughs. He was then a comic. Rock argued with Stan but found him adamant. The irony of Stan's fear of Babe's comedic strengths is that in less than five years Stan would be searching for ways to expand those strengths.

The Joe Rock–Stan Laurel Comedies were unqualified successes. Rock was very pleased at Stan's sense of thoroughness in his work. Stan took infinite pains, sometimes physically, to bring the shorts to perfection. He spent long sessions with the director, acting as his own gag man, willing to spend many hours before and behind the camera to get a laugh just so.

Meanwhile, between films with Semon, then in the last throes of his career, Babe made a few films with Bobby Ray, a talented comic who might have become his comfortable partner in a comedy team. In a 1925 two-reeler, *Stick Around*, Ray, physically a small man, played Babe's helper. They were paperhangers, Babe as boss, Ray as helper and fall guy. Babe always regarded *Stick Around* as another precursor of Laurel and Hardy, and it was in this film that Babe developed the comedic habit that was to do him such valiant service in his days with Stan – looking directly at the camera to express a variety of emotions. Taking the film audience into one's confidence this way is something like the old theatrical aside whereby the actor speaks in direct confidence to his auditors.

Shortly after *Stick Around*, Babe and Bobby Ray made *Hop To It*, a direct steal from Semon's 1921 two-reeler, *The Bellhop*, in which Babe played the larcenous hotel manager. In *Hop To It*, he has been demoted to bellhop, albeit the chief bellhop, but the film (made by a quickie outfit, Arrow Pictures) is in vivid contrast to the Semon original. *In Hop To It*, Babe is nothing more than a bully, and one has no time to reflect even on that, so feverishly forced is the tempo. Films like this made Babe glad he was Larry Semon's friend.

Stan meanwhile was working hard on the twelve Joe Rock two-reelers, beginning the spring of 1924, averaging one every three weeks, considerably ahead of schedule. The director of the films was a Rock employee, Percy Pembroke, and for a time Stan was a house guest of Pembroke and his wife. For reasons unknown, perhaps jealousy, Pembroke told Stan that the portion of his contract with Rock guaranteeing him fifteen per cent of the films' gross would never be honoured. Stan tended not to believe this because he knew Rock was a thoroughly honourable man, but Pembroke's 'information' came at a time when Roach had approached Stan about coming to work for him. Stan took Pembroke's word at face value.

Still a warm friend and trying to spare bad feelings, Stan told Rock he wanted to go back to vaudeville, and that Hollywood was out. The world of film comedy was then very small and Rock soon knew that Stan was talking with Roach. To protect his investment, Rock asked Stan to put in writing his assurance that he was not going to make any more films in their contract time. Stan did so, and went directly over to Roach – but not to perform. He was deathly tired of vaudeville by now; he wanted to fashion gags and direct for Roach. His taking the job with Roach was breach of contract with Rock who, with typical generosity did not throw any legal blocks at his buddy Stan when he went to Culver City. Stan began his duties at Roach Studios in May 1925. He was sure he would never perform again, this conviction abetted by Roach's telling him that his blue eyes did not photograph well.

Stan then had the pleasure of directing Babe in a 1925 one-reeler, *Yes, Yes, Nanette!*, starring the ineffable Jimmy Finlayson. Beetle-browed Finlayson was to become Babe Hardy's own comic foil in years to come. Babe was now being sought by a number of studios.

If his career was on the upsurge, Babe's financial condition was not. Shortly after arriving in California, the gambling bug had bitten him. Hard. He had no such temptations in Florida because there he was mostly impecunious and there were no handy race tracks. The opposite prevailed in California where, once his career began to flower, he followed the horses and sought out gambling casinos. He loved horses of any kind and envied people who owned them. Early on in his Hollywood years Babe and his friend, Charlie Lamont, together with Mrs Lamont, an Atlanta girl, got in the habit of going to Caliente every weekend to play the horses and the roulette wheels.

At first Babe's gambling was temperate. Then, perhaps as relief from his wife's growing dipsomania, he spent more and more time at the races. By 1926 most of his money was dissipated this way. He had by then become very friendly with Joe Rock, a man of generous spirit, who was always good for a sizeable loan. He and Babe became golf partners and would take frequent weekend trips to Ensenada, Mexico, where a hotel owned by Joe Schenck became headquarters for the betting gentry. Rock, who was well known not only as a performer for Vitagraph but as an independent comedy producer, had unlimited credit at Schenck's and similar places. He enjoyed gambling but did so moderately. Babe began to let it get out of hand.

In desperation he finally came to Rock and said that he needed cash badly, that he was unable to meet even rent and car payments. He was broke, and he was scared of being broke. Rock calmed him, gave him cheques in full for rent and car payments, and supplied him with $300 for immediate living expenses. Shamefaced, Babe took it all and resolved to do better. But he found it terribly difficult to stay away from gambling halls, and repayment to Rock was sporadic, and this mostly in the form of five dollar bills given to Joe's brother, Murray, for handing over. Babe was too ashamed to face his benefactor.

With typical directness, and showing a practical sense of charity, Joe went to Babe and said, 'Babe, look. You're not doing so well. Forget about the money. Just get yourself straightened out.' Rock refused further payments, and the lively golf games they had shared for months went on as before.

Rock found it easy to forgive Babe's debts because he saw in his friend a sensitive compassion for those in need. This was amusingly demonstrated in their golf. When Rock and Babe played against comparative duffers, Babe, who consistently played in the low 70s, could never bring himself to play at full skill. There was an understanding between the two friends that they would never play for money, only for beers.

If Babe's opponent was a particularly inept player and seemed thereby in need of psychological uplift, Babe would lose deliberately. He only opened up full range competitively to good players like Rock. When Babe's skills were so naturally strong that he could not choose but win, and a heavy beer pay-off had to be made by the loser, Babe would let him pay for only the first round.

By 1926 Myrtle Hardy had begun what was to be a long battle with alcohol. Babe was deeply moved by her attempts to stay sober, and for long periods she was. In a very meaningful way she became his errant daughter, and this carried over into their speech. She called him 'Daddy', and he used child-like diminutives in reply to her, usually 'Baby'. Myrtle was indeed a good-hearted and pleasant girl, devoted to her husband, but even the slightest nip of Scotch would send her off on a modest tear. These became less modest as the years went on.

In counterpoint, as this problem grew, Babe's professional life reached its most rewarding stages.

On February 6, 1926, he signed a long-term contract with Hal Roach. In carrying this news, the *Los Angeles Times* also noted that Babe would 'play various types of supporting roles in Charley Chase and Mabel Normand comedies and feature roles in the All-Star series, with the prospect eventually of being featured in his own right'.

This last prospect was closer than anyone, and especially Babe, realized.

4

Roach

If anyone writes a history of Hal Roach Studios – and it surely is waiting in the wings – it could well be described by reversing the phrase about policemen in *The Pirates of Penzance* to 'happy lot'. Those who worked there in fact called it 'the lot of fun'. For so it was, both in ambience and product. Stan Laurel said:

> When I got to the Roach lot in 1925 to write and direct, I hadn't been there more than two or three weeks before I realized this was the place for me. Without knowing until it actually happened, I was where I always wanted to be. I liked Hal. I liked Dick Jones who supervised production, and who taught me how to put a movie together, I liked all the technicians, I liked all the performers. They knew their business and I learned from everyone. There just wasn't a nicer job in the world than getting together with a great bunch of people and working your whole day so you could make people laugh, thousands of people to laugh. I used to love going there every morning, and at night I always hated to leave.

Babe felt the same except for the bit about leaving at night. Mid-afternoon during his years at Roach he would usually get a little tense trying to guess if he had time after work to play eighteen holes of golf at his club. Or a minimum of nine. A day without nine was a wasted day for him.

The Roach lot in 1926 offered ample opportunities for one of Babe's inherent versatility. He acted – mostly as comedy foil – with several performers Roach thought might turn into leading comics – Finlayson, Clyde Cook ('The Kangaroo Boy'), a small, athletic, sharp-nosed Australian who became Hollywood's archetypal cockney in scores of films in the 1930s; Snub Pollard, another Australian, who left Roach to start in his own films, failed, and returned to the kind of roles Cook did; and Glenn Tryon, a handsome light comedian who became a director for Roach. Babe more than held his own with these in Roach two-reelers. He also had the challenge of acting with several former leading Hollywood lights in what was called the Roach All Star Series, a catch-all name for a number of two-reelers featuring stars on the downgrade (like Mabel Normand and Theda Bara), and putative stars on the upgrade, like all the other actors in the studio. In theory the All Star films were so designated because the players all deserved top billing.

F. Richard 'Dick' Jones was the man in charge of production. His talent for talent, his ability to spot the right man or woman for the right job, was never better proven than in his choice for the All Star Series supervisor, Leo McCarey, the man who created Laurel and Hardy.

McCarey was relentless in his search for laughter. He believed laughter should always come, or at least mostly come, from some human well-spring, and that it should be savoured rather than merely enjoyed for the moment. He built comedy to last. Larry Semon, for instance, was not his kind of comic. McCarey said:

I enjoyed Semon – up to a point. I was greatly taken with many of his gags because they were usually original, and he pursued those gags with thoroughness. But after a while, they palled. You laughed at the unusualness of the way real skill went into executing them, but just like that cliché about Chinese food, a half hour later – nothing. There was nothing there in retrospect. I always wanted to do comedy that people would *remember*. With Laurel and Hardy I was able to do that. Wonderful men, Stan and Babe. How lucky we were to have them.

As was once observed in a sentence Stan learned to repeat as short response to the inevitable and frequent question asked him, 'How did you two get together?', Laurel and Hardy were joined by accident and grew by indirection.

The accident occurred in the summer of 1926. On a Friday Babe was preparing the evening meal as he had been doing all that week. Myrtle was in bed, quite sober, where she had been for several days with torn ligaments of the right leg. She had been visiting a friend in Laurel Canyon, and there, in a path leading to the friend's house, she saw before her a rattlesnake coiled to strike. These were not infrequent visitors to the Canyon. Terrified, Myrtle screamed, turned quickly and ran, falling several times as she fled from the snake. Her injuries were painful, and Babe, without strain, became their cook for the week.

On this Friday, in taking a leg of lamb from the oven, the folded towel serving as protective pad for his right hand was inadequate, and as he adjusted it on the handle, it slipped and his palm was burned. He dropped the entire pan and the hot juices spilled on his arm, causing terrible pain. Not wanting to disturb Myrtle, he delayed his shout of agony until he got outside the kitchen door. Here he fell, turning his leg sharply, bruising it. 'It was really,' he recalled later, 'an unfunny Laurel and Hardy catastrophe.' He was hospitalized.

The following Monday Babe was due to begin work in an All Star picture, *Get 'Em Young*, featuring Harry Meyers, one of the Roach fading stars who later found a degree of screen immortality as the drunken millionaire in Chaplin's *City Lights*. Dick Jones tried to find a substitute for Babe over the weekend, to no avail. He talked with Stan, who was to direct *Get 'Em Young*, and asked him to play the role, that of a timid butler. Stan declined, saying that he was now a writer/director and had absolutely no wish to get in front of a camera again. Jones explained he was the only one available to do it; Roach gave Stan a hefty raise in pay. Stan did it.

It was in *Get 'Em Young* that Stan inadvertently developed one of his key comic mannerisms, the cry, which he simply ad-libbed to extend the idea of the timidity of his character.

He never enjoyed doing it the rest of his career but it worked as a laugh-getter, and that for him was always the determinant of a gag's worth. This film convinced Dick Jones that Stan should continue as an actor, seeing in him a curious kind of comic vulnerability that boded well. He gave Stan another $100-raise, and told him he had a much fuller future as a performer than he realized. Stan was not convinced but one thing persuaded him that acting was to be borne for a while – his marriage. He could use the money. He married Lois Neilson in August 1926, and the following week began work on his first Roach film with Babe, *45 Minutes From Hollywood*. 'With' Babe in a very reserved sense.

Babe had great fun on the Roach lot, by the summer of 1926 having appeared with every actor there, including Our Gang. Of all the Roach actors he had a special fondness for Charley Chase, from whom he learned much. It was one of life's mysteries, Babe always claimed, that such a wonderful actor, writer, director, musician and all-round creative talent as Chase never became a top star. 'I don't mean later,' Babe said, 'when I'd see him at a studio party pretending he was just drinking Coke and you knew half of it was gin. Leo McCarey himself was the first to say Charley taught him basically everything he knew about making comedy pictures.'

A month after his encounter with leg of lamb, Babe was back at work. In *45 Minutes From Hollywood*, a Glenn Tryon firm, the Hollywood in the title derives from the hero and his family visiting Los Angeles to sightsee such Roach stars as Our Gang and Theda Bara. In the film, Babe plays a hotel detective with a fondness for dunking himself in a bathtub. Stan, inexplicably made up in moustache and bald head, is an unemployed actor living at the hotel.

He and Babe do not meet at all in the picture. The closest they come to it is when Babe and two cohorts try to break down Stan's door, but by accident break down the door opposite his. As a Laurel and Hardy picture, this rather fails to meet that designation, but then it was not so designated. Nor was their next film, which might best be called the Laurel and Hardy picture made before there were Laurel and Hardy.

Duck Soup is already primal if somewhat crude Laurel and Hardy, with the two appearing almost full-blown as a team. Here, it seems, are Stan and Ollie as ever were, or soon to be — the looming, dominant Hardy, and ingrained with delicate courtesy, opposite slight, simpleton Stan.

The story — two vagrants fleeing the law and finding refuge in a millionaire's mansion during his absence — derived from *Home From the Honeymoon*, a sketch written in 1908 by Stan's dad, A J Jefferson. Stan indeed had played in the sketch under his father's direction in England. In *Duck Soup* Stan has more footage than Babe but they are manifestly a duo, following the general structure of the Jefferson sketch. This teaming was done rather casually and purely on a one-shot basis. In a planning session for the picture, Stan, who was always an integral part of these proceedings at Roach, offered the plot of his father's sketch and it was accepted with enthusiasm.

Roach, then on his way to New York for a meeting, told Stan to write the script. It was the unanimous opinion of all the gag writers that Stan should play the role of the leading vagrant. Syd Crossley, a Roach contract player from England (and soon to return there), was to be his fellow tramp. Shooting was almost about to begin when Dick Jones substituted Babe for Crossley. This was done on the plainly pragmatic grounds that he considered Babe the more versatile actor of the two.

In *Duck Soup* the two tramps — fleeing a forest ranger trying to draft them as fire-fighters — find a vacant mansion and take up residence. Colonel Blood, the owner, has gone hunting to Africa, and the new tenants settle in comfortably, Babe the very picture of dilapidated gentry — elegantly scruffy and sporting a bedraggled top hat. Then a young married couple with ample means arrives to rent the mansion, and Babe and Stan assume the guise of the house's owner and his servant. Babe becomes the lordly *seigneur*, with incongruous five-day stubble on his cheeks, and Stan is the giddy, somewhat rickety maid. They are at the height of their masquerade when the real owner returns and the tramps flee.

The question had been asked, since even in unpolished form, the Stan and Ollie we all know appeared in almost the first film Stan and Babe made at Roach, why did they not so continue? Why, the question persists, did the Studio directly after *Duck Soup* cast Stan and Babe, unteamed, in eight other films — and in wildly heterogeneous roles — before returning them to the original mix of Stan and Ollie? The answers are easily given.

First, and obviously, no one thought of them as *our* Stan and Ollie because *Duck Soup* showed them only in rudimentary genesis, and seeing them this way initially, rather than with the advantage of hindsight, would not particularly lead anyone to regard them as unique comic treasures. They were playing a couple of bums, and very well too, but a team of bums was not likely to excite much artistic interest in the higher echelons of Roach. And even if they had, affirmative answer would have to come in from the box office showing public approval before such a liaison could possibly be effected. As ultimately proved to be the case. Too, *Duck Soup* was simply one comedy of a number already lined up in pre-production on a long and well-established schedule of shooting. Finally, the studio did not at once team Stan and Babe despite their manifestly harmonious appearance in *Duck Soup* because the All Star concept needed fuller testing and ventilation. It could not be abandoned before being fully tried, and it had not yet exhausted its possibilities as a structure of entertainment.*

So it was that nine months would pass after *Duck Soup* was finished and shooting began on the first film to be organically a Laurel and Hardy picture, *The Second Hundred Years*.

In this interim the growth of Stan and Ollie had begun — principally by indirection and use of a sensible ground rule that McCarey always followed: if a gag gets a good laugh — a laugh rooted in something basically human — keep it, nurture it.

---

*In his 1957 interview with Arthur Friedman, Stan said of the All Star series: '. . . [The Studio] ran out of stars, and finally we just kept making comedies with Laurel and Hardy in them until finally Roach decided to make them Laurel and Hardy comedies.'

After *Duck Soup* was finished, Leo McCarey became more actively Stan and Babe's champion, particularly after Dick Jones left Roach late in 1927. Speaking of Jones, McCarey said:

Jones saw Stan's great potential as a performer, and by 1927 Stan was reconciled to being a comic, although he never gave up his function as gag man. That's the year when I came into the story. When I contributed to the gag and story sessions of the Comedy All Stars, I commented from time to time on the particular suitability of Hardy as Stan's comic foil. They seemed to fit together so well, I said—not only because they were such contrasting figures but also because they had this solid instinct that top-flight comics all have of the *reality* underlying a gag. They were both superb actors, of course, and could have played the classics quite easily, although such a thing would never have occurred to them. I encouraged their getting larger parts in the films. Gradually their parts grew larger and the parts of the other players grew smaller. This was the evolution of the team of Laurel and Hardy.

If Dick Jones first recognized the potential of Stan and Babe as a team, and Leo McCarey developed their unique identity, it was Stan who first gave to Babe and himself the attributes of invincible dumbness, unconsciously patterning the two of them on the dumb servants of old Roman comedy, a type brought to finest flower in some of Shakespeare's comics – Dogberry, Bottom and Sir Andrew Aguecheek. But there was, of course, something else, very warmly something else — the individual personalities of Stan and Babe that gave Stan and Ollie their ultimate quality, that totally indefinable attribute: charm.

After *Duck Soup*, Babe and Stan were cast in another All Star production, *Slipping Wives*, with the old cardboard lover plot so popular in French farce of the wife hiring a surrogate lover to make her inattentive husband jealous. Stan is the lover, about as likely a gigolo as Nanook of the North, and

Babe a haughty butler. They rarely have a scene together. If *Slipping Wives* was slight, it looked like a redaction of *Private Lives* compared to the next pictures the boys (as Leo McCarey always called Laurel and Hardy) were thrust into. *Love 'Em and Weep* involves a married man blackmailed by an old love who shows up at his home, leaving tension and embarrassment in her wake. Stan and Babe are not only not teamed but it looks as if director Fred Guiol said ten minutes before the first shot, 'Hey, Babe has to have a part in this somewhere.' So, for who knows what reason, Babe appears, artistically suppressed by bushy sideburns, glasses, large moustache, and the fact that he is called on only to sit around and look at people. Even one with Babe's genius for reacting can hardly create anything out of nothing. Principally, he gapes. Stan, as friend of the woman-plagued leading man (Finlayson), is also mostly an onlooker. He cries a lot. Not much for the boys here.

Their next, *Why Girls Love Sailors*, is at base a Stan Laurel comedy, much in the tradition of his earlier ones with Joe Rock and others, in which he is snappily ebullient, and does an inordinate amount of running around. In this case he does so in order to rescue his kidnapped fiancée from a tough sea captain and his mangy crew aboard a dubious vessel. Stan accomplishes this by posing, convincingly, as a pretty and winsomely flirtatious girl. Babe, as second mate of the ship, has a minor role and he needs only to look tough, which he does splendidly.

In their next, *With Love and Hisses,* Stan and Babe get a trifle closer to their final screen selves. Babe is dominant, unpleasantly so, as a rowdy, nasty sergeant; Stan is a not-very-bright but epicene private. Essentially they are playing the film roles of their pre-Roach days — Babe the heavy, and Stan the aggressively silly dolt. The plot line is of the kind found in most army training camp comedies, with just enough gags to evoke a thin smile. The film following, *Sailor Beware!*, shows yet again little partnership for Stan and Babe. The latter is a flirtatious ship's steward; Stan is a dim-bulb cab driver-turned-steward.

The level of reality in *Sailor Beware!* is attested to by its principal plot line; a glamorous lady jewel thief and her midget husband, masquerading as a baby, try to con other passengers on a cruise liner. Yet this film contains a significant Laurel and Hardy device that was to grow into one of Babe's key mannerisms. At one point he is doused by a pail of water and he looks into the camera, fluttering his fingers embarrassedly. In later films he would compound this by twiddling his tie. Babe had looked reactively into the camera in pre-Roach days but here for the first time he does it in tandem with self-conscious fluster. It was done spontaneously. Although expecting the pail of water in his face, it threw him for a moment and not remembering what he should do, he waved his fingers.

Despite this development of a device that was to serve Babe well all his film life — and Stan himself does a few camera looks in the film while crying — this is not yet Stan and Ollie.

They are almost born, however, in the next All Star film, *Do Detectives Think?* Cast as detective partners, they display invincible ignorance in everything they do. More significantly in respect to their Stan and Ollie growth, they now sport derbies — as film detectives of that era invariably did. Moreover, for the first time anywhere, they do what would become their staple hat mix-up. Bareheaded, Stan picks up both their derbies, and hands one to Babe, who puts it on. It is of course Stan's and Babe sweeps it off his head angrily, hands it back, and Stan, eternally confused, hands the same hat back, and Babe is once more discomfited, the whole thing occurring all over again.

This kind of repetition simply would not work in the hands of anyone less skilled than Babe, who structures his rising anger so that it becomes a seamless natural progression. This is acting, not simply the execution of a gag.

Their next film, *Flying Elephants*, was one of a then standard comedy film genre, the Stone Age Farce, and Stan and Babe as two primordial rivals for a girl's hand do not actually meet until the end of the film. A goat conveniently bumps Babe off a cliff and Stan gets the girl. Next in the All Star series was *Sugar Daddies* in which Stan and Babe support Jimmy Finlayson again, here a dyspeptic roué, who employs both Babe as his amiable butler, and Stan as his lawyer (described in a title as one 'who went through medical college and came out a lawyer'). Finlayson has married an unlovely schemer when drunk, and the boys spirit him away to a fun house to evade the graceless bride. The film seems mainly an excuse to get comic footage from the fun house, a real one, Pike Park in Long Beach.

Up to this point in their Roach career – May 1927 – the All Star films featuring Stan and Babe had been released by Pathé, but Hal Roach now concluded a profitable deal with Metro-Goldwyn-Mayer to take all his output. In the Pathé releases, even under the All Star label, Stan alone was billed as the featured player. Now the MGM–Roach All Star Comedies were giving star billing to Stan and Babe together. Leo McCarey and Roach made that decision, and it was in the next All Star film that Leo McCarey made a commitment to himself that the boys would not only be stars but would indeed become the principal adornments of the Roach lot.

The Second Hundred Years marked a giant step forward in the creation of Stan and Ollie. They are not yet, however, using their real names in the films. In every All Star film up to this time they sported comic strip names like Ferdinand Finkelberry and Sherlock Pinkham, and this continues in *The Second Hundred Years*. But in the choice of character names for this film Stan added a refinement that specifically intensified the robust dumbness of their evolving characters. At a gag session for the film, he suggested that he be called Little Goofy, Babe by implication to be Big Goofy. Stan now looked for all kinds of ways to make themselves substantively dumb.

'By dumb,' he said to McCarey, 'I mean I think we should be *dumb* dumb.' Stan and Babe had both played ignoramuses in earlier films but henceforth, Stan suggested, they should be forthrightly, immeasurably, definitively dumb. McCarey was pleased. The concept fitted in perfectly with his plans for the boys. A man always well ahead of his time, he had found the push-push, frenetic pace of most film comedy rather boring. With Laurel and Hardy as eternal and profound dimwits, he saw that their natural and untainted ignorance would provide not only the rationale for slower pacing in comedy film but also the base for comic exploitation of it. He made their pace in subsequent films leisurely, a total innovation at the time.

Much comedy, at least in climactic scenes, was then shot at twelve frames per second. This slow cranking speeded up the action. McCarey with Stan and Babe began to shoot at fifteen or sixteen frames per second, what he called 'normal speed'. With this naturalness there was a consequent lack of need to pack the plot with incident. At last one could savour the gags, thereby getting the most out of them. One could 'see' more of the comedy.

In *The Second Hundred Years*, the boys are convicts, and they look like convicts. It was suggested in gag session, again by Stan, that they both get butch haircuts. The film takes them from prison escape to disguises — first, as house painters, then as visiting French penologists — and ultimate return to jail. The highpoint of the film is a McCarey-inspired gag, their odyssey in disguise as painters just outside the prison gates where, with paint buckets and brushes in hand, the boys whitewash everything in sight. This includes the street, a car at the kerb and a pretty girl's posterior.

What now appears in this film, and it is for the first time, is a sense of their inevitability as a team. After this one, who else could they be but Stan and Ollie, or something very close to? In everything that had gone before, they either performed well in ensemble or they had worked essentially as singles. In *The Second Hundred Years* they at last look not only very much together but as if they belonged together.

Yet Stan at this time was not thinking of himself as part of any team. He was glad of the extra money that performing brought him but he still hoped for permanent posting as a director and writer. Babe, on the other hand, now thought of himself as half of a whole. He felt the chemistry between them as they performed.

After *The Second Hundred Years* and their next film, *Call of the Cuckoos*, in which they did very brief cameo roles, Babe took Myrtle to Cuba in July 1927 for a long-delayed second honeymoon. They were both on their best behaviour, he mostly ignoring the tempting roulette wheels, she taking only Spartan sips in the way of drink. During the trip he told her fervently that he hoped the liaison with Stan would become permanent, conceding that Stan very much wanted to remain a director. When Babe returned to the studio he put the question directly to McCarey. Would Laurel and Hardy become a team? McCarey said directly that he did not know, but that he was going to do his damnedest to see that they did. He was as good as his word.

In writing their next film, *Hats Off*, McCarey took a personal experience and unknowingly built it permanently into the entity that was now becoming Stan and Ollie. Early in 1927, while preparing for a night on the town in New York, McCarey got into his formal attire only to find great difficulty in getting his black tie properly adjusted. Someone in his family had always tied it for him, but this night, alone in his hotel room, he had the devil's own job trying to get the sides even. After great effort, he got the tie in middling order and joined a group of friends at a party.

The life of that party, as always with any party she joined, was Mabel Normand. McCarey arrived a bit late and explained the reason for his delay. 'I don't know how to tie these damned things,' he said, touching his tie. 'But I finally got it together after about an hour of hard work.' It was a triumphant boast. Mabel looked at him sympathetically, walked over and pulled the tie apart. Loud laughter from everyone, and a very unhappy McCarey.

If that was the kind of fun they wanted, he was ready. He reached across to the black tie of a friend and tugged it open. That man did the same to another, and tie snapping became the game of the moment until all the men were undone.

Thus began McCarey's tit-for-tat gag that was to become a living part of the Laurel and Hardy infrastructure. A wide variety of changes would be rung on this simple concept,

ranging from mild personal retaliation to reciprocal destruction of an automobile and a house. In *Hats Off*, no longer
extant but retrievable through a preserved cutting continuity,
one finds tit-for-tat in well-shaped order. Made not long after
Babe returned from Cuba, this film shows Stan and Ollie just
about to be. For one thing, they are playing without character
names, using simply their own, a custom that in the days of
sound would grow into Ollie's frequent introduction, 'I am
Mr Hardy, and this is my friend, Mr Laurel.' Using their own
names in films was in any case a quick form of insurance.
No one could ever steal their real names from them whereas
fictional identities usually belonged to the studios.

Hats Off also saw the birth of perhaps Stan's most effective
comedy mannerism, his scratching hair pull. After getting the
convict crew cut in *The Second Hundred Years*, Stan let his
hair grow. One day on the lot he took his hat, and instinctively
brushed his hair back. Not fully grown in again, it persisted
in standing on end, and both Babe and the crew standing by
laughed at his ludicrous appearance. Knowing a good thing
when he saw it, Stan realized he had just created a natural
fright wig, and he insured this thereafter by scratching his
head and pulling up his hair simultaneously.

But it is the tit-for-tat device in *Hats Off* that remains the
most memorable segment of the picture. The boys have one of
their hat mix-ups and angrily kick each other's derbies down
the street. This grows to knocking off each other's hats, in
turn spreading to the knocking off of *others'* hats, and then
into an orgy of hat knocking, with a policeman finally caught
up in a giant free-for-all. Police reserves arrive to drive all the
combatants away — all, that is, except Stan and Ollie, who
now both for the last, almost uncountable time, put on the
wrong hats.

This, told, seems repetitive repetitiveness, but done on the
screen in varying nuances is cumulatively hilarious, and the
public said so at the time. One Los Angeles film house
found *Hats Off* such a powerful attraction they billed it
over the feature attraction. The film had an enthusiastic
press, and the public flocked to it. Now and only now,

could the Roach studios see clearly what it had in this new team.

More importantly, *Hats Off* triggered something vital — Stan's realization that Babe Hardy was not only his other half artistically, but a half worthy of great admiration. Unlike other Roach comics — the very funny but strictly one-dimensional Jimmy Finlayson comes to mind — Babe was a performer of deep and stylish dimension. Babe had brought to the Roach lot his own unique creative authority. Stan realized this. Hal Roach said of Babe later:

> The gestures that Hardy did were *his*. The tie, his looking into the camera, and the way he did things individually, nobody told him. I never heard anybody, including Laurel, direct him in anything. You didn't have to tell Hardy what to do; he was a hell of a good actor.

Stan, coming to some self-accounting in the autumn of 1927, made a twofold decision. He relinquished his plan to become a Roach writer/director, and he committed himself again to performing. He had come to know that, after all, he was blessed with a fellow comic his unique and complementary equal. Listening to audiences laughing uproariously at *Hats Off* told him that. 'I never heard laughs — so many laughs — in so short a time before,' he said. As for Babe, he also knew, in some indefinable but indelible way, that he had come home.

5

Silent

One summer afternoon in 1927 Babe was feeling poorly, and since there was no urgent need for him at the studio that day, he went home early, shortly after lunch. As he entered the living room he saw Myrtle sitting on the overstuffed chair that was his favourite place of repose, her feet up on the square footstool before it. His heart fell. Whenever Myrtle sat in that chair, she had been drinking, and for her to be there so early in the afternoon meant that she most likely had been hitting the bottle that morning.

He stopped, looked at her, and lifted his hands in a gesture of despair. She leaped up to say she was entirely sober, and fell across the footstool to the floor. He helped her up and she went into his arms, weeping. Babe knelt, put her down on the footstool, and asked her what they were going to do about all this. 'I don't know, daddy,' she said. 'I surely don't know.'

There were some avenues of approach he could take to have Myrtle use her time more profitably. That, after all, was the crux of her drinking problem — what to do with her time. Babe at this point in his career did not want children, and he thought Myrtle felt the same way about it. They had not even talked about that — symptomatic of a defect in their marriage. She was an actress, and perhaps a job or two occasionally would give her satisfaction. But Babe regarded two film careers in a marriage as potentially divisive. He had seen it happen frequently. And how does a woman go into the picture business to carve out half or quarter of a career?

He told her gently that she was in need of professional help for her drinking, a thing he had previously suggested.

It was a subject that had deeply distressed her when he mentioned it previously, as it did now. She rose unsteadily and wept uncontrollably. Babe put his arms around her and she began to kiss him fervently, over and over. Alcohol on a woman's breath was particularly repellent to him, and although he returned her kisses, he felt deep repugnance. For Babe, as he always asserted, was very much of the old school of Southern gentlemen. He had what he was proud to call a reverence for womanhood, and especially for Southern womanhood. One of the reasons he had been attracted to Myrtle — not an unusually attractive woman physically — was that in many ways she epitomized that womanhood.

Her accent was pure Atlantan, her tones genteel. Babe endorsed King Lear's praise: 'Her voice was ever soft, gentle and low — an excellent thing in woman.' More, Myrtle's manners were impeccable. For Babe Hardy, every woman he met was a lady until she proved herself otherwise, and if otherwise he could not wait to get out of her company. Here, at this moment, with his wife's whisky breath revolting him to his depths, he felt his life had taken a savagely adverse turn, and at just the moment his career had turned the corner to great success.

Yet he loved Myrtle very much, and he could not for the life of him imagine how all this would be. She was capable of sobriety for months. Then he would come home after a few hours at the golf club to find her in the big chair, frequently asleep, curled up in sodden condition. She had tried to play golf with him but found the game only mildly diverting.

On this particular day he told her to take a nap while he prepared dinner. She nodded.

'Daddy?'

'Yes, sugar.'

'I'm going to be a good girl.' Yes, but when will that be, and where will I be, he thought. She went dutifully off to bed and woke a few hours later to find dinner waiting for her.

It is something of a parlour game among Stan and Ollie buffs to select the 'first' Laurel and Hardy film. The clues are both several and contradictory, as is perhaps inevitable in defining an artistic entity that grew by indirection, very much by indirection. The simplest and most likely answer is that there is no 'first' Laurel and Hardy film. In the process of evolution definite progressions are rarely discernible, and this applied here. Babe and Stan appeared in thirty-three silent films together, thirty-two of them at Roach. That studio's records are not helpful in attempting to determine the first official Laurel and Hardy picture. The Roach press department at different times labelled films number 12 and 14 (*The Second Hundred Years* and *Hats Off*) as Babe and Stan's 'first starring vehicle', and studio records also show that film number 22, *Should Married Men Go Home?*, was the first in the newly labelled Laurel and Hardy series.

But let someone who was there identify Laurel and Hardy's first film — someone not only there, but one at the very heart of Laurel and Hardy. In a letter to this writer, Stan Laurel did not hesitate to identify the film he considered their first as a team — number 15, *Putting Pants on Philip*, the next in sequence after *Hats Off*. Paradoxically it is a film in which the characters Stan and Ollie do not appear.

The inspiration for *Putting Pants on Philip* came from an incident in the life of a friend of Stan's. Stan remembered:

> Years and years ago when I was with the Karno troupe, a chap called Alan I worked with told me of something that happened to him, and I never forgot it. I always thought it would make a good music hall sketch, and later when that didn't happen — I had been thinking of doing it myself on the halls — I got it made into *Putting Pants on Philip*. What happened to Alan was this. He lived in the south of England, Brighton or Worthing, one of those towns, and he had a cousin from Scotland he hadn't seen for many years. Hadn't seen him from boyhood, in fact. But they had corresponded all that time, and when Alan was grown, he invited his cousin down to see him, and the cousin accepted. This cousin, whose name was very Scottish, Angus or what the hell have you, arrived at Alan's, and Alan couldn't follow

a word he said because Angus was from a part of
Glasgow where even the average Scotsman could barely
understand the dialect. Alan planned to take him out to
dinner, and Angus got all dressed up in a pair of kilts, and
Alan damned near died of embarrassment. He had made
reservations at a fancy restaurant where he was sure kilts
wouldn't be looked on as just the proper thing to wear.
But they went anyway.

By that time Alan could half understand Angus's dialect, yet he had a hell of a time trying to translate to
the waiter what his cousin wanted from the menu. Alan
started to talk to his cousin in a sort of simple English
like you'd talk to a Hottentot who could only understand
a few words of what you said, and he unconsciously
started to talk in his loudest voice, and the waiter started
to talk loudly, and Angus thought the waiter was hard of
hearing, and *he* started to talk in *his* loudest voice, and
it all grew to be one hell of a mess. As a matter of fact, I
had close friends in Scotland, and it occurred to me after
I got into pictures that it would be fun to guess what one
of them, wearing kilts, might do if he visited me here in
California.

Stan took the central idea, but not the details, of this experience to a Roach gag session, and together with other writers,
crafted a delightful two-reeler.

Putting Pants on Philip begins at a dock where suave
Piedmont Mumblethunder — Babe, nattily attired in smart
three-piece suit and straw skimmer — is waiting for the
arrival from Scotland of Philip, a nephew he has never seen.
Piedmont has been told Philip is perfectly normal except when
pretty girls are around. Then he runs — toward them. Philip,
in the person of Stan in full Scottish regalia, comes from the
ship and makes several fools of himself at dockside, including
biting down on the thermometer during medical examination.
Piedmont laughs and comments via title, 'Imagine — some-
body has to meet *that*!' His discomfort on discovering Philip's
identity is formidable, and he bluntly tells his nephew to walk
behind him as they go down the street. 'Every man, woman

and child in this town knows me. You walk behind — stay behind.' (The town in the film is Culver City, site of Roach Studios.)

As Piedmont swings up the street, Philip follows until an attractive girl goes by and he runs after her, drawing a considerable crowd. After Piedmont catches him, Philip takes some snuff and his sneeze causes his prime undergarment to fall. By now the crowd has increased, enjoying itself very much, and Piedmont has to ask them to stop laughing at his ward. Philip keeps on chasing the girls, and Piedmont in high and low dudgeon chases Philip.

He finally gets Philip and sternly hustles him along. As Philip walks over a ventilator grill, his kilt flies up — we see only part of this — and two girls fainting at the sight make us aware that, as a nearby cop puts it, 'This dame ain't got no lingerie on.' Piedmont tells the policeman, 'I'll stop this, officer. I'm gonna put pants on Philip — right now!' They go to a tailor's shop. In trying to take measurements for Philip's inseam length, the tailor discovers Philip is morally offended by the procedure. Such a thing, he suggests, could never happen in Scotland. As Philip puts it tearfully, 'I never wore a set of pants in my life!'

As the battle to subdue Philip continues, Piedmont tells the tailor to guard the doors. Piedmont is determined to get that inseam length, and he chases Philip to an inner room for that purpose. We see nothing of that encounter, but moments later Piedmont enters triumphantly, saying, 'Thirty-three!' to the tailor. Philip, crying like a newly and unwillingly deflowered maiden, enters to add, 'The Bide-a-Wee Club shall hear of this!'

Out into the street, and in a long sequence Philip once again finds the girl he has been chasing, and upon seeing her trying to get across a muddy corner, rips off his kilt — he now has 'lingerie' on — and lays it down in the mud. 'Just an old Scottish custom,' he says gallantly, bowing low. She laughs, jumps over the kilt, and runs off. Piedmont observes, laughs, and as Philip bends over to pick up the kilt, stops him peremptorily. In the haughty you-after-me vein that was to characterize Ollie so frequently, Piedmont snaps Philip in the nose and says, 'Just an old American custom.' He steps on the kilt and crashes through into a large mud-hole.

As he glares in disgust at the camera, we foresee the quintessential Ollie subjected to yet another indignity heaped on him by his partner.

Thus the film Stan Laurel considered Laurel and Hardy's first. It was certainly the first film in which Stan *felt* them to be a team, the first for which he made the total personal commitment to have a partner, the first in which both men experienced at fullest the chemistry between them that was to last their lifetimes.

Babe's appearance in *Putting Pants on Philip* generated increased respect around the studio. He was already well-liked both personally and professionally, and in the latter category he was much sought after on the lot. After *Philip*, he appeared in *Love 'Em and Feed 'Em* (there appeared to be a prejudice against the word 'them' at Roach's) with Jewish comic Max Davidson, who had his own series, and with Our Gang in *Barnum and Ringling Inc.*, in which he appears as a drunk startled by the gang's pet ostrich. Charley Chase pressed him to appear in *The Lighter That Failed*, and he accommodated gladly. But it was everywhere increasingly clear that Laurel and Hardy would soon have time only for their own films. The Roach publicity office announced that those comic powerhouses, Laurel and Hardy, were the studio's new 'Cyclowns'. Oh, dear.

In September 1927 Babe and Stan began shooting what was to be from all reports of the time one of the funniest films they ever made. *The Battle of the Century* exists now only in decimated form but what remains amply verifies studio statistics that show preview audiences laughing at the rate of seven times a minute. That, it must be said, is one hell of a lot of laughter for a twenty minute film.

The Battle of the Century was built around the purchase by the studio of a complete day's output of the Los Angeles

Pie Company, whose truck appears in key scenes of the film. Stan, in deciding to make a pie picture to end all pie pictures, took the view that pie throwing before then had been pretty thin stuff comedically because it lacked some kind of rationale. If that last seems an unlikely word to yoke with pie-throwing, not at all. Stan had always thought pie throwing the sort of thing resorted to in desperation for a laugh. But using pies in some kind of motivated fashion, however tenuous, would (he said to the gag writers) give a good reason for laughter.

Babe agreed. His comedy work, however silly the roles, had always been grounded in truth. All his life he was fond of quoting Leo McCarey's dictum that the best comedy always had reality as a base: 'In your fundamentals, you've always got to be real — no matter how far-fetched you get — and I know that sounds like a contradiction. But it isn't.'

The Battle of the Century's climax, the pie fight, begins with the hoariest of gags: Stan slipping on a banana peel. But there is a *reason* for that peel being there, a very good reason. It is to serve as catalyst for what follows, a fight. Stan is Canvasback Clump, a gloriously inadequate pugilist, whom Babe, his manager, has insured in an accident policy. Seeing Stan slip on the peel, Babe is inspired to use the peel again and again in order to bring Stan to disaster. Each time he avoids it, fortuitously. Then a pie vendor comes out of a shop and steps on the peel set for Stan.

The vendor slips, confronts Babe, and from their little battle begins the larger one, a tit-for-tat sequence from Babe getting his pie in the face to everyone else on the street getting theirs. Four thousand pies were used. Real pies.

Near the end of *The Battle of the Century*, the camera rises on a dolly to reveal an entire city block — and over three score people — caught up in the mêlée. We are entranced by this Armageddon of pies, but we are not as joyful as its instigators, Laurel and Hardy, who finally stand outside the action, chortling at all they have wrought. A cop asks them if *they* started the pie fight. Babe asks, 'What pie fight?' The cop chases them down the street.

For the next six months after they had cleaned up the pies, months during which Babe and Stan did five good two-reelers, now fully in the Stan and Ollie mode, they were billed as stars of the films, although still under the All Stars Series banner. Then in March 1928, they shot *Should Married Men Go Home?* which was released under the new Laurel and Hardy Series classification. Babe and Stan quite came into their own. *Should Married Men Go Home?* also honoured Babe's avocation, golf, at his suggestion.

McCarey liked the idea and the film began shooting, but the usual gag-abundant Irishman came a cropper on this one. *Should Married Men Go Home?* has the boys involved with a burly golfer (Edgar Kennedy) at a mud hazard on the course, and there is much sloshing about in black goo. Had McCarey concentrated on the realistic problems of golfing, a more meaningful comedy would have resulted. As it is, the film is simply a set of adults playing with mud pies, and appealing to viewers on about that level of sophistication.

Golf was popular at the studio. Roach himself played and sponsored an annual studio tournament. The best player's cup was invariably won by Babe, and he treasured the honour. Stan played golf from time to time but his place of recreation was the studio. In the afternoon, when camera work would be winding down for the day, Babe would be getting anxious to be on his way to the golf club. Stan, on the other hand, would be fretting to stay just where he was and get on with the current creative task behind the camera: looking at the rushes, or joining the gag men's session or cutting film with editor Bert Jordan.

By 1928 Stan had become the unofficial director of all the Laurel and Hardy films, without in any way impinging on the various directors' functions. Since the gag sessions basically shaped the film, and the script was the result of such sessions, the director more or less knew where he was going. The 'less' occurred when Babe or Stan would get an inspiration on the set, sometimes together while the cameras were rolling, and add something to the action. Stan always placed emphasis on a rule of directness, 'no fuss' in production. Babe wore a straight make-up which he embellished with curled bangs along his forehead; Stan's make-up was lighter, not white, but light enough to serve as a clown base. Lighting of the set was always cheery. No chiarascuro here. Art Lloyd, the team's favourite cameraman, an excellent craftsman, felt frustration with such unvarying atmospherics, but Stan believed wholly in brightness as comedy's proper ambience.

Babe occasionally went to gag sessions but most of the time he was more than content to leave all artistic decisions about the team to Stan. 'After all,' he said, 'it's Stan's business.' On the very few occasions when Babe thought an artistic decision wrong, he tended not to bring the matter up, believing — as was almost always the case — that a poor gag or awkward line of dialogue would always show its worthlessness before the cameras, and be cut then.

Usually Babe and Stan did not socialize with each other. Outside of their talent, they shared very little, being quite different men with widely divergent interests. Stan was bone-deep show business, a born and bred communicant, in several senses, of laughter. Babe, in contrast, had wide interests if not particularly deep ones. Stan hung out only with people 'in the business', the article in that phrase showing its narrowness of scope. His closest friend was Charlie Rogers, his right hand man, an English expatriate and gag man at Roach. 'You'd think we'd get sick of gags,' said Rogers. 'But after a whole day's work on nothing but gags, we'd go out for a few drinks, and what the hell do you think we'd wind up doing? Talking about gags.'

Stan's other close friends were old pals from Karno and vaudeville days. Stan was born to make laughter. He was called to it as surely as some are called to the priesthood. Indeed, for him it was a priesthood, and he served it honourably all his adult life, and during part of his childhood as well. He lived wholly within the boundaries of his craft. It was a narrow if delightful world, and one sometimes not easy to inhabit when frustrations came.

This was not Babe's world. Unlike Stan, it would not have hurt him to be in another profession. He had a wider view of life than this partner. Babe moved easily among bank presidents, sales managers and golf pros. The golf club he belonged to occupied much of his time; it was emblematic of his approach to life. His widow said that his hobbies revealed more of him as a human being than this career did. 'I feel,' said Lucille Hardy, 'that he felt and believed deep down that his hobbies and outside interests were the real Oliver Hardy — and that his career was make-believe in every sense of the word.'

By early 1928 Babe thought Myrtle had settled down to being 'a good girl'. She had shown a tendency to go golfing with him more often, and although she was awkward, he was glad she thought of joining him. That was always a positive sign. On those occasions he would try to keep their stay in the clubhouse as brief as possible. People offered her drinks from private bottles, and that was dangerous.

In April 1928 Babe was invited to go for a week's vacation in Vancouver with Stan, Charley Chase, Jimmy Parrott (Charley's brother, and a Laurel and Hardy director), editor Dick Currier, Charlie Rogers and a few other Roach people. This was to be an auto tour, and Babe was very much looking forward to it, especially in view of the availability in Canada of legally purchased wines and liquors. Babe was never a heavy drinker but he enjoyed good liquor in the company of friends. Like most Southerners, he was a bourbon man, and he had been told Vancouver possessed ample supplies of virtually every potable whisky in the Western world.

The Vancouver trip was a great success. Freedom from the ludicrous Prohibition law of the United States was enough to make any comradely group giddy, and there was ample giddiness on the trip. As always, Babe was totally gregarious in the company of his peers, and on this trip he provided much of the entertainment by singing songs from his cabaret days. Stan was encouraged to do old English music hall favourites, ones he especially love, like 'Lily of Laguna', 'Down at the Old Bull and Bush', and 'Archibald! Certainly Not!' Babe had not realized before how deeply Stan loved music, and this became another bond between them. In later years they would commandeer the ample talents of Roach's head musician, Marvin Hatley — the man who wrote their theme song, 'The Dance of the Cuckoos' — to play old songs for them to sing between set-ups at the studio.

In returning to Los Angeles, Babe and Stan were exhilarated to realize that their series was receiving the major attention of Roach Studios. Now, under the guidance of Leo McCarey, they were entering a golden age of their comedy.

As they began shooting *Two Tars* in June 1928, their cameraman, the twenty-four year-old George Stevens, was told there would be an unusual amount of activity in the picture, much of it having to do with automobiles. Stevens recalled:

> When *Two Tars* began, I thought it would be a cute little picture about a pair of gobs who smashed up a couple of cars, maybe three. At least that was the synopsis given to me one day. How could we have known that *Two Tars* was going to be one of the funniest movies of all time, and that just six or seven months later we'd make an even funnier movie that I believe is one of the ten great comedy films of history, *Big Business*? You can call it serendipity, or fate, but I guess it's just the old classic situation of the right people being together at the right time. I, for one, never tire of *Two Tars* and *Big Business*. In my possibly prejudiced view, that pair of two-reelers contain more laughs per foot than anything Chaplin ever did.

The two tars are Stan and Ollie, on a one-day pass from their battleship, out together with blonde and brunette tootsies in tow, sharing their day in a rented open roadster. At day's end, the merrymakers come across a traffic jam caused by a road repair crew. Backing out of it, they are hit by another car. They back up into it in retaliation, ruining its headlights, that car in turn smacking the next car's headlights, and this precipitating an enormous cycle of reciprocal destruction down a long line of cars. All this is done in such a manner that the accidents, bizarre though they be, look uncontrived, and all retributions seem the result of normal frustration and anger. One might think that the tit-for-tat device being used again would induce *déjà vu* among film audiences. Not so, for two reasons: the formula was not used in every Laurel and Hardy film by any means, and when it was, as in *Two Tars* and *Big Business*, the events, as aforesaid, are made to seem either 'pure' accidents or the results of natural impulse.

There were five Laurel and Hardy films made between *Two Tars* and *Big Business* when tit-for-tat was employed again, giving the constantly growing Laurel and Hardy audience time enough not to tire of the device. The five interim films were of standard comic themes for the time: a spook-oriented farce set in a graveyard; two innocent husbands accidentally compromised by circumstances placing them half undressed in two strange ladies' apartment; a 'high-and-dizzy' adventure à la Harold Lloyd; a farce in which the boys mistake a horse named Blue Boy for the painting of the same name and put it, as directed, on a grand piano; and a domestic comedy in which Stan is forced to dress up, quite convincingly, as Mrs Hardy.

The high-and-dizzy picture, *Liberty*, was almost disastrous for Babe. Following the custom of a set for such films, the girders which the boys were to traverse in terror were part of a framework set atop a tall building's flat roof, raised high enough for judicious camera placement to give the illusion that the girders were dangling directly over the city streets. This framework was built with a safety platform just below camera range. Stan, unused to heights, was bothered by this arrangement. The safety platform looked too far away for either comfort or safety. Babe tried to reassure him, and said, 'Look, there's nothing to worry about. I'm going to show you it's perfectly safe.' He jumped down on the safety platform — and it broke in half. Fortunately Tom Roberts of the Roach construction crew had anticipated this, and had placed a safety net below the platform. Babe was extremely lucky to get away with a few bruises.

Following these five films, and made in the incredibly swift time of a week at Christmas 1928, Stan and Babe created their silent chef d'oeuvre, *Big Business*.

The heart of drama, serious or comic, is conflict, and in *Big Business*, conflict is brought to vigorous, hilarious apotheosis. This is a great (an adjective used judiciously and firmly) motion picture.

Babe and Stan's chief foil in *Big Business* is again James Finlayson, the master of comic irascibility. Bald, rather resembling a full-size gnome, Fin possessed eyebrows of astonishing virtuosity. They seemed to do takes of their own. Babe recalled:

> He particularly knew how to use that left eyebrow of his the way Kreisler used the violin. Fin could lift that eyebrow to express horror or resentment or disbelief, and Stan and I would have a tough time trying not to break up. Sometimes we *did*. The most hilarious guy we ever worked with.

Fin, in real life a merry and parsimonious Scot, was to appear in approximately a third of the Laurel and Hardy canon. He was their perfect comedy nemesis because his frenetic over-reactions were a balanced counterpoint to Stan and Ollie's low-key, leisurely shenanigans.

Big Business opens with a title reading, 'The story of a man who turned the other cheek and got punched in the nose.' Next we see Stan and Ollie driving along in the 1928 equivalent of a Model T pick-up, a spunky-looking little truck, loaded with Christmas trees. They are in business; it is Christmas week both in story and fact. They pull up to a house and get out. With lordly gesture, Ollie orders Stan to take out one of the trees. Stan pulls off his gloves, removes the bristly tree from the pick-up, then puts his gloves back on. Ollie shares his incredulity with us by looking at the camera. With an imperious 'follow me' gesture, Ollie leads Stan, who is carrying the tree, up to the house where he asks the chubby lady who opens the door if she would like to buy a Christmas tree. She says no, smilingly. 'Wouldn't your *husband* like to buy one?' Ollie persists. She giggles and says shyly, 'I have no husband.' Ollie thinks for a moment, scratches his head, and Stan now gets an idea: 'If you *had* a husband, would he buy one?' The lady slams the door indignantly.

The boys drive around the corner to the next house, and once again Ollie leads the tree-bearing Stan up the path to the porch. ('By this time in our stories,' Babe said, 'we had established the principle that Ollie almost always took the initiative — this usually leading to disaster, a disaster that hits *him*.') As Ollie is about to ring the bell, Stan points out a little sign, 'Positively no peddlers or solicitors.' Ollie in turn points to himself with smug pride, saying, 'It's personality that wins!' As he doffs his hat courteously, the door opens, and the camera's side-view placement allows us to see only an arm brandishing a hammer conk Ollie on the head. 'Come on, personality,' Stan says, and carries the tree off the porch. Ollie looks angrily at the door; he pushes the bell again, the door opens, and the hammer more quickly this time crashes down on Ollie's skull. He walks away, feeling badly used.

Next, the salesmen pull up before Fin's house and walk up to it, passing a coiled garden hose. Ollie rings the bell, and Fin, looking the very model of domestic comfort, comes to the door, pipe in mouth, newspaper in hand. Stan brings the tree forward to show him, but — no. Fin shakes his head briefly, and closes the door — on a branch of the tree. Ollie rings the bell, Fin opens the door, and Stan forgets to pull the tree away, and when Fin slams the door, the tree is still caught. Ollie rings the bell again, Fin opens the door in mounting irritation, Stan pulls the tree away and in so doing hits Ollie in the face with it. Fin slams the door again, Ollie angrily orders Stan to leave with him, but as they turn to go, Stan can't move. His *coat* is now stuck in the door.

Ollie rings the bell. Fin answers, tells them with emphasis to clear out. Stan brings the tree back to Fin to show him its charms, Fin slams the door once more — again on a branch of the tree. Ollie rings the bell, Fin comes out, seizes the offending tree and throws it out on the lawn, telling the boys to leave. Muttering, he goes back into the house, as the boys go.

'I don't think he wants a tree,' Ollie tells Stan. Stan cogitates — a momentous thing for him — opens up his order book and says, 'I've got a big business idea.' He walks back to the door as Ollie looks on sceptically. When Fin opens the door, Stan says brightly, 'Could I take your order for next year?'

Fin, indicating that Stan should wait a minute, goes back into the house. Stan turns exultantly, and here Stan the actor commits a minor *faux pas* for the silent camera by saying 'Babe!', easily mouth-read by any careful viewer. This was an indication that Stan was entering wholeheartedly into the reality of the scene. 'It's a sale!' he goes on to say.

Ollie rubs his hands gleefully and carries the tree back to the house, setting it down at the door, utterly delighted. Fin emerges from the house with large garden shears, clips off the top of the tree, then cuts the tree in half, and with a gloating look of 'That should hold you!' goes back into the house.

The boys look incredulously at their tree. One sees the birth of retribution in Ollie's eye, and it dawns in Stan's, too. He takes his pocket knife and carefully prises off the three house numbers at the side of the door. Then he attacks the door itself, cutting off several large strips of moulding. Fin appears in the door window, lifts his left eyebrow in astonished horror, and comes out. Stan holds up the moulding strips in triumph, breaks therm, hurls them to the ground. Fin's eyebrows both go up, and he shakes Stan in fervid agitation. Ollie twists Fin's ear, and after hitting him in the tummy with an elbow, takes Stan's knife, pulls up the single long hair Fin still has on his bald head, and gleefully cuts it off.

Stunned at this personal indignity, Fin picks up the single hair from the ground, looks at it longingly, then smirks craftily at Ollie. He walks over to him, and with cool deliberation takes the watch and chain drooped over Ollie's vest, holds the watch to his ear to hear if it is working, nods and smiles, reassured, and swings it by the chain in circles several times before smashing it against the wall of his house. He throws the pieces to the ground, stamps on them, and goes joyfully into the house.

There is a close-up of the scattered watch parts. Ollie,

removing his gloves, takes the knife, digs the doorbell from the house, pulling out its long wire several feet, and after giving it a final, vicious ring, pulls the bell mechanism completely free of the house.

He throws the entire jangled mechanism down before Fin when he bursts from his home. Fin rushes inside, to reappear in the doorway holding his telephone receiver in right hand, earphone in the other. 'Give me the patrol wagon.' He nods smugly to Ollie. Stan cuts the receiver off the phone and hurls it afar. Ollie pulls the rest of the phone out of the house and throws it away as well.

Now *Big Business* slows down even more into the leisurely-paced tempo that Leo McCarey invented for Laurel and Hardy — thus giving the audience more time to savour the lunacy of the action, the very slowness of pace itself becoming a source of laughter.

Fin, without haste, produces a pair of scissors, carefully pulls out Ollie's shirt-front and cuts off its tail. He walks away for a moment but comes back, unhurriedly, to cut Ollie's tie in half, throwing it on the ground in a defiant gesture. Ollie looks on all this with considerable surprise, and he is positively chagrined at the truncated shirt-tail. Here, had Babe expressed anger in the instant shock reaction that old-school film comedy dictated, all this would simply be minor excitation. But deeper laughter comes from Ollie's almost bemused state of *interest* in these horrible things that are happening, and this quiet pace perfectly fits the slow-thinking pair we see.

Fin leaves. Stan, under Ollie's guidance, aims the coiled lawn hose at Fin when he returns, the water blast leaving him gasping. The boys go to their truck and sit in it.

Fin rushes down to them, and the boys share cosy laughter as they regard their victim. Fin goes into his left eyebrow up, right-eyed squint; Stan mimics him perfectly, outraging Fin even more. He grabs one of the little truck's headlights, pulls it off and hurls it through the windshield.

By now a score of neighbours have gathered to watch this three-man Donnybrook. Stan and Ollie get out of the vehicle, remove their overcoats, push their derbies forward in determination as they walk toward the house, the crowd following in fascination.

Stan removes the porch light and is about to throw it on the lawn when Ollie points to a window in the house. Stan obliges. Crash. Fin, shocked at this, wheels in steely determination, runs back to the boys' truck, falling over a skimpy mid-lawn shrub as he does so. The boys follow.

Fin pulls off the vehicle's right door, throws it on the ground, and plants his foot on it victoriously, glaring at his opponents. They rush back to the house, he scurrying after them, again tripping over his skimpy shrub. Stan pulls the shrub out of the ground. Fin tries to replant it on the run but fails to do so. The boys go into the house, shut the heavy front door and hurl themselves against it until it crashes down on the front lawn in huge splinters.

The camera now goes across the street to where a massive cop (Tiny Sandford, another Laurel and Hardy foil in over a score of films) pulls up in his one-man squad car. He observes all that is going on in great wonder, but does not move.

Fin, in tense excitement, rushes to the boys' truck and standing on the front seat, pulls the steering wheel completely out of its casings, then throws it away. A shot of the cop in his car, looking amazed. Fin pulls out the truck's gas tank, and throws it in the street. He grabs one of the Christmas trees from the truck, and twisting and turning it, wraps it around himself frenziedly, repeating this with another tree. The boys rush to the house and Ollie, grabbing an axe, whacks away at a fruit tree mid-lawn. The film's pace is no longer leisurely; it now gets progressively swifter.

Stan meanwhile is pulling down the awning over the front window. Another shot of the cop, still in his car, his astonishment growing. Stan urgently pulls a vine lattice down from the house wall. Fin is still madly attacking the trees in the truck. Stan seizes a garden trellis and shoves it through the front window. Fin jumps down from the truck, proud of the havoc he has wreaked. Again a shot of the cop, still in his car, laboriously taking note of all this in his report book. Ollie succeeds in felling the tree on the lawn. Anger again aroused, Fin bends up one truck fender and pulls it off to the ground, then rips off another.

Stan destroys bushes around the house. In an excess of energy, Fin pulls off the entire bed of the truck. Stan pulls down another trellis. Fin rushes to the front of the truck and succeeds in pulling off its hood. A shot of the cop, *still* in his car, his incredulity now almost at its height. Fin runs up and down the running board, his weight causing the entire vehicle to undulate. He jumps off, takes a match, throws it on the by now gas-soaked truck — and it explodes in complete devastation. Another shot of the cop in his car, incredulity now replaced by horror. Obviously this is serious.

Rubbing his hands in jubilation, Fin dances around the car in an ecstasy of gleeful vengeance. Meanwhile Ollie has found a shovel and begins to dig up the well-kept lawn as Stan heaves a chair out of the paneless front window.

The cop now deigns to get out of his car, crosses the street and walks slowly up the lawn to observe all this intensely interesting activity.

Stan and Ollie have created a little game for themselves. Stan, standing in the living-room, hurls lamps, vases and assorted bric-à-brac out of the open front window to Ollie, who with feet planted firmly on the lawn in batter's stance, shovel held at the ready, breaks the artefacts as Stan sails them out of the house. Out they come: one, two, three, four, five — Ollie is really quite good at this, at one point swinging so heartily he falls to the ground — six, seven. Fin, having nothing more to destroy and needing vengeful satisfaction, beats the ruins of the car with a long stick.

The pace of the film is now quite frantic. Ollie, seeing the chimney on the house is intact, hurls a loose brick at it, and it falls apart, tumbling down off the roof. Then back to his game, he swings around to smash a vase as it goes past him. It lands on the cop's foot, and not realizing this, Ollie brings his shovel heavily down on it. The cop pulls his foot up, holding it in agony. The camera cuts to the front door of the house and shows us Stan pushing out Fin's upright piano on to the lawn, where he proceeds to destroy it happily with the axe. The cop crosses over to look at this closely, hardly believing what he sees. Stan does not see the cop; Ollie motions him to desist. Ollie, to mollify the policeman, goes into a demure, finger-twisting pose of regretful embarrassment. Stan, smiling, turns from the piano, sees the cop and assumes the vacant look of a chastened innocent. In propitiatory gesture, he picks up the bar of felt hammers from the piano's innards lying to one side and delicately replaces it in the wreckage. Meanwhile Fin is on the ground near the ruined truck, wrestling frantically with a Christmas tree.

The cop looks sternly at Stan and Ollie, then at Fin with his tree, and orders him to join them. 'Who started all this?' Fin points to the boys. Stan, in sudden shy embarrassment, cries. He explains as he weeps, pointing to the house, then to Ollie, who at once pulls out his handkerchief and bursts into a gale of tears. The cop, much moved by Stan's story, whatever that might be, turns to Fin and says, 'So *you* started this!'

Fin now begins to weep, and he tells his side of the story, breaking off to sob into *his* handkerchief. The camera cuts over to the assembled neighbours nearby and they are all weeping, too, some crying in each other's comforting arms. Fin gallantly offers his hand to Stan, then to Ollie. The boys shake hands with him manfully. The cop crosses over to the neighbours, shoos them away, and goes back to his tiny squad car, weeping. Stan offers Fin a cigar which he takes gratefully, much touched. The boys renew their crying, but — finding the cop gone — look at each other and break into sunny smiles of mischievous guilt. The cop sees this in horror. Stan and Ollie flee down the street. The cop gets out of his car and runs after them. Fin sits wearily in a battered chair on his ravaged lawn, determined to have some pleasure in these proceedings, and lights up Stan's cigar. As one rather expects — and it is the only predictability in the film — it explodes. The scene fades.

With *Big Business*, Laurel and Hardy touch comic greatness for the first time. Nothing perhaps reveals more about the essential character of these two men as when at career's end, in 1954, told separately by the present writer that their work had indeed reached greatness, they showed considerable embarrassment in different ways. Stan laughed it off; Babe shook his head hurriedly and went on to talk of other things.

But even had they believed this, either in 1954 or 1928, it would not have much mattered to them. From the time they reached personal and artistic maturity, they had other more important matters to concern them, deeper things: Stan, how to make funnier movies; Babe, to know just who he was.

6

Sound and Gentle Fury

Babe and Stan made thirty-two silent films, most of them very funny in an interesting variety of ways, and all of them perfectly calibrated to silence.

Mime is indigenous to Laurel and Hardy's style. Stan's flat-footed walk in wide-spaced step (abetted by his use of heavy shoes with heels removed); his folded arms set in defiance (when caught in a naughtiness) that fall repeatedly as he tries to keep them in place; his slow take of recognition, or more usually non-recognition, as he blinks his eyes slowly, then opening them wide as if his lids had just come unglued; his lifting his arms in vague outward gesture to signify hopeless finality — these movements are set in silence.

Ollie's best moments, mostly of comic dignity, are also basically mimetic: the embarrassed flutter of his tie-twiddle; his grandiose bows; the gallant doffing of his derby, consigning it in a rococo sweep to the curve of his left arm; his takes which range from a head-lifting jerk to the shaking of his entire body; his incredulous camera-look after one of Stan's aberrations; his joyous use of a pen when, after several baroque flourishes in the air, he signs his name imperially.

Stan and Ollie were characters attuned to the silent film, and when sound came — for them in the appropriately title two-reeler, *Unaccustomed As We Are* — Babe and Stan had no difficulty adjusting. They used sound as punctuation, not as focus.

In Hollywood of the late Twenties, controversy over the coming of sound was rampant. Hal Roach saw sound as the future, and with hardly a change in production stride, he let Laurel and Hardy speak. Stan had sensed the danger of speaking too much in the films. 'Babe and I,' he stated, 'said just enough to motivate what we were doing.' Speaking was hardly a novelty for them as performers. As children of vaudeville, learning lines was no chore. In *Unaccustomed As We Are*, released in May 1929, they are again in domestic comedy. Ollie brings his friend home to dinner, to Mrs Hardy's deep disgust. The film features as Mrs Hardy another durable Laurel and Hardy foil, the sharp-voiced Mae Busch. Steely-eyed Mae (in life very soft-spoken) came to represent the truculent wife in many Laurel and Hardy family situations. She was still playing Mrs Hardy seventeen years later.

The short sound films of Laurel and Hardy — they flourished from 1929 to 1935 — are probably their finest work. With the exception of several remarkable silent two-reelers like *Big Business* — the sound shorts are perfect vehicles for their talents. Twenty minutes is close to the ideal time for placing the boys in a single interesting complication, ring in the needed comic changes, and resolve them on a high note without a frame of waste or padding. Stan was always of the opinion, backed by Babe, that they should have remained in the short subject category. They felt there was only so much comedy they could do along a certain line before it began to be unfunny or repetitive.

It was in the early days of his growing fame that Babe began a gradual voyage of self-discovery. Fame brought realization that he really did not know himself at all well. His world had become almost entirely make-believe; he had wrapped himself up in the protective cocoon of his profession. He was a funny man off-screen and on, but he frequently did not feel very funny. Too often he felt removed from himself — whoever that self might be. He was also removed from his family, physically and psychologically. His mother had always been a distant and remote figure, for all her intense love of him. Dedicated to her children, her pressing duties as hotelier kept her from close contact with them. Babe had been principally brought up by his black mammy and his mother's sister, Susan Norvell, his deeply loved Aunt Susie.

Although he adored her, Babe never grew close to his mother. That inevitable distancing that hotel work brought between her and the children was to last many years. As compensation, Babe was spoiled by Lizzie and Emily, his two sisters, and his brother, Henry Lafayette Tante, nicknamed 'Bardy', and this cosseting, much as he enjoyed it, left its mark. Babe as a child, as a boy, as a young man, was pretty much alone, for all the company he was given. This, combined with the singularity he felt as the town fat boy, meant that self-isolation was a well-ingrained personality trait. In that, he was following a long-established psychological path into his profession.

Many actors take on their calling because it gives them identity — or quite frequently, a variety of identities — and as they mature in both craft and personality, self-search becomes a normal process of growth, as it does with everyone. But with actors this is intensified. The successful actor has the special added burden of trying to mature psychologically while he is being rewarded with security and esteem for never being himself. This is even more arduous for the comic actor who is expected to be funny offstage as well as on. Who, he begins to ask, is he?*

By mid-1929 this query began to shadow Babe. Stan had no such problem. He was a born comic, a born comic writer. He never had a doubt about that his entire life. With Babe it was very different. His acquiescing to the studio-made biography that his father was a prominent Georgia lawyer, and that he, Babe, had attended the University of Georgia Law School before becoming an actor, was a form of identity support he needed. His self-esteem in the late Twenties began to

---

*Sad instances abound of successful actors who never find their essential selves. One particularly affecting example is the late Peter Sellers, who discovered the nearest thing to personal identity only in the characters he played. He found nothing of himself in himself.

suffer because he increasingly felt his lack of education. One afternoon playing golf, a friend's friend in their foursome talked at length about a current national problem. Everyone except Babe offered a reasoned opinion on the matter, and his inability to do so severely embarrassed him. Next day he subscribed to two national magazines, *Time* and *Literary Digest*, and thereafter read them religiously even when he did not feel up to it. He read the *Los Angeles Times* every day, front page to last. This was the first, and weighty, step in a personal programme of learning he drew up for himself. It was a programme, initially very tenuous, that grew into a lifetime regimen of reading that concentrated on news magazines. He developed his reading habits in order to (in his words) 'get a little smattering of everything'.

In 1929, and later, his programme of self-discovery and education was unwittingly hindered by Myrtle. He had to become *her* guide in life, and in no wise, he realized, could she ever become his helpmate. This realization, coming as it did when he had determined to know who he was, or improve whoever he was, was unfortunate. Obsessively he pondered the apparently trivial incident on the golf course when he was unable to utter a single word on the current affairs matter. That incident was to remain an intellectual watershed in his life. It kept bringing sharply home to him something more than his inadequacy as a conversationalist on current affairs. He realized, or thought he realized, that he did not have a personal identity at all, certainly at least not one that satisfied *him*.

He was proud of his success as an actor, but more and more that success seemed dependent on his physical appearance, on the fact of his contrariety with Stan. It placed Babe in an immovable bind. He was Fat of Fat and Skinny — and in 1929 he hated — as he had always hated — being fat. Yet what else could he be?

Once he won success as a fat man, a success he had worked so hard for, it was unthinkable to relinquish it. If Babe possessed a tragic flaw — the 'vicious mole of nature'

Hamlet speaks of — it was his love, his deep, abiding, almost orgasmic love of food. Overeating was his way of life. His older sister, Lizzie, always believed this was a compensation for the early loss of his father. There is something of Falstaff's 'Thou seest I have more flesh than another man, and therefore more frailty . . .' in this. As a nearly-spoiled child, adored by his siblings, Babe always (in his words) 'got the best pork chop on the plate'. Yet he knew excess weight was bad for him. Thus he was set into a continuous and self-perpetuating framework of victory and defeat. He had to be what he hated to be in order to be what he wanted to be.

'It's just like the old Mother Goose rhyme,' he once told his lawyer, Ben Shipman. The one about "Where I would be".' Ben remembered it, and felt he could do little more than nod his head in sympathy.

> O, that I was where I would be.
> Then would I be where I am not.
> But where I am I must be,
> And where I would be, I cannot.

Myrtle knew and understood this truly tragic dilemma, and to the extent that her personal affliction allowed, helped him. She always encouraged his golfing because she knew it kept him fit; she saw to it that he was well nourished, and instituted periodic diets for him. But alcohol, as it always seemed to, kept defeating her, and that was defeat for him as well. It did not make him eat any the less.

Another worry surfaced at this time, a somewhat ludicrous one, dramatized by the *Los Angeles Times* under the heading, 'Actor Got Cue, But Wrong Kind, He Says in Suit'.

Instead of playing the six ball in the side pocket, Oliver 'Babe' Hardy got reckless with a pool cue and poked Tyler Brooke in the arm, causing a fracture of that member, according to a suit filed yesterday [14 March, 1929] in Superior Court by Brooke against Hardy. Both Hardy and Brooke are motion picture actors.

Brooke, who had appeared in Roach films with Babe, went on in his complaint to assert that Babe, while playing pool with him, had 'negligently, carelessly, recklessly and wrongfully' struck him. Without going into the extremely subtle difference between 'carelessly' and 'recklessly', the former was the adverb Babe himself used to describe his actions during what had begun as a friendly game of pool.

Brooke, doubtless in jest, called Babe a son of a bitch, and the son of peppery Emmie Norvell Hardy was not one to accept that designation casually. He wielded the weapon nearest at hand, and Brooke suffered a fractured arm in consequence. Babe told a friend that since Brooke had been careless in his language, it was not to be wondered at that he, Babe, had been equally careless with the cue stick. Brooke sued Babe for $109,570 damages, getting a sum settled out of court for very much less than that.

Actually Babe was doing well financially, averaging $700 a week in 1929, a time when the dollar was strong. Stan was only a bit ahead of him financially. As the years went on and Stan's creative contributions to their films became more marked, his salary grew to about a half more than Babe's, something that bothered the latter not a whit. 'For all the work Stan does on our behalf,' Babe said, 'he deserves all the money he gets, and more.'

In any case, Babe always felt well-compensated for his work. He usually had ample money for his needs. In 1930 one of his friends at the studio was cameraman Art Lloyd who, with his wife Venice, grew especially close to Babe through the years. One Saturday night after working late at the studio — typically late because Roach's was a non-union studio where scheduling was free and easy — Babe invited the Lloyds to dinner. He selected a little restaurant in Hollywood they all liked, a place Babe fancied because it served sherbet with the entrée, a gourmet touch he appreciated.

After dinner they all drove down Sunset Strip which in those days was Hollywood's Night Club Row. They passed some of the most prestigious and well-publicized of the clubs, all awash in tasteful neon glow. Impulsively, on seeing the sign for Ciro's, the most famous of all the clubs, Babe suggested they drop in briefly. 'Just for a few minutes,' he said. 'Just to see what it's like. We'll likely get to see Loretta Young and those other famous little starlets who come here Saturday night to dance.'

'Listen, Babe,' Art said. 'Just to go *into* one of those clubs will cost you an arm and a leg. They're so terribly expensive.'

Babe insisted. 'Let's go in,' he said, 'and order just *one* drink each – which certainly can't cost much. It'll be great just to *see* the place.' Very reluctantly the Lloyds went in with him. Babe was recognized, given a good table, and as they were seated, told his friends, 'Remember now, you are *my* guests.'

They ordered a drink apiece, and marvelled at the fascinating décor of the place. The orchestra was first-rate. Glamorous people abounded. By now Babe, whose appetite never let him alone, decided to have 'a little ham sandwich' with his drink, and when it came he was surprised to find it minuscule. He explained to the Lloyds that having the sandwich on the table would allow them to stay longer.

Babe saw all he came to see. Lovely Loretta Young was there; so too were equally lovely Joan and Connie Bennett, and other famous stars, dancing and dining. It never began to occur to Babe that he was as famous as anyone there. It was an exciting visit, and Babe, who was quite starry-eyed, said he was in seventh heaven. Until the bill came, and it came the moment the waiter realized they were not going to re-order drinks.

The bill was forty-eight dollars. In 1930, forty-eight dollars in terms of purchasing power would be closer to $400 today. The Lloyds were shocked. Babe could barely speak. He had thirty dollars, which would have bought three full dinners and unlimited drinks elsewhere. Art, having just come from the studio, had very little on him, but fortunately Venice had twelve dollars she had been saving for a hat. Between the three of them they were able to pay the bill, a basic tip, and some change for the boy who parked their car.

'I don't think we had a nickel between us when we left,' said Venice Lloyd, 'but we really did laugh all the way home. And for *years* we teased Babe about his forty-eight dollar sandwich at Ciro's.'

Babe and Stan by mid-1929 were fixed into a fully active pattern of shooting mostly two- and three-reeler films. Their popularity, of which they were largely unaware, was nowhere more fully defined for them than in the studio decision to make foreign editions of their films. But there would be no dubbing. Unprecedentedly, Roach supplied Babe and Stan with four separate supporting casts, filming with these foreign actors in French, Spanish, Italian and German. Monolingual Babe and Stan wrote their lines on a blackboard, out of camera range, in their own phonetic approximation of the sounds spoken to them by a language coach. After the English version of a scene was shot, the other language versions were done. Although a costly and complicated procedure, it solidified Laurel and Hardy's appeal in foreign markets, and made great profits. 'The prices we got in South American countries and Spain were fantastic,' says Hal Roach. 'A Laurel and Hardy short in the Argentine would be like a feature picture. They'd run some other picture with it, but the big attraction was the two-reel comedy.' Ten shorts and one feature film were made in this fashion before the unwieldiness of the process ended it.

Another proof of their growing popularity as a team was their inclusion in MGM's two-hour all-star revue film, *The Hollywood Revue of 1929*, starring the brightest luminaries of that studio. Stan wrote a sketch for them as unskilled magicians, their failed tricks constituting the heart of their act. It was exhilarating to be in the company of the power élite at America's greatest film studio, even though the boys' segment was shot quickly on the MGM lot, giving them no time at all to consort with some of the great stars. Stan had particularly wanted to meet one of his idols, Buster Keaton, who had performed a very mildly amusing sketch in the *Revue*. But Babe and Stan met Keaton a few weeks later at a party and were greatly pleased at his compliments on their work.

As their films grew in number, Babe came more and more to realize that his *métier* was acting, not comedy *per se*. That, at least, was always his view of what he did. In a very real sense he was the root anchor of the team, the solid touch with reality. No matter how far from realism the team was to go, and at times this was some distance — Mother Goose, Balfian gypsy-struck operetta, selling mouse traps in Switzerland, Auber's *opéra comique* – Ollie was always the connection with the actual.

Stan, dim-wit *perpétuel,* invincibly and innocently dumb, was a blend of British music hall and Lewis Carroll — total nonsense set in a child figure. Ollie, his 'grown-up' friend, equally ignorant, was not only in great physical contrast to his slight-figured pal, but he was, as Babe came finally to understand and play him, 'the dumbest guy there is — the dumb guy who thinks he's smart'. This takes some playing.

Babe keyed some of Ollie's mannerisms from a cartoon character appearing in Southern newspapers of his boyhood, Helpful Henry. Henry was a pompous fellow, Babe remembered, '. . .always trying to be helpful but he was always making a mess of things. He was very big and fussy and important but underneath it all, he was a very nice guy. That's very much like the character I play.' Babe's triumph as an actor was that he made authentic a fussy yet charming and endearing ignoramus.

In the early films he is bumptious and authoritative, a show-off know-it-all, and had he been content to remain that, Laurel and Hardy as a team might have lasted as long as the Taxi Boys (Billy Gilbert and Ben Blue), a Roach team that broke up soon after inception. What Stan Laurel was able to see early on in their partnership — and to delight in — was that Babe brought an actor's eye to his character, which is just how Babe planned it. In Babe's words:

Stan is a great comic. He has the finest comedy mind of anyone I've ever known in this business, as I've said often enough. I knew right away that I was basically not a comic although I could do comic things. I saw when I teamed with Stan that I was to be a foil, as I had with Larry [Semon]. But at a much more relaxed pace. And the more real I made my character, the funnier he became. My reactions to Stan's dumbness, particularly since *I* was so dumb, started to get laughs themselves, so Stan tried to develop the whole idea of my reactions getting bigger and bigger — and I began to work on that entire concept. So we were getting two laughs where there usually would be only one — the dumb thing Stan did which got a laugh, then my reaction, usually right to the audience, which got another laugh.

Taking a comic spin-off from the very name of Helpful Henry to focus the eternal quandary of Ollie in respect to Stan, Babe initiated the use of a simple question Ollie constantly asks his buddy: 'Why don't you do something to *help* me?' (It was asked initially in their first sound film, *Unaccustomed As We Are*, released May 1929.) The ringing of changes on Stan's discomfiting his pal, to the latter's deep frustration, are many and various. This oft-repeated query sets this basic Laurel and Hardy theme into a situation not far from pathos, but it never enters that dimension because Stan always pulled back from it in their films. He thought his friend, Chaplin, the only one qualified to do that.

Another fundamental Laurel and Hardy note is sounded by Ollie in his not infrequent statement to his friend, 'Well, here's another nice mess you've gotten me into!' (Not 'another *fine* mess' as many people think.)* For indeed virtually every Laurel and Hardy film, following drama's first law, resolves itself into conflict, into some mess of high disorder.

*'Another fine mess' was used by the boys only twice — once as the title of a 1930 three-reeler of theirs, and again in a radio sketch Stan wrote for them.

Use of 'another nice mess' by Ollie actually began in one of their silent films, *Double Whoopee*. Ollie mouths it at the end of a fight with a cab driver, Charlie Hall, another long-time Laurel and Hardy foil. The phrase appeared in about every tenth film of theirs thereafter, making it a less than insistent theme statement, used just enough to assert its primacy as their basic situation. It even had variations. 'Nice mess' becomes 'kettle of fish' in *Thicker Than Water*, and 'bucket of suds' in *Saps At Sea*. In *Chickens Come Home*, Stan seizes an initiative and takes the expression unto himself, at least once aware of his responsibility in the matter of messes:

OLLIE   Well –
STAN   Here's another nice mess I got you into.

Babe not only used Helpful Henry as a guide in defining Ollie. He had invaluable source material in his mother and especially in his Aunt Susie.

Aunt Susie was to have a profound effect on him professionally. The slightly over-genteel mannerisms he used in his comedy were mostly hers. The extended pinky, the courtly bows, the gallant gestures of welcome and farewell, the fervid cordiality — these he had all observed in Aunt Susie, and they lived again in his acting. When he first tentatively employed them as comic devices, directors and fellow actors encouraged their use.

Just as he used his full name — Oliver Norvell Hardy — in the films for comic purposes, and with great pride, just so were all Aunt Susie's social nuances put in his personal repertoire. 'Every time I do one of those little movements of hers,' he said, 'it's like a little visit home, to my childhood.'

Aunt Susie much enjoyed her strong guiding role in Babe's raising and education. She frequently told him little stories that had moral themes, and read him Mother Goose in ringing comic tones. As a lady well set in her ways and true to her strong British background, she was very fond of afternoon tea. This she drank formally, with requisite tea cosy, silver service, cucumber sandwiches, scones and fine napery. Young

Norvell would sit in to tea with his mother and Aunt Susie, sedulously imitating their deportment.

This was the Norvell family tradition at its most operative. Both Miss Emmie and Aunt Susie were extremely proud of their heritage, and they looked on their tea time as not only properly honouring that tradition but as a way of preserving it. Consequently their conduct on these occasions took on the coloration of high society, Aunt Susie especially dominant, very much the grand lady, albeit a very amiable one.

Little Norvell was always fascinated by her extended pinky when she lifted a cup to her lips, and the beautifully precise way she set it down on the saucer, like an archbishop crowning a monarch. He loved the way she sorted out napkins, creasing them into proper folds with a firm trace of the finger down their length. All of these things, and more, Babe was to remember when Ollie came into his ken.

In time Babe came to regard Ollie as a Southern gentleman, forgoing the regional accent in order to universalize him. He thought Ollie possessed the attributes of the traditional gentleman, having all his virtues and characteristics save one, intelligence. The humour in this is that Babe had Ollie retain the profound conviction that he possesses intellect of the loftiest order. In *Helpmates*, after hosting a wild party the night before, Ollie can look at himself in a mirror and ask with great sincerity, 'Now, aren't you ashamed of yourself? A man with your supposed intelligence acting like an empty-headed idiot!'

If Ollie is a gentleman — and in the entire corpus of Laurel and Hardy, he always is — he must have the manners of a gentleman, and that is where Aunt Susie came in. Those manners are slightly in excess of need, perfectly suiting the extravagant character they mirror. Babe was always grateful to Aunt Susie for her indirect contribution to his screen persona. He remembered she loved horses, and he found a way to include her name in one of their films. In perhaps the best-known Laurel and Hardy short subject, *The Music Box*, where the boys are delivery men, he named their dray horse 'Susie'. As those who know the film with recall, this is a tribute. Susie the horse is smart, determined and with a mind very much her own.

Babe's genius as an actor is seen countless times in their films but never more tellingly than in the 1930 two-reeler, *Blotto*. The boys plan to go out on the town, Stan using subterfuge to get away from his suspicious wife for the evening. (Mrs Laurel is played enchantingly by Anita Garvin, accurately described by Walter Kerr as 'an exceptionally withering, unjustly forgotten comedienne'.*) Anita initially withers Stan into apprehensions but Ollie urges his pal to steal a bottle of liquor his wife has been saving for some nameless occasion during this arid Prohibition time.

Anita, overhearing details of the planned theft on the extension telephone, develops her own plan. She hurries to the kitchen, empties the bottle and fills it with a deadly elixir of tea, spices, pepper sauce and other caustic ingredients. After she replaces the bottle, Stan steals it, and goes with Ollie to the opening of a new nightclub where one can order glasses, ice and soda syphon, no questions asked — as long as one keeps the bottle out of sight.

The body of *Blotto* concerns their antics and the reactions of others as the boys drink their 'liquor'. Increasingly more intoxicated by the power of suggestion, they ultimately convince themselves they are having the time of their lives under the influence of Anita's bitter concoction. The great moment in the film comes when Ollie takes the first two drinks of the stuff. With high and gleeful anticipation, he knocks back his first healthy swig, and then in a reaction that lasts only a few seconds, he registers his feelings.

He frowns as the liquid fire goes down his gullet. His eyes close, he shakes his head like a whip, breathes an agonizing 'Whew!', then holds his head carefully as if to contain the pain. His eyes open and he looks at the drink incredulously.

---

*But well-remembered and actively cherished by the many members of The Sons of the Desert, the international Laurel and Hardy Appreciation Society, who have brought Anita out of retirement to become a principal adornment of their biennial conventions.

The potency of this annihilating liquid he cannot believe. He takes another long swig. His eyes close in contorted pain, he rolls the entire top of his torso around for relief from the agony. He shakes his head several times, holds his forehead once more, and emits a passionate 'Whooo!' When, at last, the hot lava steaming down his oesophagus can no longer be felt, he has enough faith in what *must* be to lean back in triumph, look at the glass admiringly and, with a lovely smile, tell Stan with deep conviction, 'You can certainly tell good liquor when you taste it!' Delighted at this new knowledge, he slaps the table in high glee. Their fun has begun.

This, quite simply, is acting of the first order.

While Babe was creating Ollie in all his compact parts during the heady days of the new sound films, Myrtle began to grow away from him. He came home early one day to find her slumped down in his chair, stupefied from drink. After he spoke angrily to her, she retorted bitterly that she smelled another woman's perfume on his coat lapel. He had indeed lunched that day with one of the Roach *ingénues,* but it was an entirely innocent occasion. Not that he did not wish it had been otherwise. Myrtle brooded about the perfume for a few days and then decided to act.

On 25 July 1929 she filed for divorce, charging seven years of cruel treatment, saying in her deposition that her husband returned home on occasions 'refusing to explain the evidence of his close proximity to persons using powder and cosmetics'. This somewhat coy assertion Babe did not understand since he had rather overwhelmed Myrtle with reasons for his being near persons using powder and cosmetics. A movie studio, as he hold her and as she knew quite well, had powder and cosmetics around by the barrelful.

In her complaint Myrtle went on to say that Babe had not returned home from several days at a time, and that moreover he had said he was through with her. He had certainly told her that at moments when it seemed they were making no progress in overcoming her alcoholism, but invariably he withdrew the threat when she burst into tears. When she wept he always went into a ritualized procedure of babying and comforting her. As to his absences from home, these were real too, but they were trips down to the Caliente racetrack, usually with studio personnel. Usually, but not always.

Babe accepted the idea of divorce rather stoically. The idea of it, on reflection, both alarmed and comforted him. He had fears for his wife's safety if she chose to live alone, and he was human enough to feel some relief at the thought she would no longer be a burden to him. However, and this was the sticking point, he still loved her. Despite the divorce application they stayed together at their home on Fredonia Avenue, Los Angeles, agreeing to separate when further judgment was made on her suit. The suit went into abeyance.

On a Wednesday, the last day of July 1931, Myrtle took their car while drunk, planning, as she later explained, 'to go shopping'. Never a sure driver at best, the car weaved down the street from her house, at one point going over the kerb, continuing erratically until, with great difficulty, a motorcycle cop stopped her. Unable to give coherent answers to his questions, she gave her name to the jail matron as Mrs Myrtle Hardy, address 3687 Fredonia. In the phone call allowed her, she called her sister, a Los Angeles resident, not Babe. The sister, Mrs Mary Pense, of Ben Lomond Drive, Hollywood, came to furnish bail, making the astounding statement that Myrtle had been prescribed alcohol by her physician for an unspecified ailment. If so, this was tantamount to dousing fire with kerosene.

Babe visited Myrtle at her sister's, again in comforting fashion, to take her home. She once more made promises, and all seemed well. Myrtle accompanied her husband to the Stanford–USC game in November that year when Babe and Stan went to San Francisco for public appearances at the new Fox Theatre there.

As a publicity ploy and to please partisans of both teams, it was announced that Stan was betting on Stanford, Babe on

USC. Babe had indeed bet on USC which he regarded as 'his' team through the years, going to their games when he could, and always ready to lay a little wager on behalf of his boys. Usually though, such wagers were not little.

In San Francisco this time he kept the bet modest out of deference to Stan's setback in the Wall Street crash, a loss of $30,000. Babe had never invested in the stock market. 'I do my gambling when I can see and enjoy the action,' he told a friend. Something good came out of Stan's loss. So psychologically scarred was he by the crash that he invested thereafter largely in trust funds which were to leave him well off in his old age despite the depredations of alimony.

It was about this time that Babe's half-brother, Henry Lafayette Tante, re-entered Babe's life. Babe had encouraged him to move to California. Tall, heavy, looking much like his brother except for his somewhat Roman nose, Henry — known to his family as 'Bardy' — was a man of quiet charm. When he reached California he had not yet set his sights on what he wanted to do. In 1930, the year he arrived in Los Angeles, he was 42, four years older than his famous brother, possessing a pleasantly lethargic manner and an excellent sense of humour. Babe got him extra work on the Roach lot, and Bardy appeared in *The Laurel–Hardy Murder Case* and others of the films, always in non-speaking roles.

In June 1931 Bardy asked the Superior Court of Los Angeles to change his surname from Tante to Hardy — 'that being the name by which he has been known for several years', according to the petition. The name change was allowed. Babe was greatly touched by his brother's decision, regarding it as a wonderful way to bring them closer.*

Some years after Bardy had been in Los Angeles, his and Babe's nieces, Margaret and Mary Sage, also came out from Georgia to do extra work at Roach's, again at Babe's invitation. Margaret recalls Bardy as a most affable and personable

---

*In the same court just six weeks before, Arthur Stanley Jefferson had his name changed to Stan Laurel.

gentleman, a man of decidedly strong feelings on most matters, in that way much resembling his mother, Miss Emmie.
Margaret says:

> Miss Emmie, that is, Emily Norvell Hardy, Norvell and
> Bardy's mother, came out to Hollywood to visit her two
> boys. She loved them both, of course, but I think she had
> a special feeling for Norvell, which by the way is what
> we and she always called Babe. And still do! Now, living
> diagonally across from Norvell in Los Angeles was a very
> wealthy lady, a widowed lady, named Frances Rich, who
> thought the sun just rose and set on Bardy. She was about
> twenty years older than he. Frances didn't hesitate in
> making her feelings known to him, either. She adored
> him. It's fair to say she absolutely lavished gifts on him
> — a new red Cadillac, a government bond worth several
> thousand dollars, and a beautiful suite, all his own, in
> her lovely home. This was all a series of wedding gifts
> to Bardy. After they were married, in fact the very *day*
> they were married, they separated. It had been a lovely
> wedding — Norvell, Miss Emmie and Myrtle were there
> — and just a few hours later, Bardy came to his mother
> and said, referring to his new wife, 'Mama, do you know
> what Frances did?' 'No, dear,' said his mother. 'Well,'
> said Bardy, 'I was in my suite at her house, resting by
> myself shortly after the wedding. And she came —
> and *knocked on my door.*' Bardy paused, and added
> pensively, 'I didn't care for that.'

Without a further word of explanation, Bardy returned
the Cadillac and government bond to his new spouse, and
quitted his lovely new suite forever. It was received family
opinion that Bardy, genial and fun-loving though he was, was
a remarkably sensitive soul. To uncomplicate his three-hour
marriage, he had it annulled, left Hollywood, went home to
Georgia and promptly married a childhood sweetheart who,
according to his family, 'had been waiting many years for
him'. They were very happy together but Bardy died not long
after. 'He never really took good care of himself,' one of his

nieces said. 'He favoured highly seasoned foods, and didn't watch his diet.'

She might have been speaking of his brother. Babe's long love affair with food never really stopped, but he always made periodic efforts to slim down and succeeded at times in the 1930s, most likely at some cost to his health. His niece, Margaret, remembers that in 1934 when she and sister Mary came out to California, Babe went through several cycles of yo-yo dieting — gain, lose, gain, lose. In the loss phase he would take five grains of thyroid compound to slim down, and after reaching his goal, glory in it for a few weeks, then gain it all back in an eating binge.

Babe loved having his family visit him. He always found Bardy's company enjoyable, encouraged Margaret and Mary to stay on in Los Angeles, and because they were comely, had some hope for their future in pictures. He told them candidly they needed to take acting lessons before trying to get anything other than the walk-ons and crowd scenes he arranged for them in his films. Mary, like Bardy, had her own childhood sweetheart back in Georgia, and she returned to marry him. Margaret also went home shortly after that to become her mother's companion in Atlanta, living with her and Babe's mother for many years at the lovely Royal Georgian Hotel, where Babe insisted they stay indefinitely at his expense.

Babe succeeded in getting his mother to California twice. She found the weather comfortable and the living easy, but California had one serious lack. It was not Georgia. During the first visit, Babe set her up comfortably at the old Hollywood Hotel, providing her with car and chauffeur. She stayed six weeks, then left saying she missed old friends back home. Two years later Babe talked her into coming out again, hoping this time he could persuade her to settle in for good. To further that plan, he found a beautiful apartment for her, close to his new home in Beverly Hills.

Mrs Hardy had been in her new place two weeks when Babe, giving up his golf game for the day, went to see her after work. She was gone. He asked the building superintendent where his mother was, and learned she had left that morning — for good. She took the car Babe had provided her, directing the chauffeur to drive straight home to Georgia. She never returned. She called Babe and told him that as 'a true Georgian' she could never live in any other place. He understood.

Babe's family grew increasingly aware of Myrtle's condition. The *Los Angeles Times* of 27 March 1931 carried a story that she was once again in the care of her sister. Myrtle was, according to the report, the victim of a nervous breakdown — the medical definition given was 'melancholia' — and had been reported by her husband as missing. She was found by two detectives at the St Paul Hotel, West Sixth Street, in Balboa, Panama. Myrtle's sister told reporters the invalid would be placed under the doctor's care. Babe was glad she was at her sister's. There would be someone home most of the day to keep her company, one of her great needs.

Babe did not want children at this phase of his career; perhaps, he thought, he might never want them. Although he liked them, children tended to make him nervous. In any case Myrtle was clearly unfit to have children until her problem was suitably addressed.

Babe tried to do that. Early in 1931 he had put Myrtle, with her approval, into Rosemead Lodge Sanitarium in Temple City, a drying-out facility which also provided psychological guidance for alcoholics. She left after a few weeks there to visit the Balboa hotel, a place she had known in earlier days when working for the Balboa Film Company. There would be similar excursions. These disappearances of Myrtle were hardly sordid descents into revelry. She wandered away to places she had formerly known just to drink and reminisce with old friends. She was lonely. She loved Babe; Babe loved her; but wherever they lived was (it seemed to her) *his* home. She was a guest there, she felt.

Shortly after moving in with her sister after the Balboa episode, Myrtle was bound over to appear, according to the *Los Angeles Times*

... before Superior Court Judge Gould in psychopathic court yesterday and was placed on parole with the provision that she enter a private sanitarium for rest. On the representation of her attorney, Ben Cohen, that there was nothing wrong mentally with his client, and that the family is anxious to have her placed in a private sanitarium, Judge Gould ordered her paroled to the psychopathic parole officer with the provision that a sanitarium, suitable to Mrs Hardy, be selected where she might go.

Rosemead was the place she agreed to, and Babe took her there. She remained placidly at Rosemead for a few weeks and then went to join Babe at what he emphasized was 'their' new home in Beverly Hills on North Alta Drive.

As Laurel and Hardy's prominence grew, they seemed to become a fixed part of the Hollywood scene, fitting easily into national consciousness. Yet in the years 1927 to 1935, when they made seventy-one short subjects in the two- and three-reeler format, they did so to scant critical attention. This is not to be wondered at, given the need of reviewers to address themselves to the thousands of full-length films being made those years. In a sense Laurel and Hardy were beyond review. They had become a part of national life both in the United States and beyond.

Yet one critical recognition came to Babe and Stan, in 1932, and it was all the more heartening to them in that it came from their peers. Their superb three-reeler, *The Music Box*, was the Academy Award winner for 'Best Live Action Comedy Short Subject of the Year, 1931–1932'. *The Music Box* shows vividly how Laurel and Hardy could evoke unforced laughter, truly well motivated laughter, from a single, simple object — a boxed upright piano which they must deliver to a house atop a high terraced rise of steps.

It was early in 1932 when Stan decided to visit his dad and stepmother in England. After five years of unremitting hard work, Stan felt entitled to a holiday. He had spent most of those years not only performing but acting as the director's director. 'Stan was very clever about it,' says Anita Garvin. 'The director was never cognizant of the fact that he was not doing all the directing. Even Leo McCarey — and there was no director better. Stan's mind was going all the time; I don't think he had one waking moment when he wasn't thinking of something.' By 1932 that mind was very tired.

Babe felt the need to relax too. Although he did not — purposely — work on the films to the extent Stan did, he played hard, mostly as relief from the tensions Myrtle brought him. These same tensions brought another woman into his life. Viola Morse, a very attractive divorcee with a small son, was also a Southerner and a woman of genial, easy charm. Babe was captivated, and stayed captive a long time. His sense of responsibility to Myrtle was strong, and although he felt no compunction in making Viola his 'close companion' (the words he used to describe her to Stan), he was a Southern gentleman, and such a man would never desert a lady in need.

As for Viola, she was not Babe's mistress. 'Close companion' was a phrase he used unambiguously; it was meant to be taken literally. His relationship with Viola was not a sordid one, even if it might have been sexual.

Stan's decision to visit England gave Babe a thought. Several thoughts. The first was that it would provide Myrtle the kind of adventurous activity she had long been seeking in their marriage. As Babe saw it, her frequently expressed complaints that as a couple they did hardly anything together could now be countered by a trip abroad, a new experience for them both. Moreover, Babe had been told by fellow golfers that Scottish courses were the finest in the world. He suggested the trip to Myrtle and she was enthralled. He asked Stan if he would mind their company. Stan was delighted.

Stan had been having his own marital troubles. These were as nothing compared to Babe's. Stan's difficulties stemmed principally from his having the old (and in this case almost to the year) seven-year itch. Married since 1926 to Lois, a lady low key by temperament and little involved in any of his professional ventures, Stan was usually too busy for extra-marital liaisons, and at least in principle disliked the entire idea of unfaithfulness.

Lois had been a good wife. She handled their money well and at times acted as Stan's agent in contract dealings with Roach. When called on to be hostess to Stan's old cronies and new studio friends, she did so willingly. She bore him a daughter, Lois Jr, in 1928, and for a while this seemed to settle Stan.

But he was still a bachelor at heart, so much so that in time he also found a 'close companion' in Alyce Ardell, an attractive French actress who had worked in a number of Hollywood studios. Alyce did not want to marry Stan. She simply enjoyed his company, and for a little over ten years became his uncomplaining *petite camarade*. By 1932 Stan was feeling less and less of a married man. Lois did not go to England with him.

When the Hardys and Stan left for their holiday, they found almost immediately that the anticipated vacation was to be everything other than that. Metro–Goldwyn–Mayer arranged a publicity barrage about their visit, and admiring mobs overwhelmed Babe and Stan wherever they went: Chicago, New York, Southampton, London, Glasgow, Blackpool, Birmingham, Manchester, Leeds, Sheffield. 'Mobs' is the right word. Dozens of people were injured in the mêlées caused by the public appearances. No one, least of all Babe and Stan, had any idea of the fervour their admirers would show in trying to get near them. This disquieting adulation shocked and surprised the two men. 'We could never figure it out,' Stan said as late as the last year of his life.

Stan's dad, Arthur J Jefferson, and Stan's stepmother, Venetia, greeted the Hardys and Stan with great warmth. 'A J', at heart rather an old ham, revelled in his son's great popularity and enjoyed sharing it. Stan found this secretly amusing, and he gave his dad all the tether he wanted when newspapermen came around for interviews. The fact was that 'A J' became something of a bore in this respect, much given to pointless reminiscences of his own glory days, but Stan was fully forbearing. He always felt grateful to his dad for giving him the encouragement he needed as a boy comedian.

Metro–Goldwyn–Mayer had arranged so thorough a personal appearance tour for Babe and Stan in Britain that Babe had hardly any chance to golf. On one of the occasions when he did, at the splendid Gleneagles course in Scotland, he bought at the clubhouse a tartan umbrella to go with the tartan suspenders and socks he had purchased earlier in Glasgow. 'I don't expect I'll be using this pretty thing very much,' he said, flourishing the umbrella, and walked out of the clubhouse into a deluge of rain. Babe readily identi-fied with things British. Not only did the Hardys consider themselves descendants of Nelson's Hardy, but there was a Norvell family tradition that Babe's grandfather had at one time attended Edinburgh University.

In England a popular woman's columnist in Blackpool's leading newspaper, working under the nom-de-plume of 'Sylvia', interviewed Myrtle during the visit to that city, and despite the gush in the piece, one can enjoy Myrtle's evident delight in being sought out. Under the heading, 'I Meet Mrs Hardy', Sylvia enthused:

I met famous Mr Laurel and Mr Hardy and discovered two things. One is that Mr Laurel has an attractive young daughter, and the other that Mr Hardy has a very pretty wife. A very pretty wife. She has fair curls, pink cheeks and blue eyes which twinkle behind dark eyelashes, has Mrs Hardy, and she was wearing a smart blue flecked tweed coat with a blue stitched hat when she arrived in Blackpool. Mr and Mrs Hardy found there was a romance in film work some considerable time ago. That was when they met one another.

'I was in drama and he was in comedy, and so we met and were married,' she said with her gay little smile. 'My husband is just a big, shy boy. He would like to spend his holiday taking great rides into the country. I am afraid we shall all get back home again needing another holiday to get over the effects of this one. But we won't get it. The sad part about it is that they start work again one minute after they get back.'

There was genuine poignancy in those last two sentences. Therein was contained the principal burden of Myrtle's unsatisfactory life with her husband. Myrtle went on to tell Sylvia that Mrs Laurel did not come on the trip because 'she doesn't like crowds and travelling, and is not over-strong, so she preferred not to make the trip. Mrs Laurel is a very beautiful woman.' Sylvia went on to describe Stan's pride in his young daughter, then four-and-a-half, and that Stan

... was smiling gaily and talked happily all the time. His smile is a surprise after his mournful escapades on the films. But then he is the most charming and courteous of men. Mr Hardy, however, heaved his famous bulk along, blinking through his horn-rimmed spectacles, and, clutching a huge tartan umbrella, he solemnly surveyed everyone without a twinkle or a word. 'I have never been to Blackpool before,' admitted Mr Laurel, 'but I have always meant to come.' 'So have I,' said Mr Hardy, and they looked that famous look at one another. On the films it is Mr Hardy who does all the talking. In real life it is Mr Laurel . . . Mrs Hardy thinks there is nowhere in the world like California. She lives in Beverly Hills among the stars and knows almost all of them.

So she did, and — sadly — had a not real friend among them. Had she possessed even one close friend, Myrtle's life with Babe might have been significantly different.

After a brief visit to Paris, the threesome returned to the States and as Myrtle had forecast, work at the studio began directly they returned to Los Angeles. Babe was in fine form. He had lost weight on the trip; Stan had gained twenty pounds.

It was inevitable Myrtle would begin drinking again. The Hardys had not been back six weeks before she left the house one morning, neatly dressed and coiffed, and did not return for three days. When she did, still neatly dressed and hair precisely in place, but with dark circles under her eyes and whisky on her breath, Babe did not say a word. He looked at her expectantly. 'What do you want me to say?' she said.

Without a word, he turned, left the house and went to Lakeside. It was his one sure place of comfort. Lakeside Golf Club in the San Fernando Valley had increasingly become the golf club of the stars during the 1930s. Bing Crosby joined Lakeside in 1931, the year Babe did, and they quickly became friends. They were cut from the same bolt of cloth, possessing the interesting mix of genuine loner and hearty bon vivant. Crosby admired Babe's singing voice for its purity, and while golfing would sing duets with him, picking old, near-forgotten songs.

They both liked Lakeside not only for its amenities but because its upper middle class membership, all men well along the path to success, would never dream of asking for autographs or in any way treating movie stars deferentially. Crosby, Babe, W. C. Fields, Don Ameche, Guy Kibbee, Frank Craven, Adolph Menjou, Jimmyo'z Finlayson, Charles Coburn — and others of the Hollywood contingent among the Lakesiders — were treated like every other member.

A big reason why Babe was well regarded at Lakeside was his skill at golf. In the film world he had only one real rival as golfer — the ever immaculate and slightly overdressed Adolph Menjou. In the mid-Thirties Babe and Menjou were serious contenders for the club championship, gradually making their way to the finals — just the two of them.

Menjou had a reputation for subtly unsettling his opponents verbally during a match — nothing overt, just a casual unbarbed phrase that would put a rival slightly off his form. He tried this with Babe in the final round, and got nowhere. With great composure, Babe played impeccably on this occasion and defeated Menjou to become Lakeside's champion. It was one of the greatest moments in Babe's life. He won one-up.

Eddie Gannon, for decades the starter at Lakeside, has very strong memories of Babe there, both as golfer and member. As a boy, Eddie caddied many times for him:

Billie Dove signs an autograph for Mr Hardy.

(bottom left) Babe at the 1931–2 Academy Awards with Margaret (Mrs Hal) Roach and Thelma Todd, who is mugging at a friend off-camera.

(bottom right) Babe, as semi-acrobat, clowns around with Stan in front of the Roach studios, early 1930s.

The 1932 tour, en route from the *Aquitania* to Waterloo Station,
23 July 1932.

(bottom left) The first triumphal Laurel and Hardy tour abroad,
1932. Babe jokingly carries Myrtle (sober) off their train in New
York.

(bottom right) Showing off their plaid sock suspenders, atop a
Glasgow distillery, 1932.

Babe and Myrtle at the twentieth anniversary party of the Roach
Studios, 7 December 1933.

Using his chum, Guy Kibbee, as a tee. Clowning for the press at a Motion Picture Golf Tournament, around 1933.

Kibbee ostentatiously eavesdrops while Babe chats with chief rival in Hollywood golfing ranks, Adolph Menjou.

Babe with his mother ('Miss Emily'), his oldest sister, Elizabeth, and his niece Margaret, circa 1934. Margaret was an extra in several of his films.

Babe occasionally ventured into Stan's favourite sport, tuna fishing. With Guy Kibbee off Catalina Island.

Jimmy Durante, kibitzes Buster Keaton, Chuck Reisner, Babe and Stan at MGM in 1932. Keaton and Durante were teamed, in artistic disharmony, at the time.

Avuncular Guy Kibbee lets the little boy pick his pocket with Babe's gun in his back. Aiming his gun, Douglas Dumbrille. A hunting/gambling excursion to Mexico, December 1934.

Babe bikes around the Scottish village built by RKO for Katharine
Hepburn's film, *The Little Minister,* and borrowed by Hal Roach for
Bonnie Scotland, 1935.

Babe at Santa Anita
Race Track with Viola
Morse.

Babe, in favourite
relaxing position, with
unit manager Bill
Terhune on the Roach
backlot during the
filming of *Way Out
West,* 1937.

PERFUMES

Babe was, of course, a terrific golfer, and it was a pleasure to watch him play. For a big man, he was very light on his feet, and he seemed to *flow* as he walked. So smoothly. No heavy lumbering steps like so many large people take. His golf swing was a thing of beauty. He swung efficiently, effortlessly, and after hitting the ball he would bend at the knee three times, very gracefully, and on his third dip, he'd point his club at the hole as if to say, 'So there!'

Naturally he played golf with all the etiquette the game demands. He was the soul of courtesy. I saw only one exception to that, and he had good reason to lose his temper. One member he had been playing with had been giving Babe a hard time. Riding him verbally about something. I forget what it was for, but Babe was getting more and more angry over the nagging this guy was giving him. Finally Babe could take it no more, and in maybe the most gracefully alliterative cuss phrase ever uttered — which described his opponent's face perfectly — Babe called him a 'chiselled-chin cocksucker', and a few other things. This was all the more powerful language in that Babe was a real gentleman, even among men, and just didn't use that kind of language. His opponent's jaw dropped in astonishment.

As his problems with Myrtle grew, Babe spent more and more time at Lakeside without her. In addition to golf, he loved bridge and tried to get in several games a day. His old friend, Charles Coburn, did not play golf but he, together with another Hardy chum Guy Kibbee, loved bridge too. This was rather odd because both Coburn and Kibbee were perfectly awful bridge players.

Babe enjoyed playing with them, and although he usually won, he 'played them gently', to use his own phrase, so that their drubbing would never seem excessive. After dinner, the Lakeside orchestra played, and then Babe became much in demand as a dancing partner. The wife of one member remembers:

Babe Hardy was the best dancer, the best ballroom dancer, you ever saw. It was nothing for women to walk over to his table and ask him to dance. It happened all the time and he got used to it. The reason they asked him was NOT because he was a movie star. Those ladies wanted to dance with him because he was just the best dancer in the club. Bar none.

As pleasurable as his days at Lakeside were, Babe always had to go home at night, usually never sure if Myrtle would be there. On one of the occasions when she was not, he impulsively went on vacation to South America between pictures — alone. While he was gone, in April 1933, Stan and Lois, in an attempt at reconciliation, took a four-week auto trip to Victoria, British Columbia. On their return, Lois filed for divorce on the grounds of mental cruelty and incompatability. That must have been some auto trip.

Three weeks later Babe and Myrtle separated. He filed suit for divorce on the grounds of mental cruelty, stating that she had absented herself from their home 'for several days at a time', had drunk liquor to excess and was plunging him in debt. Myrtle replied in a divorce cross-complaint that he had lost $30,000 in one day at the Caliente track, had gambled away $3,000 at roulette, and on a daily average at Lakeside would lose over a hundred dollars betting on golf and cards. The latter accusation had basis in fact. Myrtle had no way of proving the Caliente losses since she did not go with him. Viola had become his invariable companion in Mexico. The trip to Britain had neither severed that connection nor made any improvement in the Hardy marriage.

Babe moved to a hotel, Myrtle stayed on at their Beverly Hills home. In an attempt to discuss their financial situation, Babe visited Myrtle, only to find her sister, Mary, there. Mary was very protective of Myrtle and insisted on listening to Babe's discussion of their financial picture. When Babe made the point that conversation with his wife on this matter was completely private, Mary demurred, telling Babe that she 'represented' her sister. She had some of Myrtle's papers in her hand, and at one time flourished them aggressively in Babe's face. Angered, he grabbed the papers and flourished them right back in Mary's face, hitting her nose. The strength and intent of that blow was the subject of great dispute two days later when Mary brought suit in Superior Court against Babe for $50,000, charging assault and battery.

The suit was dropped a month later when the *Los Angeles Times* of August 3, 1933, carried a double-barrelled story about Babe and Stan.

FAMILY RIFTS PATCHED BY LAUREL AND HARDY

With a few feathers missing but nevertheless flying high, the dove of peace is hovering above the Roach comedy team of Laurel and Hardy. Stan Laurel with radiant face said yesterday that he and Mrs Laurel, who has filed a divorce suit against him, have become reconciled, are living together again and that she will drop the proceedings. He credited their baby, Lois, now 5 years old, with having led them together into the old path of happiness again.

'And,' he said, 'the Hardys are doing the same thing.'

'It's news to us,' chorused Ben W Shipman and David H Cannon, attorneys respectively for Mr and Mrs Hardy. 'We are in the course of agreement over a property settlement, and if they are to patch up their troubles, they have not yet let us in on it.'

But nevertheless on the Roach lot the rumour persists that 'the Hardys will too.'

That dove of peace was to prove a very flighty bird.

7

Tide at the Full

The Hardys did follow the Laurels in reconciling.

Two months to the day after the dove of peace article, the *Los Angeles Times* was trumpeting the news in a heading, 'Hardys Kiss and Make Up in Love Tiff'. Babe moved out of the Beverly–Wilshire and back to 'their' home. He told the press that he and Myrtle had made 'a big mistake', that they were going to correct it, and that in consequence they would 'have more happiness than we ever had before'.

Ben Shipman, his lawyer, on reading this, said fervently to his wife, 'I hope so. God almighty, I hope so,' and sighed. It had been a hard road for Ben, trying to do his best for Babe and Stan. Benjamin W Shipman, a quiet-mannered, intelligent and very unpretentious lawyer, had been business manager of the Hal Roach Studios in the Twenties and early Thirties. Even before Babe and Stan attained renown, they were in the habit of taking personal problems to him. He seemed to have a knack for getting them out of scrapes. A man so soft-spoken he was sometimes regarded by fellow lawyers as innocuous; Shipman cultivated and encouraged this reputation, using it as a ploy to disarm opponents in court.

There was great affection between the three men, and in the last twenty years of his life Stan talked with Shipman every day on the phone. When Laurel and Hardy became a legal entity in later years, they insisted Shipman become the third unit of their partnership. He gave up his work at Roach in the Thirties to expand his legal practice, and to become Babe and Stan's full-time lawyer and accountant. At that time he little anticipated that his work for them would become the principal task of his working life.

Speaking of them in 1966, Ben said:

> Such sweet men. But oh, the problems they could get
> into! Particularly Stan, but Babe too. And most of it was
> woman trouble. I remember once, in Stan's checkered
> marital history, when it looked as if things couldn't get
> much more mixed up than they were, and I expressed my
> wonder at the very complexity of all this to Stan, he tried
> to soothe me by saying, 'Ben, don't worry. I know you'll
> work it out. Things are fine.' I said to him, 'If things are
> fine, how the hell do you explain why I'm so screwy?'
> That made him laugh, which is just why I said it. That
> was the blessing of being the lawyer for those two fine men.
> Somewhere, somehow, we always found time to laugh,
> and sometimes there was precious little to laugh about.'

Babe disliked writing anything, even personal letters, and it
was Shipman who composed the statement Babe gave to the
press in 1933 at the time of reconciliation with Myrtle:

> I am glad to announce that the difficulties which existed
> between Mrs Hardy and myself have been definitely con-
> cluded. It is most happy that both of us have had the
> good fortune of being enabled to consider our seemingly
> great difficulties separately and impersonally, and thus
> be able to see them in their proper light. Both of us felt
> that if some adjustment was possible, it should be done
> to save the true comradeship which has sprung through
> years of devotion and common struggle. We are making
> a new start, realizing that we owe to each other the
> duty of taking our just share of blame for any past
> misunderstanding, with the acknowledged determina-
> tion to achieve and preserve our new-found happiness.

This is attorney's rhetoric, but it was heartfelt by the
Hardys. This was Shipman's expansion of Babe's words: 'It's
both our faults. We've been through too much to give up now.'

Although Babe wrote occasional love notes to Myrtle and
short periodic letters to his mother, that was the extent of
his correspondence. Too aware of his deficiencies in syntax

and spelling, he left the fan mail, which was considerable, to Stan. Stan's own spelling and punctuation were uncertain but that did not overly concern him. He believed that anyone who wrote to Laurel and Hardy should receive a personal response, and to that end answered literally thousands of fan letters over a thirty-year period.

He always made it a point to include the correspondent's first name in the body of the letter or postcard for added warmth. Babe was greatly relieved that Stan took over this duty. On their standard Laurel and Hardy picture postcard, Babe's signature was duplicated, but Stan added his each time, individually. He grew to enjoy the task, and typically on the day before his death sent out five postcards and two letters to fans who had written.

By the early 1930s Stan and Ollie had become almost mythic in Hollywood, celebrated in cartoons and comic books, firmly placed in the pantheon of stars. Their physical identities were by now classic. Fat and Skinny wore clothing distinctly lower middle class, slightly out of fashion, but raggedly neat. They favoured stand-up collars, thereby giving them a faintly formal touch, Ollie wearing a four-in-hand, Stan a bow tie slightly askew. Their literally crowning hallmarks were the derbies. Stan said of them:

> Derbies have always seemed comic to me. They always suggested a man who was a little ritzy. Charlie [Chaplin], of course, always wore one, for the same reason we did: to give his character some dignity. Someone dignified doing something comic makes it more comic. The derbies Babe and I wore were smaller proportioned than regular derbies. They were actually boys' derbies – kids did wear them years ago – so we bought our first derbies in the children's section of a Los Angeles clothing store. They had all sizes for kids, just like adult derbies. But finally we had to have our own derbies specially made, not only because they stopped making them for kids but also because we would destroy quite a few in the course of the pictures, getting them smashed, and what have you, in the course of action.

*

By the early Thirties Stan and Babe had fully mastered the deliberately scaled-down pace of their reactions to each other. When, earlier, Stan and Leo McCarey had their inspired notion of deliberately reversing the traditional gallop of film comedy to a drawn-out tempo, they were also doing themselves a favour creatively. 'The longer we did that slower pace,' said Stan, 'the more we realized we were under less pressure to produce gags. We could cut down on the sheer number of them, and that was a relief come gag session time.'

This slowing down is seen to best advantage in their sound shorts, and particularly in *Them Thar Hills*, 1934. Stan and Ollie are confronted by an indignant Charlie Hall who is frightfully offended that they have allowed his wife, Mae Busch, to get inadvertently tipsy. This sparks off a series of mutual humiliations that flow along almost sedately – Stan, for instance, cutting hair from Charlie's head and affixing it to his chin with molasses, unhurriedly. Charlie quietly pours kerosene from a lamp over Ollie, and asks Stan politely for a match. Just as politely Stan obliges, and Ollie goes up in flames. The slow pace of this retaliatory process was so well received by the public in *Them Thar Hills* that it became the first and, as it turned out, only Laurel and Hardy film with a sequel. *Tit For Tat*, the title speaking for itself, filmed the following year, marks the zenith of the reciprocal destruction device. In *Tit For Tat*, Stan and Ollie open an electrical appliance shop which they are very surprised to find is next door to Charlie's grocery. Charlie remembers them very well indeed, and the goings-on, crossings-over and crossings-back, are a litany of retributive insult. With this, Babe and Stan realized they had gone just about as far as they could go with the device, and thereafter it appears hardly at all in the Laurel and Hardy canon.

In the early Thirties Laurel and Hardy's short sound films were tremendously successful, but exhibitors were asking for more and more full-length films. It was the day of the double feature, and Roach knew that inevitably the boys would have to accommodate to this need. In 1931 the team had begun a short prison picture, *The Rap*, with the boys as small-time bootleggers put in prison on perhaps the lowest level of blame conceivable: selling a bottle of beer to a policeman Stan took for a street-car conductor. Inside prison they incur the enmity of a rogue convict leader, and the boys unwittingly foil him and a prison break, winding up uncertain heroes.

Roach was never fussy about the length of his short subjects. If the film was doing well during creation, and the laughs were consistent and hearty, he did not object to a two-reeler becoming a three-reeler or even a bit beyond that. There was such good comic material in *The Rap* that Stan found it stretching easily to four reels. This gave Roach pause. 'Look,' he said to Stan, 'why should we give the distributors a four-reel picture for the price of a two? To hell with that. Add two more reels, and we've got a feature-length picture that we can sell at full-length price.'

The two reels were added, the title changed to *Pardon Us*, and Laurel and Hardy were in the big time, no longer an extra added attraction. Fortunately they continued with the two and three-reelers for a while, alternating with feature films until cartoons took over the short-subject field leaving Roach no alternative but to make longer films.

One of the short subjects made between their features shows Babe at his splendid best, in full command of his skills. Ollie-as-victim was never more delightfully realized than in *Helpmates*, 1932, where he is at the mercy of three aberrant forces of nature – a shrewish wife, his vacuous partner, and himself. The film begins with Ollie as the victim of his own foolishness. Spectacularly hung over, he looks disgustedly in the mirror, in stern self-chastisement, to accuse himself of 'pulling a wild party . . . Now, aren't you ashamed of yourself?' A telegram comes, saying his wife will be home at noon from a visit to her mother, so Ollie, desperately needing help to clean the party-strewn house, phones Stan. Stan had been unable to attend the party because a dog bit him and he was afraid of getting 'hydrophosphates'.

He comes over to Ollie's and sets briskly to work, helping his pal, turning every bit of aid into a personal disaster for

Ollie. That this is done in the name and deed of friendship only increases the fun. Babe's mastery as an actor lies in the reality of his reactions of horror and comic disgust at the cascading series of catastrophes his partner leads him into.

After ten minutes of such typical disasters as Stan's opening a cupboard, thereby causing a large bin of flour to fall down on Ollie, Ollie is sufficiently prepared to leave the house to meet his wife at the station. Before leaving, he tells Stan to get the house in apple pie order. Stan sets his mind to this task, an ominous matter. As a homely touch for Mrs Hardy's arrival, he places several logs in the fireplace but is a little surprised that a single match lit beneath fails to get them going. He then soaks the logs heavily with kerosene and takes a match from his pocket. The scene fades.

Fade-in. Ollie returns, and as he crosses up to the front of his house, he is sporting a very large black eye. He is considerably alone. He opens the front door of his lovely house, only to see Stan hosing down its smoking, roofless interior. Ollie steps forward incredulously, and crashes through the charred floor. With a show of Job-like patience, he asks what has happened. Stan blubbers, 'Well, I wanted to make a nice fire to make it comfortable for you!' Ollie ponders this, finding it hard to summon up appropriate words for the occasion.

'Well, I guess there's nothing else I can do,' Stan says thoughtfully.

Ollie ponders that one. 'I guess not.'

'Well, I'll be seeing you,' Stan says as he prepares to leave.

'Hey –' Ollie says. 'Would you mind closing the door? I'd like to be *alone*.'

Stan takes his departure in hopeless fashion, but the gods are not through with Ollie yet. It starts raining while he is sitting meditatively in a large chair, the only one left in the house. As the rain comes down, he sighs and carefully removes a piece of lint from his pants. This little bit of business, which Babe contributed, is a master touch. Ollie's neatness and precision in the face of disaster is thus highlighted, and the last shot in the film is quintessential Ollie – battered, resigned, yet impeccable in his dignity, beaten but indestructible. Fade out.

Helpmates may be the most representative of all Laurel and Hardy films. It certainly is in respect to who gets the most laughs: Babe.

Because Stan either created their gags for them, or shaped gag men's ideas to the Laurel and Hardy formula, and also because he dearly loved to get a laugh, it initially surprised some people at the studio that he almost always in their films tried to give Babe most of the laughs. But Stan understood, and just as importantly, Babe understood, that their structure of ignorance-causing-disaster needed a rest point of reaction in order to be appreciated at full. That point was Ollie, the fall guy quite literally, the invariable recipient of the sticky end of the gag. Babe's tremendous skills of reaction, as he hoped, frequently doubled the laughs in their films and this thrilled Stan. One wonders if he ever recalled his fear of years before when Joe Rock suggested Babe as comedic support for him. Stan now spent many hours thinking of ways for Babe to get the climactic laughs in all their episodes.

It is likely the greater number of laughs he evokes between them that causes some admirers of Laurel and Hardy to consider Hardy the funnier of the two. This is like saying H of H_2O is better than O, but it is not an uncommon statement. 'Some rather undiplomatic guy once asked me if I thought I was funnier than Babe,' Stan once said. 'I told him the truth. I told him I laugh a hell of a lot harder at Babe than I ever did at myself – and I'm sure never afraid to laugh at myself if I think I'm really funny.'

In his autobiography, Dick Cavett makes the interesting point that although he finds Stan the more sympathetic of the two, and '. . .even though I adored him and Hardy when I was a kid . . . I have to agree with Woody Allen that Hardy is probably superior from an artistic point of view – the finer screen comedian. Laurel came from a broader stage tradition, and his gestures and reactions are sometimes a bit too large for the screen, whereas Hardy's are precise to the fingertips, scaled perfectly to the distance of the camera.'

There is truth in this. Stan's gestures are larger than

his partner's. Babe's are certainly more precise and more accurately shaped for the camera than Stan's. But without dismissing the Cavett/Allen theory, it must be remembered that Stan is playing a creature loose in body and thought process, not at all well self-contained. His loping saunter and deep vagueness would inevitably make him wider and more open of gesture than his ever-fussy partner. Ollie, in deliberate contrast, is a fuss-budget, devoted to useless precision. He is one who adores the exactness of small effect for its own sake. This is seen nowhere more memorably than in use of his hands.

In *Be Big*, 1931, the utterly prosaic task of ringing a doorbell becomes for Ollie a happy act of manual affirmation. Before he pushs the bell with one finger, he revolves his entire hand in a precise circle, then triumphantly puts his finger forward. Ollie is alone; he does not do this for effect, that is — for anyone else's effect but his own. Ollie does this because manual movement must ever be ritualistically fancy. In *Them Thar Hills*, setting up a little table for dinner, he unfolds it, then strokes his stretched fingers three times across the top in a centre-to-side movement, in soothing caress, topping it all with a quick downthrust of his extended fingers. This is a coda of blessing, a joyous ultimate. Next, Ollie puts the table cloth on, repeats the movements, but now for his coda efficiently removes a speck of dust. This is all movement for the *joy* of movement, in rococo.

Cavett, in speaking of his opinion that Babe is a finer film artist than Stan, adds however this appealing thought:

> But somehow this is an admission I make only reluctantly. There is some kind of affectionate edge to Laurel. I suppose you could evoke a theory that we all feel picked on as kids, and that, since Stan seems more picked on than Ollie, we identify with him.

If Stan is more picked on, Ollie certainly suffers more. That is a delicate kind of comic balance while these two wait for their own Godot.

*

Although Babe agreed with Stan that in terms of artistry, it would have been better to have remained in the short-subject category, it was undeniable that they were getting more critical attention when they entered the feature market. The most attractive aspect of the feature films was the salary increase they brought, but there were other compensations. Of Laurel and Hardy's twenty-three feature films, Babe always preferred the ones with what he called 'production', films containing more than comedy – usually good music – and set in something of a cultural milieu.

Like Stan, he insisted that the production values be kept high, values seen throughout most of *Fra Diavolo (The Devil's Brother)*, a laugh-packed version of Auber's 1830 opera, laugh-packed, that is, when Stan and Ollie are around. The film is like a good racing car forced to half engine power when the straight sub-plot surfaces. Yet it has exquisite moments of comedy that make one almost forget the soggy musical numbers which are largely flat and uninteresting. The best of the comic moments is Stan becoming drunk while filling up a large pitcher from flagons of wine passed to him by Ollie, who draws the wine from a barrel above. When the pitcher is full, Stan cannot think of where to put the wine except to drink it to make room for more. As usual, Ollie's look of incredulity on realizing his friend is besotted is directed to the camera, and it is profound.

Ollie has similar moments of stunned disbelief when Stan plays little tricks of physical dexterity with his fingers that Ollie cannot duplicate. The standard Hardy camera-look had by now grown into a wide-encompassing range of reactions: angered disbelief, stunned horror, injured anger, and total incredulity. The audiences grew to love these extensions, and they still live on in contemporary performers who cherish them, notably Johnny Carson who uses the Hardy camera-look as he stares into the television camera in comic astonishment at a guest's *faux pas*. Carson also profitably mimics Stan's reactions on occasion. His ultimate tribute to Laurel and Hardy is that he does not have to identify the source of these reactions.

*

As Babe's success in the feature films grew apace, so too did Myrtle's problem. Just after reconciliation in 1933, she would go off occasionally to drink with old friends but these visits were far between and not protracted. Then gradually they grew in number and duration. Certain afternoons Babe would come home to find her unusually vivacious and talkative, always a bad sign. Quietly, he would hunt for the bottle, usually finding it in the toilet tank. He never confronted her with his discovery. But increasingly he grew tired of coming home. Mostly he was able to steer her back to Rosemead Sanitarium.

Babe was not alone in his troubles. In the Thirties Stan's personal life was entering the realm of the bizarre. His wife, Lois, got a divorce in October 1933, California law stipulating that the final decree become binding a year later. This was the year Stan met and actively wooed an attractive blonde widow, Virginia Ruth Rogers, marrying her in Mexico on April 2, 1934, a marriage completely invalid in California. Stan hastened to assure the press that he and Virginia would not live together until his divorce decree became final in six months. This did not sit well with Hal Roach who asserted, quite accurately, that he ran a 'family' studio. Newspaper accounts of Stan and Babe's marital troubles disturbed him greatly.

Roach also began to argue with Stan about Laurel and Hardy scripts. *Babes in Toyland,* the charming 1903 Victor Herbert musical extravaganza, was Roach's choice as a feature vehicle for Babe and Stan, and to that end he wrote a plot outline on which he spent much time and creative energy. In keeping with its Mother Goose orientation, he conceived of Babe as the Pieman and Stan as Simple Simon. He gave the treatment to Stan who found it flat out unsatisfactory.

Roach found Stan's reaction just as unsatisfactory, and acrimonious wrangling began on the matter to the point where Roach gave up in disgust, and told Stan to do what he wanted with the film. Roach's plot for the film was a clever one and might have made a most satisfactory script. We shall never know. But what Stan finally put together was a delightful film that has won respectful critical notice through the years. It also won Roach's ill-will, and thereafter he and Stan clashed on artistic matters.

Through the years, indeed to the very present, Roach has maintained that Stan was a gag man virtually without peer, and absolutely dreadful on story. Stan, he says, '. . . in story construction was just impossible. His things were – hell, a ten year-old kid could have written better.' If Stan was so dreadful at story construction, one must ask why the films he made, with few exceptions, turned out so very well. This is not to denigrate Roach, a kindly man who gave much comedy to the world. It is possible his way may have been better. One must be grateful to Roach for allowing Stan to do things his way. Most studio heads would not in any way have countenanced such active dissent.

Certainly in the *Babes in Toyland* disagreement between Roach and Stan one finds the first impetus for Laurel and Hardy's ultimate departure from the Roach lot, something Stan admitted later quite freely was a mistake. Babe tried to remain studiedly neutral in all of this, having close loyalties to both Roach and Stan, although he always went along with whatever his partner wanted.

When they finished *Babes in Toyland,* Babe had an operation his doctor had long advocated – removal of his tonsils. After recuperating he hosted a Mexican hunting party with his friends Grantland Rice, Frank Lloyd, Guy Kibbee, Frank Craven, Douglas Dumbrille and Hal Roach. Babe developed a qualified interest in hunting. At first he shot all kinds of animals but then found himself unable to hunt deer after killing his first in Utah on a previous occasion. The sight of the animal's soft eyes in pain made him limit his hunting thereafter to creatures that farmers found predatory.

On return from Mexico, Babe and Stan did several two-reelers, *Tit For Tat* and *The Fixer Uppers*, and discussion began on a feature film with a Scottish theme. This, given Stan's Scottish background, could have been a very agreeable artistic challenge. The story, going through several working titles to *McLaurel and McHardy,* was written by others at the studio before Stan was consulted on its content. He disliked the script, and Roach, not wanting the kind of squabble that had characterized *Babes in Toyland,* reacted strongly to Stan's dissent by firing him.

There was added reason for Roach's anger. He had been talking about contract renewal to Stan, and Stan, hoping that he and Babe could be united in a single contract thus giving them more control over their future, was just not ready to talk with Roach.

The day after Stan was let go, Roach announced that the Laurel and Hardy films would be replaced by a new series, The Hardy Family, consisting of Babe as pater-familias, Patsy Kelly as his wife, and Spanky McFarland as their child. This was news to Babe.

The newspapers carried stories to the effect that Laurel and Hardy were no more, this becoming the germ of subsequent, still persistent, rumours that Babe and Stan had quarrelled and ended their friendship. A *Los Angeles Times* reporter found Babe on the golf course when Stan was fired and asked him if the team had broken up. Honestly bewildered, Babe said:

> We've not broken up. We're the best of friends. [Stan] and I have been together longer than seven years and our team must not be broken up. I spoke to him today and he can't understand it either. I think the difficulty is between him and the studio. His contract expires in May and mine in November.

Babe had put his finger on the problem. In addition to the artistic differences between Stan and Roach, the latter had always made a point of keeping Babe and Stan under separate contract, in this way giving himself an advantage in contract negotiation. He continued this kind of jockeying for years.

Babe and Stan got together and decided that in view of Stan's dismissal by the studio it was imperative they show unity publicly and dramatically. They accomplished this by getting into their tuxes and going to dinner together at the

Ambassador Hotel's Coconut Grove, a popular film colony hang-out. To make sure everyone got the idea, they walked into the dining-room arm in arm.

Roach cooled down. Within a week, Stan and Roach were reconciled, the fictional Hardy Family evaporated and plans were announced for *McLaurel and McHardy,* soon to undergo a title change to *Bonnie Scotland.* This film, like several to follow in a vein begun with *Fra Diavolo,* might best be labelled dichotomous, splendid Laurel and Hardy mixed with unsplendid sub-plots usually featuring a pair of young lovers frustrated, then unfrustrated. The double plot, two interwoven stories – one funny, one straight – will work when the straight story is interesting, which in *Bonnie Scotland* it is not. The prevailing studio thinking was that Babe and Stan were not quite up to sustaining a whole full-length film by themselves, a curious theory when one considers that a previous Laurel and Hardy film, *Sons of the Desert,* a single plot film featuring the boys in hilarious high jinks away from their wives at a convention, was a great success.

There were certain difficulties in the making of *Bonnie Scotland.* The juvenile originally cast for the love story, Barry Norton, made the mistake of arriving on the set with all his lines fully memorized, a futile procedure in a Laurel and Hardy film where plot and gag improvisation was rule of thumb. Norton could not accommodate to this kind of shifting activity, and he was let go, replaced by versatile William Janney who could. The love story was given so much prominence in the film that at its preview it seemed Laurel and Hardy were supporting players. Twenty minutes were duly cut from the love story at the expense of the flow of the film and *Bonnie Scotland,* despite some charming Stan and Ollie segments, is flawed.

William Janney recalls the shooting of one of the best bits in the picture. Stan, Ollie and Janney as British soldiers in India are marching along, Stan hopelessly out of step. His uncadenced hops trying to get into the others' rhythm gradually forces everyone else to fall out of step, too. For this scene Babe and Stan used rifles made of balsa but Janney insisted on a real one, to his sorrow that very hot day. During a break, a grip came over to well-perspired Babe, handing him an ample canteen from which he took several swallows. Consumed with thirst, Janney asked Babe if he might have a drink. Babe nodded, and Janney drank eagerly. 'It almost took the top of my head off,' said Janney. The flask was full of straight gin. Babe exploded into mischievous laughter. He was not a heavy drinker but he did use alcohol on occasion during difficult shooting to sustain his energy.

Myrtle, on the other hand, needed alcohol constantly for release from her own pervasive fears and apprehensions, fears she could never articulate either to her husband or psychiatrist. In the summer of 1935 Babe again persuaded her to enter Rosemead, then took a vacation he badly needed. *Bonnie Scotland* had been unusually hard work. He bought a new eight-cylinder car, of which he was extremely proud, and drove to Seattle. He explained to a *Seattle Times* reporter that there was no disagreement between Stan and himself, in answer to a query he was to hear unendingly thereafter. He explained patiently to the reporter that he and Stan had never had 'one cross word in eight years. We both realize that one without the other would be like salt without pepper. I attribute our being together to contrast. My stuff wouldn't suit Stan and his stuff wouldn't suit me. We're staying together.'

He spent two days in Seattle seeing friends and visiting the local race track, an invariable homing ground wherever he went. At the track the judges invited him to come up and see the races from their stand. 'No thanks,' he said. 'I'm on my vacation and I'm having fun right where I am.' After Seattle he left for a fishing trip at Diamond Lake, near Crater Lake, then back to Los Angeles.

There he found Myrtle had been a pretty good girl. She seemed to be doing well enough at Rosemead and told Babe so proudly. He began work on another dichotomous film, *The Bohemian Girl*, based on Balfe's 1843 opera. Myrtle sent Babe a note from the sanitarium expressing her love, and asking him to visit her despite an agreement they made that he would not see her until her current regimen of treatment was over. His reply – and it is the only extant holograph Babe Hardy letter – shows why he disliked writing them. The lack of punctuation and spelling errors were typical, as was the wholehearted love:

> [From Roach Studios,
> c. Nov. 20, 1935]

Dear little girl –
I was so pleased to get your sweet letter and invitation today at 4³⁰. I don't think it advisable to see you as it would make matters worse. For that day, I am going to the desert hunting, But I have gotten you a little something which I hope you will like particularly the inscription on the inside. I will be with you as always in *mind and heart* as you are never out of my mind. I would have written you before, but your letter is the first that I knew you could receive mail there. Regardless of the future dear to try and be the strong sweet little baby that you will always be in your daddys heart. Have been working awfully hard there has been so much illness on this picture. Stan was layed up for 2½ weeks Mae Busch for 4 weeks it seems we have been on it for a year – Happy anniversary dear and I hope you like what I have gotten for you – I will send something to the house Wed morning – Be sweet, think sweet and know that my devotion had never changed and never will But we must go *up hill* and *not back* so consequently why that next time must be the time – *I love you darling* everlastingly

> Daddy
> X

The X occupies a large portion of the page and is, of course, meant to be a big kiss. The gift mentioned has not survived. Their wedding anniversary, the fourteenth, was immediately pending. The 'next time' refers to their forthcoming reunion which, like all the others, was a success – for a time. In the end it was time itself – the constant pattern of Myrtle breaking from constraints, physical and mental, into temporary wanderings – that finally wore both of them down. In essence, Myrtle got tired of being forgiven and Babe had no more forgiveness to offer.

The occasion for their final separation was a triviality. One Sunday in July 1936 she asked Babe to take her for a drive, 'a long drive', she specified, but he said he wanted to play golf, and that he would return that evening and take her out then. She was adamant; so was he. 'He became very upset,' she testified at a temporary alimony hearing shortly after, 'so I took a little trip by myself.' She went to church, then disappeared for two weeks.

In her complaint for separate maintenance she said she had proof that Babe, a year before, had entered a woman's apartment at 2:25 am, carrying bottles of liquor. He left at 3:45 am. In her suit for the maintenance Myrtle was asking $2500 monthly, a hefty sum for the time, 'payable in advance'.

Babe had certainly been dating other women whenever the need for undemanding female companionship arose. During the making of *Our Relations*, a marvellous non-dichotomous film in which he and Stan find themselves in a *Comedy of Errors* relationship with their twins, Babe approached a member of the cast. Iris Adrian, the ebullient archetype of the wise-cracking chorus girl, played a tart in the film, and Babe was attracted to her – as what normal male would not be. After shooting a scene with her, he asked if she would go to dinner with him. She agreed, and that evening got dressed for the date. Her phone rang. It was Babe. He had come home after work, quite tired, and after a few drinks began to feel not unusual symptoms of his general worthlessness as a swain. He told her she really didn't want to go out with him. 'I'm an old fat fellow,' he told her. 'You wouldn't like me.' She did not think of him as an old fat fellow, and told him so. But his lack of self-regard won out.

Myrtle, in suing for her $2500 a month allowance, following the advice of her lawyer, claimed 'extreme mental cruelty', the usual charge in a case where physical violence was not

involved, adding that she and her husband had separated and
reconciled 'eight or ten times', that her husband's 'grouchy
and ugly attitude and demeanour' had given her a nervous
breakdown, and that he had 'fraudulently' caused her to be
confined in a sanitarium against her will.

In reply to these total inaccuracies, Babe specified in detail
instances of Myrtle's drinking, of her attendant drying-out
periods at Rosemead and of her departures from there
('escapes' he termed them), on one occasion breaking her
ankle while doing so. He spoke of her once leaving their
home quite drunk, with $35,000 on her person, this causing
him great anxiety as he began an exhaustive six-week search
for her. Myrtle counter-charged that on one of her 'trips' from
home, she returned and was turned away by guards Babe had
hired for that purpose. Babe admitted this.

The emotional strain of testifying to all these wretched
events in public hit Babe powerfully when he took the stand.
It was one thing to say these things in a lawyer's office. It was
overwhelming to do so in public court facing many strangers
and a row of reporters. While testifying, the years of agony
with his wife overcame him, and he began to weep. Myrtle,
in the chair facing his, began to weep, too. The judge ordered
the court cleared until Babe regained control. After further
testimony, the judge gave his decision. He allowed Myrtle
separate maintenance but gave her $1000 a month instead
of $2500.

One week later Madelyn Hardy, Babe's first wife, appeared
in New York claiming fifteen years' back alimony. 'I landed
the jobs he got as extra, and the first real movie positions
he had were all my doing,' she said incorrectly. 'I was
well known and earning lots more than he was in those
days,' she declared with considerable more accuracy. She
claimed they had signed an agreement giving her thirty dollars a week from 1921 in perpetuity, but that the document
had been destroyed by fire. 'But I have witnesses,' she said.
Ben Shipman sighed and talked at length with her lawyer,
an agreement was signed, and Madelyn left Babe's life in
comparative affluence.

At times it seemed Stan's marital troubles marched hand-in-hand with his partner's. Stan's two-year marriage to Virginia Ruth Rogers was ill-starred from the beginning, and he was divorced the same year Babe got his freedom from Myrtle, in 1937. Stan's life was further complicated by an old flame from *his* past, Mae Laurel, his former vaudeville partner and common-law wife, who suddenly appeared from Australian exile to sue for alimony. Ever-patient Ben Shipman settled this one out of court, too. The fact that Stan remarried Virginia Ruth four years later and divorced her five years after that – to an even more complicated set of alimony claims – gave Shipman, as he told Stan, 'a permanent case of the triple conniption fits'.

The Hardy divorce case was uncomplicated. The heart of it was a simple exchange between Babe and Shipman. Babe was asked on the stand, 'did [Myrtle] say she no longer cared for you, and wanted you to get a divorce?' Babe replied simply, 'Yes.' Myrtle was given a good property settlement, and the alimony was satisfactory to her. With typical concern she sent Babe a telegram wishing him well, and he responded with one of his own:

THANKS FOR SWEET WIRE THAT LADY COULD ONLY BE SWEET ANYWAY ALWAYS KEEP IN MIND THAT THERE IS ONLY ONE THING IN ANY LIFE AND THAT IS YOU AND YOUR WELFARE THIS MOVE IS BEST FOR BOTH

ALWAYS YOUR HONEY

OLIVER

It is to be noted that Babe never thought of himself as Babe. He signed that name, which he never cared for, in cards to friends and working acquaintances, all of whom knew him only by that designation. To his family he had always been and always would be Norvell. But to himself he was Oliver, son of a Civil War hero and courtly Georgian of that name he had never met. But under any name – Oliver, Norvell or Babe – he knew himself just about as well as he did his dad.

With his divorce, Babe felt a relaxation of spirit. Looming were other stresses just ahead. It is sometimes said, and validly, that a real pro is one who can do his job well even when he is not inclined to. This obtained in the span 1936–1940 for Babe and Stan who, in those years, had enough personal and professional troubles to swamp them several times over. Yet those were the golden years of their feature film making. In those years they made such excellent movies as *Our Relations, Way Out West, Swiss Miss, Block-Heads, The Flying Deuces, and A Chump at Oxford*. During those years Babe got divorced, Stan got divorced *three* times, and both made a series of headline-getting court appearances they found demeaning and ludicrous. It was also a time of great stress for them professionally in that bit by bit they were leaving the homely studio that had given them birth.

Stan felt compelled to challenge Roach again on several artistic matters. A key plot device in *Swiss Miss* was cut from the film without explanation to Stan. In the film, a tipsy Stan and a determined Ollie push and pull a piano across a swaying rope bridge high above a deep Alpine chasm. Midway they meet a gorilla. Ample laughter in this situation, one would say, yet as originally written by Stan the comic tensions were far richer. As first shot, a jealous rival of the man who needs the piano plants a bomb in it. It will go off when a certain key is struck. It was planned that the many twistings and turnings of Stan, Ollie and the gorilla on the swaying rope bridge – especially the accidental falls of the intoxicated Stan against the keys – would deepen the suspense.

Before release of the film, however, and without Stan's knowledge, the scene showing the rival planting the bomb was removed by the studio, and the rope bridge scene now contains shots of Stan crashing meaninglessly against the keys. The deletion, without either his knowledge or consent, upset him considerably.

Moreover, in their next film, *Block-Heads*, Stan was again thwarted by Roach, this time in altering what could have been the funniest moment in the picture. Here there may be allowable argument that the scene, as Stan planned it, had overtones of the grotesque. Today it would be considered mild indeed.

Block-Head's comic villain, big game hunter Billy Gilbert, finding the guiltless Mrs Gilbert in what seems to be a compromising situation – in Ollie's pyjamas, in Ollie's flat, in the absence of Ollie's wife – chases Ollie and Stan with his elephant gun. He blasts away at them as they run out of their apartment building. Then comes the film's final scene as conceived by Stan: Ollie and Stan are in separate trophy mounts over Gilbert's fireplace. Ollie turns his face to Stan and utters his by now classic lament, 'Well – here's another nice mess you've gotten us into!'

Roach cut this scene after previewing it, substituting his own choice for the ending, one that had been used for a 1928 Laurel and Hardy short, *We Faw Down*, in which shotgun blasts at the boys as they run between two buildings cause men in various states of undress to jump out of windows, thus making it a very busy afternoon for miscellaneous adulterers. This same shot was remade to end *Block-Heads*, with Babe and Stan portrayed by doubles. Stan's living-trophies-over-the-mantel is surely funnier and more appropriate than the one by Roach, and he felt understandable resentment at this encroachment on his artistic rights.

This episode, plus Roach's keeping Babe and Stan under separate contracts, finally caused Stan to rebel. In 1939 his current contract ended and he resolved not to sign again with Roach unless it was with Babe in a team contract. Babe's own contract had several months to run.

In that interim Roach took what first seemed tentative steps to team Babe with the once great Harry Langdon who had been working as a writer at the studio. Tentative is the word. The result was an undistinguished film, *Zenobia*, in which Babe plays a straight role, a warm-hearted country doctor, most capably. He is not in any comedic sense teamed with Langdon in the film, thus quashing newspaper reports that Roach indeed was trying to create a new pair of comics. The humour in *Zenobia*, a rural domestic comedy, was not stressed, although Babe did not allow a few Ollie-isms to appear, such as camera-looks, double takes and at one point saying, 'That's a *fine* state of affairs,' a variation on his best-known lament to Stan. The film failed at the box office.

During the making of *Zenobia,* and for most of 1938 and 1939, Stan experienced the worst months of his existence. In January 1938 he married Vera Shuvalova, a very tall, husky Russian singer and dancer using the stage name Illeanna. Illeanna, a self-styled countess, was in Ben Shipman's words, 'a dame who gave the word "dame" a very bad name'. She and Stan made a strange pair.

She drank prodigiously, quarrelled loudly, embraced violently, sang emotionally overwrought songs on request and not on request – and this was only in public. Privately she was even more intense – in sum, a one-woman mob scene. Stan's Beverly Hills neighbours complained periodically about the noisy quarrels coming from his house, usually accompanied by smashed window panes and other rude sounds of the night.

Illeanna once upset Stan so much that she drove him to drink. No one, man or woman, had ever done that to this most genial man. During a fight, he sought relief in liquor, jumping in his car to get away from her. He wound up speeding crazily down the wrong side of the street, was arrested, charged with drunk driving, sent to trial and got a hung jury, mostly in his favour. Later the charges were dropped.

A few days later, Illeanna got drunk herself during one of their set-tos, got into the same vehicle, drove off and smashed into two cars parked nearby. She was given a five-day sentence, and when Stan came to collect her, they kissed passionately, and argued violently all the way home. The next week the Laurels had such a calamitously loud fight that the police were called to quiet the din. The newspapers made merry note of all these caterwaulings, week after week, and Hal Roach ground his teeth.

Quiet little Ben Shipman finally could take no more. He went to Stan and said, 'You are probably my best friend in all this world. So I can tell you quite frankly that you are making a complete and total ass of yourself. You are ruining your health, and you are ruining your career with this woman. To tell you nothing more and nothing less than the truth, you are acting like a God-damned fool.'

Stan listened. He divorced Illeanna a few weeks later, in May 1939.

Babe felt enormous sympathy for his partner. During all the troubles with Illeanna, he felt that he was hardly the man to give his friend advice, but he was greatly pleased that Shipman had taken the initiative in that mater. Stan's spirits were considerably lifted after he shed Illeanna. Relationships with Roach improved.

Shortly after *Zenobia* was made, Babe and Stan signed with Roach to make four pictures described by Roach as 'streamliners', or four-reel films, a length halfway between short subject and feature film. Roach also agreed to lend Babe and Stan out to independent producer Boris Morris for a film, *The Flying Deuces*, to be released through RKO.

First of the Roach four-reelers was *A Chump at Oxford*, which because of its short length was able to concentrate on the boys instead of a soggy sub-plot. It is in consequence first-rate comedy. Babe and Stan then went to work for Morros in a studio new to them, the independent General Service Studio, on Melrose Avenue. Shooting for *The Flying Deuces* began the summer of 1939.

It was the most momentous move of Babe's life. There was a script clerk on the film – not just a script girl who follows continuity during the shooting – but the script clerk, who in addition to keeping continuity types the script in direct consultation with the writers and is present on all phases of its creation. For *The Flying Deuces* this was Virginia Lucille Jones, a very pretty, very petite brunette.

She became Babe's world, and for the first time in his forty-seven years – as he told Stan in wonderment – his personal life had meaning.

8

Lucille

Lucille's first encounter with Babe was unpleasant – for her. The very first day of shooting on *The Flying Deuces*, just minutes after meeting him, Lucille had a run-in with Babe. She says:

> The master scene had been shot, and the camera had moved in for an individual shot of Babe. His hat, which had been off in the master scene, was on. He wasn't holding his gloves and cane as he had been doing in the previous scene so I started to tell him this just before the shooting began. This is a part of keeping everything in the film in continuity and was an essential part of my job. In a very gentlemanly way and with an almost courtly gesture, he stopped me by saying, 'I know how it was, my dear. Don't you worry. *I'll* take care of everything.' I was so humiliated that I was speechless. My face turned red as a beet and I walked away thinking that somebody as pompous and conceited as that was just bound to mess everything up. But the minute the camera turned, I saw how wrong I was. He became the character he had been portraying. The dialogue, the mannerisms, every little gesture was flawless and matched the master scene perfectly.

Lucille did not at once get over her irritation, and Babe sensed this. He tried to win her over her by little acts of kindness and extra consideration. He was attracted by her beauty but also began to realize she was a person of substance, a caring, no-nonsense lady with an engaging sense of humour.

Within a matter of days he fell in love with Lucille but kept it to himself. He would even come to writers' sessions just to see her. He rarely went to these meetings except during those times when he felt he could offer meaningful reactions. She had no idea of his feelings for her.

Lucille came to Los Angeles from her native Phoenix, Arizona, where she was a secretary, then briefly an acrobatic adagio dancer. She loved dancing but a mishap while performing at the Biltmore Hotel, Phoenix, seriously affected her sacro-iliac, and she had to look elsewhere for work. She was interested in writing, and with some secretarial skills in hand, had worked for various authors as a secretary. From there it was a natural progression to become a script clerk. She got a job with Sol Lesser in that capacity, and later worked free-lance as one uniquely skilled in her field. Ellen Corby, who began her life in films as a Roach script girl, was working for Boris Morros, and when she left for a better job, Morros called Lucille in to become script clerk for *The Flying Deuces* the summer of 1939.

She was fascinated by the way Babe and Stan worked, noting two special things about their *modus operandi*. First, they tried to work in sequence as much as possible, creating as they went along, instead of in the usual Hollywood pattern of shooting all interiors at once, going to exteriors when done, for reasons of economy and facility. This was not Stan and Babe's way, their best films growing organically, one scene begetting another in natural progression. The second thing Lucille noticed about the team was that they used two cameras operating simultaneously. They did this because, as so frequently happened, they would not know just how one of their routines would end. To catch their improvisation, they needed both a long shot and a medium or close shot to capture every action.

Lucille enjoyed the script sessions on *The Flying Deuces* very much because she felt herself to be in the very heart of its creativity, and was in some small way contributing to it. The writers, among them Harry Langdon, sought to coalesce their thoughts, and one of the writers finally dictated dialogue that Lucille took down in shorthand. She read it back to them and a final draft of dialogue was agreed on. This she would type up at once, sometimes staying up all night to do it for the writers' final scrutiny in the morning. While typing these evenings, Lucille was pleased when Babe frequently brought her cups of coffee. She regarded this as most friendly and told her mother how 'very kind' Mr Hardy had been to her.

Lucille did such excellent work on *The Flying Deuces* that Stan asked Roach to hire her for their next film, *Saps at Sea*. This was done and Lucille fell into the by now familiar mode of writers' sessions – the note-taking, script-typing and revision periods. She also enjoyed the days of active production in her other capacity as script girl.

After *Saps at Sea* had been in work a few days, Roach stopped production on it because *A Chump at Oxford* in its four-reel length had been so successful in preview that he wanted two more reels added, thus bringing the picture up to regular feature length. *Saps at Sea* was put in abeyance and the added footage of *A Chump at Oxford* was shot. This was successfully completed and shooting was resumed on *Saps at Sea*. The very last day of its shooting was the first time Lucille had any inkling of Babe's feelings for her.

Babe and Stan were not on the set as she was watching some process shots with a number of crew people. Invited to look through the camera, Lucille did so, then stepped back on a roll of carpet and fell heavily. She felt little discomfort but half an hour later a blinding headache struck her. It was a minor concussion but a very painful one.

She was sent home, and Roach prop man Bob Sanders and his wife stopped by to see how she was, carrying a big box of chocolates from Babe. 'He is quite concerned about you,' Sanders said. A few days later a large bouquet of American Beauty roses came from Babe, and Lucille, although pleased, thought the gifts a bit unusual. Properly grateful, she resumed her duties at Roach, thanked Babe, and work began on editing and retakes of *Saps at Sea*. Babe developed the habit of coming into the script office and watching her type. Thinking he wanted to look at script revisions, she would push what she had typed across the desk to him. He usually ordered coffee for them, and did some desultory reading of the script.

One morning he said to her, 'Lucille, I want to talk to you. There's something personal I'd like to say.' She stopped typing. 'I don't want to shock you, but this is something I can't hold back any longer.' He got up and paced the floor. 'I just want to tell you the longer I know you, the more impressed I am. Just don't take this the wrong way, but it would make me the happiest man in the world if you'd be my wife.'

Lucille's mouth opened, her jaw dropped in astonishment. She was completely caught by surprise, then stammered a few meaningless sounds.

'That's all right,' he said. 'Don't answer me now. This must be a shock. I'm so much older than you. I just had to let you know this.'

They had never had so much as a single date, even for tea or coffee at the Roach commissary. Lucille told him to sit down and drink his coffee. She sat quietly, and let him talk, then told him she had a lot of thinking to do. Back home she told her mother of the proposal, and that cheerful lady said, 'Well, *I'm* not surprised. You've talked a lot about the studio in recent months of course, but you always stress Babe's doings more than anyone else's. You must be getting interested.'

Lucille had not realized that. She began to think about Babe and became very unsure of her feelings. One morning over their coffee in the office, he asked her if she had made up her mind.

'Well,' she said, 'I guess I hadn't realized it. My mother told me I was more interested in you than I realized. Maybe it could work out.' Lucille was nothing if not cautious, and Babe dexterously and quickly took what she said for agreement. 'What kind of wedding do you want?' he said. She replied, 'Well, if we do get married – and I guess you'll think this is crazy – I want to elope. But I want to tell my mother and take her with me.' She was quite serious.

'I'm so thankful you don't want a big wedding,' he said.

By now Lucille was realizing that she had more or less

committed herself to matrimony, and she did not find the thought displeasing. All retakes on *Saps at Sea* had been completed, and early in December 1939, Babe came to the studio and gave her a beautiful engagement ring. Two weeks later he visited her house for the first time, met her mother and formally asked for Lucille's hand. New Year's Eve 1940, Babe and Lucille, now comfortably engaged, had their first date at the Roosevelt Hotel, which featured the music of Harry Owens and his Hawaiian Orchestra. Thereafter their music was the couple's favourite.

There was – as he was apprehensively aware – one unfinished part of Babe's life. He had been very close to Viola Morse for a long time, but his commitment to her was never total, not pledged in any way. He regarded her with utmost affection but had no plans to marry. He had the excruciating experience of telling Viola that he had found the girl he wanted to marry. This was more than excruciating to Viola. According to newspaper reports, she took thirteen sleeping pills, went out for a drive and crashed into three cars, one of them a police cruiser.

In time Viola recovered, both physically and emotionally and this took some little doing. She had, moreover, the added trauma to bear of her young son's unexpected death. But valiant was the word for Viola. With great strength of character she left Los Angeles, took up new endeavours and became a successful businesswoman. One could always see in her the personable integrity that had so greatly attracted Babe through the years.

Babe and Lucille were married in Las Vegas the afternoon of March 7, 1940, attended by 'one of the largest elopment contingents on record', as one newspaper described it. With the two were her mother, sister and brother, the latter serving as Babe's best man. Also present were Ben Shipman and Stan's secretary, Jimmy Murphy. Stan was sent a telegram advising him of the event, and responded with an enthusiastic wire of congratulations. He had grown very fond of Lucille. The Hardys were married by Judge Roger Foley at the home of A W Ham, Las Vegas attorney, an old friend of Ben Shipman,

Babe giving his age as 48, Lucille hers as 26. After the ceremony they went to Riverside, California, and a bridal suite at Mission Inn there, returning to Los Angeles a few days later.

Babe almost immediately bought a three-bedroom ranch home on Magnolia Avenue in North Hollywood, on three pleasant acres with pool, guest house and stables. The newly-weds settled in comfortably, and found their neighbours most friendly. Next door was orchestra leader Horace Heidt, and across the street was Western star, Buck Jones. He and Babe were old friends, Babe having appeared with Jones in a picture years before.

Laurel and Hardy were entering a new phase of life, and they felt confident albeit a bit homeless. At the completion of *Saps at Sea* in December 1939, they left Roach, hopeful that their new company, Laurel and Hardy Feature Productions, incorporated three months before, would find backing somewhere in Hollywood. Ben Shipman, secretary-treasurer of the company, began to inquire at the major studios. Stan was president of their company, Babe vice-president.

Babe felt more secure financially in 1940 than ever before. He had given up horses and that saved him many thousands of dollars. Gambling until now had been his dark mistress, his secret and sometimes not so secret vice. The race-track was always his passion, so much so that in the Thirties he became a founding investor in Del Mar Race-Track along with his buddy, Bing Crosby. When that commitment was made, he decided to go all out and start his own stable, complete with racing colours of green and white. He hired a top contract trainer and an excellent jockey, supported by a stableman and exercise boy.

But Babe was ruled in this game by his heart, not his head. Typically, one day when the trainer, Frank Childs, told him that one of the Hardy horses racing that afternoon just needed the experience and couldn't possibly win, Babe bet to win, and considerably more than a sawbuck. He loved every horse he owned and felt great if unwarrantable pride in each one. The saying at the track was that Babe's horses were the equal of any until the time came to run. One of his horses, Miss Chase, according to sports columnist Henry McLemore, 'went to the post six times and loving it so well, stayed there six times'.

Manny, Babe's favourite among his horses, was a far cry from Miss Chase. Manny was worked up into a top claiming race, a big and prestigious money affair. That day Babe was detained at the studio and could not find anyone to bet on Manny for him. Once out of the studio and dying to get to the track, he was held up by traffic and, maddeningly, got there just in time to hear that Manny had won, paid a big price, and had been claimed by someone else. That was the end of Babe's love affair with racing. He sold his stable and retired his colours. By 1940 he knew that his race-track days were distinctly over.

By 1940 he had become a great homebody. Either home or Lakeside were his hang-outs; he tended to favour the former. The Hardys rarely went to night-clubs. Babe had had his fill of those, what with singing nightly in the cabarets of his youth. 'I've had enough,' he told Lucille – to which she, still very much a young woman, was tempted to reply, 'But I haven't!' She never did because, deep down, she always enjoyed doing what he did. He was fond of bringing home card-playing buddies from Lakeside, unannounced, for dinner, apologizing to Lucille for it. She did not mind, and actually thrived on it. Her explanation for not getting upset at what would vastly irritate most wives was simple. 'They were all such *good* company,' she said.

Lucille did most of their cooking but Babe would create special gourmet dishes on which he spent much time and care. He made ethereal waffles ('Too good for the gods!' Ben Shipman described them), great hamburgers of a special blend, a superb Caesar salad, and spaghetti and meatballs that were a triumph, the sauce taking all day to prepare. The Hardys had a fruit orchard on their property, growing four kinds of plums, three varieties of peaches, in addition to apricots, figs, and an extensive range of citrus fruits. Many of these fruits they bottled and Babe helped sterilize jars and tighten lids.

Once in the midst of this extremely domestic chore, he looked lovingly at Lucille and said, 'Oh, you don't know how happy I am just to be doing this. It's the exact opposite of my life with Myrtle. With her it was stress, strain, stress, strain. Now here I am putting lids on a jar of tomatoes, and feeling just like a kid let out of school!'

The Hardys would visit friends' homes, usually Lakeside members, people from a wide variety of professions, unlike Stan's friends, all of whom were show people. At times Babe and Stan would co-host a party at the little theatre on Babe's property he had named The Laurel and Hardy Fun Factory. Guests on these occasions were principally old friends from the Roach lot. Babe and Stan did not mix a great deal socially, their general interests being so different. They shared birthday celebrations together as a rule, usually in the form of barbecues at Stan's home in Canoga Park. He called his place 'Fort Laurel', explaining it was his one retreat from ex-wives. Stan loved barbecues. 'I'm used to them. I've been roasted enough by the women in my life!' he told Shipman.

One of Babe's favourite guests before he married Lucille was his school-teacher sister, Emily Crawford, who came to Los Angeles in the late Twenties. She gave her life to youth, becoming supervisor at the Los Angeles Orphans Home, teaching without salary. Babe would often take her out to dinner, but rarely had her at home when Myrtle was in his life, for obvious reasons. After he married Lucille, he looked forward to having Emily out to the North Hollywood house, but she became seriously ill and died three months after his marriage. He paid her funeral expenses, and went with Lucille to her funeral, considerably upset at his loss. 'A gentle, sweet and giving lady,' he described her.

Finished with their Roach contract, Stan and Babe set about looking for employment, and not finding immediate interest in them by the studios, decided to strike out on their own. Asked to do a Red Cross benefit at Treasure Island, San Francisco, Stan quickly wrote a fifteen-minute sketch featuring Babe and himself at a driver's licence bureau. This was so well received that it made them think the sketch might be used profitably for stage appearances. Stan expanded the sketch, and it became the heart of *The Laurel and Hardy Revue*, a series of vaudeville acts, including a line of girls, capped by the sketch, that went on tour in September 1940 to a number of American cities.

The flavour of their sketch can be found in these two brief excerpts where Stan and Ollie confront a cop at the licence bureau.

OLLIE	If you don't mind, I'd like to renew my driver's licence.
COP	(*hands form to him*) Just fill out the application.
OLLIE	(*whose arm is in a sling*) I'm sorry, sir, but owing to a slight accident, I don't write.
COP	Well, get your friend to fill it in for you.
OLLIE	I'm sorry, sir, but you see, he can write, but he can't read.
COP	If you can't write, and he can't read, how come?
STAN	Well, you see, we both went to different schools together.

After further confusing the cop, they confuse him altogether. The British strain in this is strong:

COP	You say your name is Oliver N. Hardy?
OLLIE	That's correct, sir.
COP	What does the N. stand for?
OLLIE	*En*ry.
COP	*En*ry?
STAN	Yes, *En*ry *Ar*dy.
COP	Enry Ardy?
STAN	Yes. And you spell the Holiver with a 'Ho'!
COP	Enry? Now see here, you do *not* write Henry with a N.

STAN   (*indignantly.*) Of course you don't. You
            write it with a pencil!

Rehearsals of the *Revue* were held in the Laurel and Hardy
Fun Factory, and the show opened in Omaha. There the boys
were given the key to the city, but in a situation right out of
their world, they had to give it back. An embarrassed city
official realized there was only one such key, and it already
been promised to Presidential candidate Wendell Willkie, due
in the city later that day. The *Revue* was greatly successful
in Omaha, and went on to full houses in Minneapolis,
Milwaukee, Chicago (where they read the Sunday funnies to
the kids over station WLS), Indianapolis, St Louis, Columbus,
Pittsburgh, Philadelphia, Newark, Hartford and, concluding
their engagement, Buffalo, in mid-December 1940.

Babe found 1941 a bad year. He was sued twice by Internal
Revenue Service for back taxes, and twice by Myrtle for back
alimony. In all these instances he had followed what seemed
to him clearly defined delimitations of the law. Myrtle's
weekly alimony was $250, applicable only when his salary
was $1000 a week or over, and she contended that he
conveniently forgot the zero in $250, since she had been
receiving that pittance weekly for some time. She asserted
that even *that* amount arrived irregularly. Ben Shipman, a
master at patchwork, satisfied both Government and Myrtle
temporarily with funds to each party. Both the IRS and Myrtle
had inadvertently overstated their cases, and Shipman knew
he had his work cut out for him as future reckonings loomed
in Babe's future.

These debilitating experiences of Babe in 1941 seemed
to be counter-balanced by bright hopes for his and Stan's
professional future. Ben Shipman, in persistent shopping
around at the major studios, had awakened interest in his
boys at Twentieth Century-Fox. Babe and Stan were equally
interested in Fox because, as a studio considerably larger than
Roach's, they would almost certainly have budgets and sets on
a higher plane than at their Alma Mater. It was much to look
forward to. On April 30, 1941 a contract was signed by Laurel

and Hardy Feature Productions to make a film with Fox. If that proved satisfactory, more would follow in a five-year sequence.

This contract – and all the painful events consequent to it – existed in a milieu of assumptions, and therein lay frustrating dismay something rather close to heartbreak for Babe and Stan. These assumptions, both on their part and the studio's, were cardinal to the disastrous events that followed. Also, Ben Shipman, a crackerjack lawyer, was not a Hollywood agent, a role circumstances forced on him. He made the first assumption. An honourable man, he believed the Fox executives meant what they said when they agreed to his verbal stipulation that Stan should have 'artistic' control over their films. Stan, in turn, assumed that Ben had secured such a right for him, assumed it because Ben said he had. On the other hand the studio assumed Stan and Babe understood that ultimate artistic decisions were the studio's. Ben and the boys' assumptions were ephemera, binding as the air. A good Hollywood agent would have nailed them to the mast in five minutes.

Babe and Stan had an initially heartening talk with a Fox executive, Sol M Wurtzel. This gentleman, in detailing the studio's hopes for Laurel and Hardy, said he thought this new opportunity for them would result in 'a deepening' of their art. They would, he said, be given the best Fox writers to help them turn out comedies of 'stature'. Babe, in years to come, would remember that phrase. 'By stature, I guess he meant as tall as a dog kennel,' Babe told Stan.

Babe actually had higher hopes for the Fox films than Stan. Stan had grown slightly apprehensive when he heard that a single writer, and not a team of gag men, had been assigned to write their first film, *Great Guns*, an Army comedy. Stan's uneasiness changed to horror when their assigned writer wrote a complete and unfunny script, after minimal consultation with Babe and himself.

There were other ominous, indications of change for the worst. From the very beginnings at Roach, Stan wore a very light make-up, a modified clown white, to emphasize the other-world quality of his character. At Fox he was told to wear the conventional make-up for a man his age. This did him the double disservice of revealing his real age — fifty-one — and of making him 'human'. Stan, the character, had vanished. Then, in a Fox publicity release puffing *Great Guns* came these chilling words from the highest echelon, boasting of what had now happened to the Stan and Ollie of yore:

> Their clothes, too, have been modified a bit . . . It was felt that the public taste had changed somewhat, and that the unbelievable [!] antics of Laurel and Hardy would be more amusing if they themselves were more believable characters. That is, in *Great Guns* they will be a funny and oddly-assorted pair but not completely beyond what a person might find in real life. . . . Stan and Ollie believe revisions in their style will hold their millions of old friends and find them many new ones.

Stan and Ollie believed no such thing. At least Stan didn't. Babe admitted later that he was suspicious of any producer who would talk confidently of bringing 'stature' to them, but one phrase in the press release rang true for him; 'not completely beyond what a person might find in real life'. He had always envied his old friend and fellow card-player. Charles Coburn, for his opportunities to play middle-aged men of all qualities. Secretly Babe nursed the hope that Ollie might become more like Charles Coburn. Babe knew that at Fox he would be less a comedy foil and more a character actor. Moreover (Babe reasoned to himself) if Stan's character could be equally 'humanized', while still retaining its fey singularity, perhaps these changes might be fruitful.

Babe was quickly disillusioned. From the very day they began shooting, the Fox rule of thumb was: do it the studio's way, or not at all. Do *not* do it the long and well-established Laurel and Hardy way. Lou Breslow, writer of the film, was boss, and his script turned Stan and Ollie into dopes, unqualified dopes, not the endearing dopes of the Roach days. Moreover, the love interest in the film, a young draftee and his sweetheart (roles played by uncharismatic Fox contract players), was given more emphasis than Stan and Ollie, and *Great Guns*, incredibly, presents Laurel and Hardy as supporting players in their own starring vehicle. Even the dichotomous Roach films were far better than this.

Thomas M. Pryor's review of *Great Guns* in the *New York Times* put the matter very well:

> They say a change does a man good. Maybe, but it hasn't helped the team of Laurel and Hardy. The boys have changed studios quite frequently these past few seasons [there were two changes] without any notice-able improvement in their pictures. In fact their present offering, *Great Guns* ... is the weakest thing they've been mixed up in yet. Not that the boys are slipping; but alas! how desperately do they need a script-writer with an understanding and appreciation for their particular style of fun-making. Lou Breslow obviously isn't that fellow, for *Great Guns* is a haphazardly contrived comedy about the Army which makes preposterous demands upon the comedians.

Glen MacWilliams. Babe's chum from the 1923 *Quicksand* location days in Arizona, became director of photography on *Great Guns* because of his old friend. Babe asked for him, and MacWilliams, who had been away for years in England and badly needed support in re-entering the Hollywood scene, was hired by Fox. MacWilliams puts his finger squarely on *Great Guns'* artistic failure. 'Stan and Babe would never be actually in the studio until we were ready to shoot. They had nothing to do with the production of the picture except for early meetings with the guy who was writing it.'

Notwithstanding, and purely because of the names of Laurel and Hardy, *Great Guns* made a profit, and 20th Century-Fox asked Stan and Babe to make another. Since Fox seemed to be the only studio interested in them, and hoping for better days, they agreed to try again. Stan thought wistfully of the days at Roach but the Roach studio those days was not making comedy, or very little of it in the old vein. In the early Forties Roach was producing excellent films of all kinds, among them the well-received *Of Mice and Men*. Then, as World War II warmed up, the entire studio was taken over by Army Signal Corps to make training films.

Stan and Babe took the driver's licence sketch on tour again while their next film, *A-Haunting We Will Go*, was being written for them with a then well-known stage magician, Dante, as co-star. After the tour, they returned to Fox for the picture, only to find it the mixture as before. *A-Haunting We will Go* (1942), was another débâcle, and its cheerlessness is epitomized in its chief plot line: Stan and Ollie find a job delivering a corpse by train to another town, the coffin actually containing a live gangster fleeing the cops. Once more Babe and Stan were forced to do the film Fox's way, not their way. They went through with their contractual agreement, but they resolved that in their next film they would demand some voice in its creation.

That voice was Charlie Rogers, by now Stan's closest friend, pal of his golden days at Roach, and one of the script-writers for the new Laurel and Hardy film *Air Raid Wardens* (1943). Another cause for hope that things would improve was that the film would be produced by MGM, the Cadillac of Hollywood studios. Stan also knew another of the film's four-man writing team Jack Jevne, who had written Laurel and Hardy dialogue at Roach. The MGM script centred around Stan and Ollie as volunteer air raid wardens. Essentially the boys were to present a story kidding – but respectfully – certain aspects of civil defence. The sand thrown in that machine was the dour presence on the set of a U S Civil Defence official who raised heated objections to anything in the film that seemed to make fun of the subject.

Since this was the entire point of *Air Raid Wardens*, the film came out with all the comic texture of moist Kleenex. Stan and Babe had wanted very much to contribute to the war effort. They had appeared with the driver's licence sketch at various army bases, and in 1942 they joined Hollywood's biggest stars in the Victory Caravan that went on a bond-selling tour of leading American cities. On this tour Stan and Babe received the lion's share of the applause, not a small accomplishment in view of the company they were keeping: Bing Crosby, Judy Garland, Pat O'Brien, Frank McHugh, Merle Oberon, Jimmy Cagney and others of first stellar rank. 'Laurel and Hardy stole the show,' Cagney said years later, 'and in the most gentlemanly way you ever saw. Because there was no vanity there. Just pure – very pure – comedy, and that's all there was.'

Babe and Lucille, like many Americans in wartime, maintained a Victory Garden to supplement their food supply. Babe found himself playing much less golf at Lakeside because of the really solid exercise he was getting in his large garden. He learned how to work a hand plough and cultivator with some dexterity. The Hardys grew enough vegetables to feed both themselves and their neighbours. They raised pigs with the idea of slaughtering them for meat, but as the pigs grew, they became true family pets. They came to know Babe's voice and followed him around without cease.

One sow, Geraldine, clearly adored him. The pigs finally grew so large that their affectionate nuzzling of Lucille, as she gardened, knocked her down repeatedly. There was no possibility of having these faithful old friends killed, so they were given away. That was also the fate of the chickens and turkeys the Hardys raised. With that experience, Babe's hunting days were completely over. Thereafter he devoted most of his spare time to woodwork.

After *Air Raid Wardens* at MGM, there now seemed to be a better opportunity for the boys at 20th Century-Fox because producer Wurtzel promised Stan a veteran comedy writer, W Scott Darling. Veteran he was, long past it. His comedy creaked. Darling had done scripts years before for Al Christie, a kind of road company Hal Roach. But on the plus side Stan was also promised Mal St Clair as director for their new Fox film, and St Clair was a skilled veteran, having worked for both Mack Sennett and Buster Keaton.

The new Laurel and Hardy film, *Jitterbugs*, was an improvement over its Fox predecessors, although that is saying very little. *Jitterbugs* was a fairly high budgeted film, and was given several good musical numbers featuring the very attractive newcomer, Vivian Blaine. The story – Stan and Ollie as a zoot-suited two-man band helping a young man and his sweetheart overcome some confidence tricksters – is essentially fluff, but it gave Babe and Stan a chance to do some engrossing character acting. Stan masquerades persuasively as the *ingénue*'s wealthy aunt from Boston, and Babe is positively beguiling as a putative millionaire, Wattison Bixby, oozing Southern gallantry. Charles Coburn could not have done half as well.

Jitterbugs, even on a lower Laurel and Hardy level, does entertain. Not so their next effort for Fox, *The Dancing Masters*, which although it featured several old Laurel and Hardy routines, erred by interjecting them dispiritedly and randomly into the plot. The same can be said of their next for Fox, *The Big Noise* (1944), a tired bore in which the boys have to deliver a bomb to Washington. Instead it was given to us. *The Big Noise* has at least one distinction – it is Laurel and Hardy's worst film. They simply could not do worse than that.

The question is sometimes asked: didn't Babe and Stan *know* they were making such terrible films, and if so why didn't they stop? Of course they knew. They were painfully aware of what they were doing, and as to why they did not stop, Babe's answer, although a bit too simple, was: we had to eat. And they did stop – after two more films, one made at MGM, *Nothing But Trouble* (1944), about a boy king, in which Stan and Babe are revealed as little more than cretins; and *The Bullfighters*, also 1944, for Fox – not bad, not good, but not a disgrace.

Babe particularly could not afford to stop working for Fox and MGM at this time (1941–1944) because the Government kept making threatening noises about his back taxes. The IRS was demanding $75,755 in addition to the appalling sum of $100,000 interest, and all this in the day of the sturdy and not-so-plentiful dollar. Babe, through Shipman, continued to protest his innocence, but the Government was not listening. Babe and Myrtle many years before had agreed to pay individual income tax when they were not living together, and the IRS simply assumed that they lived together uninterruptedly from 1921 to their final divorce decree nineteen years later. Actually they had numerous separations. Babe's biggest mistake was the failure to pick up his final decree when granted the divorce in 1937. He simply did not bother to get it until 1940 when he married Lucille. 'I just didn't get around to it,' he said lamely.

The tax battle dragged through the courts for ten years, placing an enormous strain on the Hardys. The IRS finally put a lien on everything Babe and Lucille owned, not even allowing them to sell their valuable home and buy a cheaper place. This made Babe both furious and heartsick with worry. He had an annuity income of $300 a month from New York Life, and the IRS attached that. Ultimately the Government settled for about one fourth of what they said Babe owed them. The final irony was that years later when Babe's tax bill was paid, and when refunds of $48,00 from the IRS and $4500 from the State of California were ordered, Myrtle received all the money.

All during this time Myrtle kept suing for money she was not entitled to. Her claims were always rejected by Superior Court but that did not stop her from trying. She persisted, without cease, up to and beyond Babe's death.

Despite all this travail, Babe soldiered on at the Fox and MGM films, waiting for the ordeal to be over. Lucille said:

> It was a great tribute to our marriage that he was able to remain so comparatively tranquil in the midst of all that turmoil with taxes, Myrtle's lawsuits, and the terrible movies they were making. Oh, he could get very upset at times! But generally, despite his hurt and anger at all these things, Babe was able to put most of his troubles to one side when he came home and closed that front door. In a strange way those were happy times for us because we really needed each other so very much, and it's true that troubles bring people closer. I came to realize how much I loved that dear man, and he said

he found strength in me. Also, no matter how bad things got, we always had time to laugh and kid one another. And he was a wonderful kidder!

During the war, Babe encouraged travelling servicemen from the USO to come over to use their pool, although he warned Lucille, when driving, never to pick up service people thumbing a ride on the street. There had been several cases of thieves and rapists stealing uniforms and masquerading as servicemen.

Lucille took care of most family business. She understood Babe's deep reluctance to write letters, so she always did this for him, composing the letters, then typing them up for his signature. Outside of little notes to his mother, Lucille recalled him writing only six letters – all to her – during their marriage. The letters, she said simply, 'were beautiful'. They were so close to her heart that, after Babe's death, when she had intimations of her own end, she destroyed them, not wanting anyone else to share their quiet, deeply loving intimacy.

Babe sometimes wondered at his own innate optimism. 'I've had an unhappy life up till now,' he told Lucille shortly after their marriage. 'I was always sad inside, as a boy and as a young man. I never knew myself. I was frustrated. I always felt I could do more.' Marrying Lucille was the turning point in his life, finally bringing him the deep peace he had longed for all his days. He was supremely happy in his home, and outside of a few personal friends he and Lucille invited over, he did not relish intrusion – particularly from the telephone. He detested it. 'Would you get that, honey?' he would say when it rang, or 'Are you near the phone?' She learned always to answer it. If it was for him, he would speak to the caller, but did not linger in conversation, coming quickly to the point and discouraging casual chat.

So deeply sentimental was he over his marriage to Lucille that Babe did something perhaps unparalleled in anniversary observance. Lucille remembered:

We celebrated our anniversary weekly, monthly and yearly. That was how much our marriage meant to Babe. We were married at 4:35 pm on Thursday, March 7th. So we always celebrated every Thursday at that time, being together, unless we couldn't possibly help it. If he was out of town, he would wire me. The one time he had to go abroad without me, he would cable me every Thursday. If he was at Lakeside, I'd go over to meet him for that time. At home, we'd have a drink together. And the same thing on the seventh of each month, and of course on the seventh of March. At the studios on Thursday afternoon if they were shooting at that time, he'd rush to the phone the minute the scene would break.

Although he liked being around the house, Babe was far from domestic in skill. He had absolutely no mechanical sense, and when anything in the house failed to function, he was helpless, even in little things. Lucille, intensely practical, took care of all these problems, and when it was a fairly big problem, say in plumbing, she would shoo him off to Lakeside, to his great relief. Lucille would study the problem and almost always come up with the answer. This skill was very important in wartime what with many plumbers and other such workers in the services. Lucille needed only a cleaning woman who came in once or twice a week.

Not long after he married Lucille, Babe wanted to get one of the Filipino house boys, then fashionable, to help in domestic work and drive Lucille around town at need. She firmly rejected this. 'I need no one to drive me around,' she said to Babe,' and I certainly don't need a house boy. *I'm* the house boy!' Babe drove quite well. In his early Hollywood days he loved big cars, especially Packards, but with his middle years he began to fancy small, unobtrusive cars and always drove them thereafter.

After completing *Jitterbugs* at Fox, that studio approached Stan and Babe in 1945 with an offer to make some new films. Their five-year contract with Fox had expired, and *Jitterbugs* was doing well at the box office. Babe and Stan did not even need a meeting to discuss the Fox offer. They turned it down resoundingly despite Babe's uncertain financial position.

Stan had been having his own financial problems. His marriage to Virgina Ruth was ending in 1945, and the final decree came in 1946, all this to much public clamour about alimony. In real need of relaxation one afternoon in 1945, Stan went to a Russian restaurant in the valley he liked, The Moskwa, and there was a lovely blonde friend of the Russian lady who owned the place. The friend was herself Russian, a White Russian born in Harbin, China, named Ida Kitaeva. She was the widow of the world's greatest concertina player, who billed himself only as Raphael. Ida (pronouned EE-dah) resembled her fellow Russian, Illeanna, only in that she was a woman of great passion, a passion chiefly expended in taking great care of her new husband. She and Stan eloped to Yuma, Arizona, in May 1946. Stan – Stanchka she called him – was her world, and she was never afraid to tell the other world so.

Stan was very moved, and frequently amused, at her unremitting care. She never smothered him but she became the keeper of the flame both during their twenty overwhelmingly happy years together and after his death.

Babe and Lucille were tremendously pleased with Ida. They knew how badly Stan needed one of her disposition. Babe never talked to Stan about his marital difficulties except once when they both had similar troubles given undue newspaper notice. One year there were many headlines about their respective failures as husbands. Babe hated this kind of newspaper attention. 'You know,' he said to Stan. 'Sometimes I'm sorry I ever learned to read.' Stan smiled and said, 'I'm sorry I ever got to like girls so much. It would have been a lot easier for me if I'd been [naming a famous homosexual comic].' Ben Shipman, who was in the conversation topped them with, 'Hell, it'd have been a lot easier for *me* if I'd gone into burlesque instead of law school – with you two guys as clients!' This broke Stan and Babe up. Ben, whose face was usually set in a grave frown that belied his truly genial nature, resembled a burlesque comic about as much as Pope Pius XII did.

When Stan married Ida, his financial situation was so bad that he was unable to buy her a wedding ring, let alone an engagement ring. She had to use her first wedding ring and minded it not at all. Stan, on the other hand, minded it a very great deal. In time their financial situation would be considerably improved, but it was galling that at his wedding he was not able to give his love even a modest diamond. Knowing how deeply he felt about this, Ida did not tell him – and would not for some time – that financially she had been left very secure by her first husband, and that in consequence the Laurels had no cause ever to worry about money. Stan's sensitivity on financial matters at the time was heightened by the knowledge the he was the only cause of his money woes.

Overall, worries about unemployment for Babe and Stan in the mid-Forties were very real. At times Stan thought privately they were through. Who would hire them? He expounded to Ben Shipman a theory that a comedy team most likely had a successful tenure of only decade or so. Under that rule of thumb, he and Babe had seen their best days. Financially, in fact, they had. But wonderful times were yet to come – and most unexpectedly – in Stan's place of artistic birth, the British music halls.

9

Ebb and Flow

Laurel and Hardy never stopped being popular in Great Britain but a highly successful revival of their best Roach films there in the summer of 1946 made English impresario Bernard Delfont much more aware of their solid appeal to all audiences. He wrote Ben Shipman and asked him to approach Stan and Babe about doing a six-week tour of England.

Stan was so happy about the possibility of the booking that he shouted when he heard the news – 'Like a little boy,' Ida described him, 'a very happy little boy going home again.' Babe was equally pleased – until December of 1946, in the planning stages of the tour, when Lucille suffered a sacro-iliac episode, a grave one. Her doctor insisted on an operation, and a carefully supervised convalescence. Going to England was out of the question for some time, the doctor said.

'Well, then, it's out of the question for me, too,' Babe told Lucille.

'Now, look,' she said. 'You are going. Too much of your future – and mine, when it comes to that – depends on your going. You know I'm pretty good at taking care of myself. So, you go.'

The Laurels and Babe sailed on the *Queen Elizabeth* in early February 1947 for a two-week engagement at the London Palladium, to be followed by a four-week tour of the provinces. They would then film a typical English pantomime, *Robin Hood*, written for their characters. The film fell through because of poor financial planning by its producers, but bookings for the music hall tour began to grow. The driver's licence sketch was used again, and 'to heavy mitting', *Variety*'s phrase for wild applause.

The act opened in Newcastle, and on to Birmingham, and so to the Palladium for three triumphant weeks. Next, to Wimbledon and Lewisham for a week apiece, and back to London for an unprecedented month's engagement at the Coliseum. Lucille arrived in England during that period. Then the provincial tour began, one not anywhere near as difficult as playing *The Laurel and Hardy Revue* in the States with its four-, sometimes five-shows-a-day schedule. In Britain they did only two performances a night with a matinée on Saturday. There were no performances on Sunday, the day they spent in travel.

After the London Coliseum date, they did their originally planned tour of Dudley, Liverpool, Morecambe, Blackpool and Glasgow (where they did the act in kilts), but they were received with such acclaim that Bernard Delfont added other cities to the tour. Theatre managers across Britain began clamouring for them.

Stan and Babe were honoured by the civic fathers of Glasgow in a lunch attended by the lovable doyen of British entertainment, Sir Harry Lauder, a devoted admirer of the boys. Stan marvelled at the fortunes of life that had brought him such great honour in the city where he had made his extremely modest debut as a boy comedian.

On 16 June, the first night of the Glasgow engagement, well along in the sketch, Stan noticed to his horror that Babe was not responding as he usually did. He was, in fact, ad-libbing, something simply not allowable within the time limits of the act. Stan was further shocked when an accordion act on the bill strolled on stage in full panoply, playing and singing. It was only when he recognized the song, 'Happy Birthday', that he laughed and shook his head in surprise. It was his fifty-seventh birthday, and he had almost forgotten it. Ida and Babe had not, and they had arranged for the interruption.

Before they left Glasgow, the boys were invited by Harry Lauder to Sunday lunch at his magnificent home, Lauder Ha', on the outskirts of the city. He had loved the Laurel and

Very much out of character, the boys high-step with Rosina Lawrence and Patsy Kelly in a publicity shot for *Pick a Star,* 1937. The scene does not exist in the film.

Ollie offers fervid blossoms to his lady love, Della Lind, as Stan stands by. *Swiss Miss,* 1938.

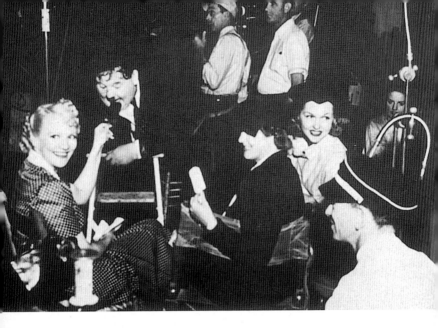

Minna Gombell, Babe's leading lady in *Block-Heads,* offers him an ice-cream bar while waiting for the next scene, 1938. Patricia Ellis, full-face, to the right.

Seconds after the previous photograph, Babe asks Minna, 'Now, just where did that ice-cream bar go?'.

(*above left*) The right girl at last. Babe and Lucille's wedding day as
reported in the press, Las Vegas, 7 March 1940.

(*above right*) A treasured Hardy photograph, inscribed to him by
'pal' Bing Crosby.

Hardy without Laurel. Here director Eddie Sutherland discusses
the work at hand with Harry Langdon and Babe under a model of
their film's eponymous elephant hero. *Zenobia,* 1939.

Stan, unidentified starlet and Babe do some publicity farming on
Stan's estate, Fort Laurel, Canoga park, mid-1940s.

Lucille Hardy, Stan, Babe and Ida Laurel dining on the *Queen Mary*
en route to one of the British music hall tours.

W H Healey, his wife Olga (Stan Laurel's sister), Babe with tray and Stan at the Healeys' pub, The Bull Inn at Bottesford near Nottingham, 1954.

Babe in his dressing room at the Hippodrome Theatre, Birmingham, England, 1954. (John McCabe in mirror.)

Babe at his heaviest. The last British tour, 1954. Babe, Ida Laurel, Stan and lawyer/manager Ben Shipman.

Babe, Lucille, ship's captain, Ida and Stan returning to the US from England on the merchant ship *Manchuria*, June 1954.

With a new partner – John Wayne, in *The Fighting Kentuckian,*
1949.

A scene from their disastrous last film, *Atoll K,* made in France,
1950–51, with Suzy Delair, Adriano Rimaldi and Max Elloy.

Celebrating Babe's 59th birthday, 18 January 1951, on location for
Atoll K.

The last portrait session, summer 1956, as it appeared in the press.
Babe's obvious loss of weight caused much public concern.

Hardy films from the first and recalled every detail of *Putting Pants on Philip* to Babe. During the Glasgow engagement, Lauder saw them perform six times, coming backstage after each show to sit on one of the big wicker theatrical hampers Babe and Stan used on tour, his little legs dangling over the side. The boys asked him to sing his famous repertoire of songs a cappella, and he did so, spiritedly, beating time with his legs against the wicker basket.

At the Lauder Ha' Sunday lunch, the cheerful little man obliged again with old songs in response to Babe and Stan's pleading. Babe was especially fond of 'A Wee Deoch o' Dorris', and thereafter sang it on a regular basis, and in true Lauder style, in his bath. 'And even out of the bath,' said Lucille. The boys discovered that Lauder did not have to be coaxed to sing. He sang incessantly to friends because it had become his only relief from pain – the pain of loss. During World War II he had lost his beloved wife and son. On the big stairway of Lauder Ha', leading upstairs from the living-room, was a beautiful larger-than-life painting of his son. That portrait was both Babe and Stan's most poignant memory of their visits to Lauder, visits that were to continue for the next few years.

After Glasgow, the act went to Skegness, Edinburgh, Hull, Bristol, Manchester (two weeks), Bolton, Swindon, Finsbury Park and Chiswick. Their originally booked tour of six weeks had grown, by exceedingly popular demand, to seven months. Meanwhile Delfont had been getting requests from the Continent for Laurel and Hardy appearances. He booked the boys into Scandinavia, and then into a Parisian night club, the internationally famous Lido, for six weeks.

On the Continent the driver's licence sketch was given in English; nothing was changed except occasionally Babe and Henry Marigny, who played the cop, would interject two or three words of the host country's language into the proceedings. There was no language barrier because the audiences were not there for instruction in English. Just the sight and sound of Babe and Stan were enough. In Scandinavia the act played the Tivoli Gardens of Copenhagen, Aarhus, Odense,

Stockholm's Uppsala University, Göteborg and Malmö, then on to the Lido.

Performing at the Lido was no fun. In a night-club an act can never be sure of an audience's undivided attention. At the Lido, although the audiences were most respectful, the noise factor was invariably high and the performing atmosphere uncomfortable. 'We never did that again,' said Babe.

It was during the Lido stay that Babe and Stan were asked to be part of the upcoming Royal Command Variety Performance in London. Deeply honoured, they consented but it proved to be a hurried affair. Too hurried. They had to make an exhausting channel crossing at night, but their spirits were revived by the suites provided them at the Savoy Hotel. There was still wartime austerity in England but the seven-foot bathtubs at the hotel were traditional British comfort as ever was, and the Hardys and Laurels loved them. 'I should have brought me toy sailboat,' Stan told Ida.

King George and Queen Elizabeth, together with daughters Elizabeth and Margaret, and the Duke of Edinburgh, were in the Royal Box during the variety performance. The King was observed throwing his head back repeatedly in great gusts of laughter during the driver's licence sketch. Despite getting the greatest amount of applause during the evening – a programme featuring the leading British music hall artistes of the day – Babe and Stan were severely disappointed. Their schedule would not allow them to meet Their Majesties because a train was being held for connection with a cross-channel ship at Dover. They had been given only one night off from the Lido. In later years Stan said, 'We should have called the Lido and told them I had a bad cold, which I easily could have had after all those years in California away from British heating. Not meeting the King and Queen was the most disappointing thing that ever happened to us.'

Lucille and Babe loved all their travel abroad. Lucille tried to get Ida to sight-see with her but Ida preferred either going to the movies or caring for Stan. She generally stuck very close to her husband because the Laurels were comparative newlyweds.

Lucille had brought two cameras with her and zealously tried to record all the places she visited. In that way she also got a close look at the texture of Continental life, and, keen observer that she was, grew saddened at what she saw. Babe liked to go with her when he could but he was too frequently recognized, and that became tiresome. 'It simply makes me tense, and even more so when I have to try and communicate in a language I don't know,' he said. He was always willing to sign autographs but at leisure, instead of hurriedly on the street, with people tugging at his clothing. Several times in Paris people ripped his coat and jacket.

For autographs he finally set up a system that worked well. On arriving at the theatre with the inevitable crowd of fans milling about, he would stand at the stage door and give a little speech: 'I'm sorry that Mr Laurel and I can't sign your books or papers just now, but if you'll leave them with the stage doorman, we'll sign them between shows, and you can pick them up later. We'll be happy to do that.'

During the Lido stay especially, the Hardys had good occasion to note the hunger and discontent that were everywhere, or so it seemed to them. Lucille in her long walks, camera in hand, could see it, and kept Babe fully informed. (When he returned to the US he told Shipman, 'I really saw Europe through Lucille's eyes, and she has pretty good eyes.')

The Hardys had been given a luxury suite adjoining the Laurels' at the Hotel Georges Cinq, magnificent rooms with all marble bathrooms, silk bedroom panelling and superb tapestries. Lucille began to feel uneasy about all the elegance. The atmosphere seemed too much like 'Let them eat cake!' She grew apprehensive, and Babe shared her feeling. They had already seen social ferment on French streets.

The very day their party arrived in Paris, they noticed, the reception for them given by the Lido was attended by a number of newspaper reporters with bandaged heads. These were people who had been caught up in the Communist riot that had swept the city that day.

Babe was further shocked to learn that the Lido even had a goon squad on nightly call to guard the performers in case of further riot. One evening, just as Babe and Stan were about to go on, they heard a tremendous uproar in the club. They peeped through the curtain and saw the big room full of people hurling chairs and dishes at each other, cursing at the tops of their voices. It was the beginning of the famous general strike.

Babe and Stan walked back to their hotel, and were told by the management to stay in their rooms until advised otherwise. Water and electricity in this, the poshest of hotels, were turned off. It was mid-December. To flush their toilets, they had to ask the maid to bring up pails of water several flights. Elevator service was gone. The maid was well tipped but in any case thought her chore was *par privilège*. Every morning Stan had to shave with his tea water; Babe learned to do that too. Garbage accumulated, rats began to appear. The strike lasted ten days.

Delfont had booked the boys into Belgium through the Christmas holidays – Liège, Charleroi, Ghent, Bruges and Brussels. The problem was how to get there. The Communists were throwing sharp, three-pronged metal bits all over the roadways, and the trains had been stopped. The resourceful Belgians, however, found a way. They got a bus, refurbished it for the Hardys' and Laurels' comfort, took them from Paris at 4 am, and by means of travelling on side roads, reached Brussels in comparative comfort. On this trip the four travellers were appalled at the sour legacy of war they saw everywhere, especially the sight of old women ploughing the fields.

At the lovely Métropole Hotel in Brussels, they found quite another world. The Hotel gave them not only their best suites but a great dinner – with a special name, 'Hamburger a l'Américaine'. Under silver covers, the four each got a Sèvres plate on which reposed a large gobbet of raw hamburger, an indentation holding a raw egg. 'What is this?' Babe asked. 'Hamburger a l'Américaine,' the two waiters chorused. When the difference between Steak Tartare and real American hamburgers was explained, the waiters took the meat back to be cooked to preference.

At least it was beef, and they were grateful. A few weeks before, in England the four of them had gone out to dinner and were served special steaks. The meat was brought, it was well cooked, it looked and tasted succulent. But Lucille, who had bought a lot of horse meat for her dog during the war, knew what it was – and said nothing. Everyone enjoyed the meal very much. Later she told Babe he had eaten horse meat, and he was not much perturbed. 'It tasted good,' he allowed. In turn he told Stan, thinking it would amuse him. It did not. Stan, who usually rolled with life's punches, large and small, was knocked over by this one. He felt retroactive nausea.

The Belgian tour concluded on 8 January 1948. Babe and Lucille, who had become good friends of a Belgian theatre manager, accepted his invitation to stay over and see more of the local countryside. Stan and Ida went back to England to visit his sister, Olga, and her pub-keeper husband, W H Healey, owner of the Bull Inn, Bottesford, near Nottingham.

The Hardys took a freighter back to the States, a longer journey than in a liner, but one they felt would give them more chance to rest. It was during this voyage that Lucille noticed for the first time any active feeling on her husband's part for children. Because his childhood was basically unhappy, Babe had never felt any strong desire to have offspring. Before they married, Lucille had said she wanted children, and he had told her, 'I'd be the proudest man in the world to have a child by you.' But after living with him a few years, she sensed that he really did not have much patience with children, and concluded it best they have none.

On the trip back to New York, the Hardys were enchanted by the two children of a Belgian immigrant woman going to join her husband in Canada. During the voyage there was a big storm, and most of the passengers got violently seasick, including the Belgian woman. Only the crew, Babe and Lucille and the children were capable of taking food. At the height of the storm, the Hardys took over the children and sat up all night with them in the ship's bar, the only place where furniture did not lurch randomly and dangerously during the tempest. A steward brought in a mattress for the kids, and Babe and Lucille watched over them solicitously as they slept.

Babe fell in love with the children, and deeply admired the mother. He confided to Lucille, 'Oh, if there were only some way we could adopt those kids!' In the months to come, the mother wrote the Hardys, sending pictures of the children. Babe would still talk wistfully of ways they might adopt them but Lucille believed that if they were around every day, Babe would find them considerably less attractive.

When the freighter docked in New York, Babe was feeling quite good. He had lost 90 pounds because of the British and Continental rationing. The first night the Hardys were back in the States, they had dinner served in their New York hotel room, and made it memorably all-American. So starved were they for home food that they ordered two big authentic American hamburgers apiece, ample apple pie and two quarts of milk.

On his return to California, Babe talked about his experiences abroad at some length to his old Lakeside pal and fellow Southerner, Hearst columnist, Henry McLemore. McLemore, who had known Babe upward of fifteen years, said in a 1948 column that when he saw his friend on return, he was scarcely recognizable, 'being about a third of his former size'. This was humorous exaggeration but Babe was, comparatively, a trim man. In Europe, Babe told him, he had 'eaten everything in sight', but there wasn't much in sight. Babe said, in serious vein:

> Those people are starving over there. Not only starving but freezing . . . If we don't help them, if we don't see that they have the bare necessities of life, then you can expect them to join any party which will make a few promises. And the Communist party is making promises.

Babe never talked party politics to a reporter, nor did he now. Very much a Democrat in the traditional Southern fashion, he did not approve of those in the limelight using their celebrity to influence votes. 'What right,' he said on one occasion, 'does a pair of half-assed comics like Stan and me have telling anyone else how to vote? They know as much about it as we do, and probably a hell of a lot more.' Stan, who was a Democratic sympathizer, although an English national, concurred.

In 1948 Babe was truly worried about the spread of Communism, and decided to talk openly about it to McLemore. He told his friend that he felt some qualification to do so because the average American abroad stays a month or less, but he, Babe, had been there a year, and felt he had seen important omens of change in the European picture.

Had he in any way enjoyed himself abroad? McLemore asked. Babe allowed that he had, that it 'wasn't all bitterness and despair. It was fun breaking records for attendance at the theatres I played. That's the ham in me, of course. And there was the day the haggis exploded in Scotland.' In telling this story to those who, unlike the Celtic McLemore, did not know what haggis is, Babe always had to explain that it is a traditional Scottish dish of the minced lungs, heart and liver of a sheep, mixed with suet, onions, oatmeal and seasonings, boiled in the stomach of the animal. Gourmets do not cry for it.

At this particular banquet in Scotland, the Lord Mayor honoured Babe and Stan by producing a formidable haggis as the main dish. But it evidently had been kept in reserve too long because when it was served, it exploded with a mighty report all over the guests. 'I picked haggis off me for a week,' Babe said.

McLemore was clearly a man of some discernment. He concluded his column on Babe with this prescient observation:

A great man, the Babe. A great comedian. Also a great cook of turnip greens. Someday someone will have the bright idea of casting him in straight roles with a slightly comic touch, and he'll be even a bigger hit than he was as an out-and-out comic.

And someone indeed did, someone, of all unlikely people, named John Wayne.

When Stan returned to the States he was deeply exhausted and had alarming symptoms of constant fatigue and persistent thirst. He was diagnosed a diabetic, and this news depressed him considerably. For a while he wondered if he would ever work again. Ida learned how to take his sugar count and administer the proper insulin daily. He improved gradually.

During this time Babe played the small but juicy part of the town mayor in a Masquers Club production of the Maxwell Anderson-Lawrence Stallings hit war play, *What Price Glory?* This all-star charity production, featuring John Wayne, Ward Bond, Maureen O'Hara and others – all under John Ford's direction – played in five California cities for the benefit of the Military Order of the Purple Heart. Babe enjoyed it, and he added one memorable bit of business that was the funniest moment in the show. In confronting a man intimidatingly, he literally bumped the man upstage with his belly.* It was,' said James Cagney who was there with an old friend, 'the funniest thing I think I have *ever* seen. Roland Winters and I had to hang on to each other, we were laughing so much.'

During the tour of *What Price Glory?*, John Wayne asked Babe if he was available for a role in Wayne's forthcoming production, *The Fighting Kentuckian*. Babe said no. Wayne and the film's writer/director, George Waggner, persisted, but Babe was adamant. He was part of a team. He mentioned Wayne's offer, in passing, to Stan who said, 'You're going to do it, aren't you?' Babe replied in the negative. 'Why don't you do it?' Stan said. 'I just don't want any stories getting out that you and I are battling,' Babe said. 'Oh, for God's sake, Babe,' Stan replied, 'just because I'm sick and can't work, there's no reason you shouldn't. You're crazy not to do it. *Do* it.'

The Fighting Kentuckian (1949), is excellent proof that Babe could easily step away from Ollie. The Kentucky accent was fun for him to do but it must have taken considerable control not to do takes in his old free-wheeling style. His

*Babe first did this gag in a Pathé film, *Fatty's Fatal Fun* (1915).

character has a number of comic reactions throughout the film but they are all realistic and entirely within the context of Willie Payne, frontiersman, proud fighting man, fiercely loyal to his pal, Wayne, and devoted to his home soil.

It is fine character acting that Charles Coburn would have been proud to do. Indeed, Coburn praised him highly when the two Georgia boys got together later over a bridge table at Lakeside. *The Fighting Kentuckian* is basic John Wayne fare set in the early nineteenth century South – blending intrigue, strong action, and a non-mushy love story. The writing is good, and Babe's finest moment in the film comes when he is reminiscing about his state, 'Old Kaintuck'. Talking to Wayne, he slips into sentimental memories of down home, trying to get his friend into a mood for return there. In soft, reflective tones, almost underplaying, Babe says, 'The grass is knee-high to a yearlin'. The blue jays are peckin' at the persimmons, and everything is peace and quiet. Down in the barn Paw is sittin' up with an old red mare that's groanin' way down deep. Tomorrow morning the neighbours'll come ridin' in to see the new foal –' when Wayne cuts him off with refusal.

There are moments, brief moments, of physical humour in *The Fighting Kentuckian*. Babe backs up into a stream and falls down amid a mighty splashing, twice; and he hits his nose accidentally, holding the injured member tenderly. But these are not done in Ollie's style, and what emerges from the film is a distinctive character, played with distinction. Had Laurel and Hardy not resumed their joint career, Babe could easily have gone on to character acting for his livelihood. Or to directing. It was at this time that he talked to Lucille about his ambition to be a director. But even there he was characteristically self-effacing. 'I wish I had the courage to go out and try it at least once. I know I can do it. I'd love to be a director.' As a good judge of character, in several senses, he would have done well.

There was always that quotient of timidity about him, said Lucille, whenever he thought of stepping into something new. 'But fate must have brought him and Stan together,' she said.

'Look at those people who were even bigger stars than they, now forgotten. So Babe's shyness was a good thing.'

Frank Capra, who had worked at Roach in the early days as a writer, and Bing Crosby both saw *The Fighting Kentuckian*, and the former asked Babe to do a cameo role in *Riding High*, a new musicalized version of Capra's 1933 hit, *Broadway Bill*. Crosby was to star, and he told Babe, 'C'mon, you've got to do it. It's perfect for you. Type-casting. It's a guy who loves horses, bets and bets, and keeps on losing!' 'Look who's talking,' Babe said. 'Unfortunately that character does sound like this particular Southern gentleman.'

In *Riding High*, Babe dramatized, comedically, the cyclic progress of the eternal bettor who spreads a bad tip that eventually claims all the suckers who hear it, even the cynical nasty (Ray Walburn) who began the false rumour deliberately. There is a slight touch of Ollie in Babe's role in that he sports a derby. But this is not Ollie. There is no time in the film for this individual to become anyone.

Stan's health was improving, and under Ida's close care he was gaining strength daily. Early in 1950 he and Babe were approached by two European companies, Les Films Sirius and Sortezza Film, a conglomerate of French, Italian and American producers, to appear in *Atoll K*, a film to be made in three months, on the Riviera, with generous financial backing from the French government. Babe and Stan were interested at once.

Stan was even more interested when he was assured by contract that he had final say on the script. As it turned out, that was rather like having final say on what deck of the *Titanic* you preferred. The film certainly looked good from afar. They signed.

Perhaps just to spend the French government's money on something pleasant, the producers asked Babe and Stan to make a somewhat pointless pre-film promotional visit to Rome. Pointless but fun. When Babe and Stan arrived at their hotel's adjoining suites, they heard a crowd shouting in the streets. The uproar was insistent: 'Cric! Croc! Cric!

Croc!' in huge waves of sound. Cric and Croc were Stan and Ollie's names in Italy. They went out on the balcony and took bow after bow. Ida and Lucille joined them and the clamour grew. Stan thought they might defuse the persistent tumult by joining with Babe in throwing the fresh flowers sent to their rooms down to the crowd, but this only increased the shouting. It ended hours later.

That evening there was a knock on the Hardys' door, and Lucille opened it to find Mervyn LeRoy holding a roll of toilet paper in each hand. The Laurels were summoned and LeRoy – in residence to make *Quo Vadis* – said, 'Welcome to Rome! I knew you would need these, because you likely haven't yet experienced the agonies of Italian toilet paper. I had a gross of these shipped to me from the States.' Le Roy was an old friend of Babe's from racing days, another investor-founder of the Del Mar track.

Next day the Hardys and the Laurels went sight-seeing, visiting all the wonders of the Roman Forum, the Colosseum, and even the big new blocks of apartments their hosts insisted they not miss. 'Looked like just a big bunch of apartments to me,' Stan said later. That night they were given a banquet at a famous night-club where the ladies were thrilled to meet Tyrone Power, an old friend of the boys. Having seen Rome in most of its vital aspects, they returned to France and the problems attendant on the new film.

Squabbles over production and personnel damned *Atoll K* almost from the start. The film (also released variously as *Robinson Crusoe Land* and *Utopia*) is seven reels of what Shakespeare called 'vain bibble-babble', a film so bad that it is worth seeing several times just to savour its awfulness. Every film lives – or dies – on the worth of its script, and *Atoll K*'s four writers began their work with something of a communications problem. Of the four, one spoke only French, one spoke only Italian, one spoke only English, and one spoke French and English. They all preferred to work different times of day, and all had widely different senses of humour.

The film's original concept, the premise given to the writers, was a good one. Stan and Ollie, two stateless persons, are shipwrecked on a Pacific atoll which by right of possession becomes theirs. They follow the example of Robinson Crusoe, living simply but well, until uranium is discovered in their little paradise. Then all the countries in the world want the boys to become citizens, but they refuse. One day the atoll slowly disappears beneath the waves, and Stan and Ollie must leave to follow their eccentric destiny elsewhere.

The writing team for *Atoll K* turned in a script that Stan accurately and kindly described as 'rubbish'. The worth of that script can be glimpsed from this plot detail: the boys plan to barbecue a stranded whale on their beach, so Ollie goes off on the ocean in a piano crate to find some matches. He is kidnapped by a crew of stowaways and disappears for almost the rest of the film.

In desperation Stan called in a couple of old gag-men friends, Monte Collins and Tim Whelan, to do salvage work on the script. They had hardly any time for this because at that moment both cast and crew were gathering at Cap Roux, a headland between St Raphael and Cannes, to begin shooting. Always photographed seawards to suggest the island that is the film's locale, this cape became the focus of much pain and worry. It was, to begin with, a hellhole of heat.

The plot of *Atoll K* in its final rewrite was considerably simplified from the one the polyglot writing team had composed. In the new version, Stan inherits a great deal of cash, a South Sea island and a yacht from his bank-hating uncle. By the time Stan and Ollie reach Marseille, where the yacht is anchored, taxes and other duties have taken away all the cash, and the yacht proves to be an infirm motor/sail schooner. They leave for the South Seas with an ad hoc crew: Antoine, a stateless chef – supposedly their engineer, imposed on them by a captain docked nearby, and Giovanni, an Italian stone mason stowaway. (These roles were to have been played by two great clowns, Italy's Toto, and France's Fernandel. Lucky souls.)

Out on the ocean, a great storm embroils them, and they land fortuitously on a newly-risen atoll, aswarm with all kinds of crustacea, particularly lobsters, one of which becomes their pet.

They revel in this new life, the happy four. Giovanni builds them a fine house, Antoine makes bouillabaisse with the regularity of morning coffee. And things get even better with the coming of Cherie Lamour, comely chanteuse from nearby Papeete, whose argument with her French Navy fiancé made her run away, finding the atoll by accident. She becomes the adored one of the four bachelors, and they all establish a tax-free, law-free, prisonless state, Crusoe Land, its flag an arrow-transfixed heart.

Then Cherie's officer boy-friend finds the atoll, charts it for France, discovers it is loaded with uranium – and the world and his brother descend on it, turning Crusoe Land into hell. Ollie institutes law and order, so the mob tries to hang him and his friends. Cherie, meanwhile, has succeeded in reaching her absent boy-friend via shortwave, and he rescues them just after the atoll surrenders itself to the sea, the sea that just minutes before washed away all the evil-doers who had flocked to it.

Most of this is just plain godawful. Symptomatic of the film's jerribuilt inadequacy is its crude dubbing. Stan and Babe are the only ones speaking English, everyone else is speaking either French or Italian, their lips completely out of sync with the English we hear. This is very disturbing when the invariably excited Continental actors utter their lines in flat, toneless Chicago accents. Nothing coheres. Outside of Stan and Ollie, everyone else seems to be shouting their lines from a nearby room.

Making *Atoll K* was an agony. The Cap Roux location was unseasonably hot for all the weeks of production. Stan had prostate trouble, had to go to Paris for an operation, dropped in weight from 170 to 114 pounds, and looks literally cadaverous in the picture. *Atoll K*'s principal creative problem, outside its script, Lucille expressed vividly in a letter to her mother of 28 August 1950:

. . . Of course the greatest difficulty is language. The cast consists of Babe and Stan, the French girl, Suzy Delair, a French actor, Max Elloy, and an Italian actor, Andre Rinaldi. The French speak their lines in French, the Italian speaks Italian . . . It makes it very difficult for cues. Also the director is French, understands English only fairly well. The American associate director does not speak French or Italian. The cameraman speaks only French. The operating cameraman understands a little English, but very little. One script girl understands only French. The other script girl however speaks French, Italian and English . . . and she works from three scripts, one in each language. You can imagine the pandemonium at all times, particularly when there is some disagreement as to how a scene should be played – each in a different language trying to get over his idea – and after sometimes half an hour or an hour of explaining, arguing and interpreting the various languages, you are worn out.

The film's director, Leon Joannon, a man without any comedy experience, had a vivid idea of himself as a director – to the extent that he always wore a pith helmet, riding breeches, high laced boots and spoke to the cast only through a megaphone. Three megaphones, of varying sizes. 'He was funnier than the picture,' said Stan. 'Although that's not saying a hell of a lot.'

Joannon was an intensely lethargic director. A film's shooting progress is usually measured by the number of set-ups done in a day. A set-up is the arranging of actors and camera in proper relationship to the setting, and the average film on schedule has perhaps fifteen or more set-ups a day. Joannon averaged four or five. One day there were ten, and this was regarded as a marvel by the French crew.

Lucille said of that crew:

They had a party every night of the shooting . . . and they all nearly dropped dead the first day when Babe and Stan were to do a scene, and – after the crew spent about three hours lining it up, lights, etc. – the director said, 'All right. Let's rehearse it.' Stan said, 'Why rehearse it? Let's take it.' Babe said, 'Sure, let's take it. We know what we're supposed to do.' [The director and crew] were all dumbfounded, and very dubious, but finally the director said, 'All right. If you prefer.' They took it, and it was perfect first take. They just couldn't understand it, and still can't when the same thing happens again and again.

To further complicate matters, Babe got ill, too, but he asked Lucille not to mention to anyone the irregular heart-beats his French doctor had discovered. Babe was heavier than he had ever been, and even in this, his last film, he could not escape a reference to his fatness. At one point Ollie explains to Stan that the emergency life-raft for both of them, when inflated, will carry four people. 'But what about me?' Stan asks. 'You don't have to be insulting,' Ollie says.

Yet for all its strident inadequacies, *Atoll K* has something oddly endearing about it. Of course, it possesses a certain poignance because it is Laurel and Hardy's last movie, and one is moved when, after Stan's comment to Ollie about his weight, Ollie says, 'Haven't I always taken care of you? You're the first one I think of.' Stan then wipes Ollie's moist eyes with a handkerchief. Although this is meant to be funny, its effect out of context is quite the opposite.

Bits in the film are, in fact, quite funny. When Crusoe Land is born, Ollie decides to write its constitution, hands a long pencil to Stan, asking him to sharpen it. Stan takes it to a machine and grinds it down to an inch-long stub. 'This'll have to be a short constitution,' Ollie says drily. When Ollie is elected president ('I vote for myself and Stanley seconds the motion'), in picking a cabinet from the country's five-person population, he selects Cherie as vice-president, Antoine as Foreign Minister and Giovanni as Minister of Construction. 'What about me?' asks Stan. 'Stanley,' Ollie says, '*you* are the *people!*' This does not move the people until Ollie explains to him that there are a lot more 'of you than there are of us'. 'Well, why didn't you tell me!' says Stan, immensely pleased.

The music in the film is fine. Several gags in *Atoll K* work beautifully. When the yacht's motor conks out, and Ollie accidentally falls in the sea and is rescued, he changes, comes out on deck to note that quite against his expectations the boat is pushing along at a great rate. Then he looks up and sees why. There, serving as supplemental sail, trouser bottoms closed, are his ample pants tacked to the mast, bellying out with the wind.

Later, in the midst of the big storm at sea, Stan sees a little oil can near his bunk. He opens the porthole, squirts a few drops out, and for a brief moment the sea is absolutely tranquil. Still later, when the household's pet lobster walks around at night in distemper, Stan takes him up, rocks him and burps him gently on his shoulder. But these are rare moments.

It was possibly someone's 'in' joke, but Stan and Ollie's little yacht is named Momus, a name Ollie mentions fleetingly in the film. Momus is the Greek god of fault-finding, the examplar of ridicule. Whoever christened that boat knew something.

And finally how many nuances of feeling are evoked in the last words of their last film, when Ollie turns to Stan – after their inherited island is taken from them for unpaid inheritance taxes – to say, 'Well, here's *another* nice mess you've gotten me into!' – as Stan sobs out his traditional cry!

In returning to the States, there was one very vital need for them both – recuperation. Babe had been frightened by his heart difficulty. Although it was clear that the Côte d'Azur's killing heat was instrumental in elevating his blood pressure dangerously and causing fibrillation, there was no question that there was cardiac impairment, and he would have to take it very easy for a considerable time. Losing weight was imperative, his doctor told him. And above all, rest. Again he and Lucille took a quiet route home, by frieghter, going through the Panama Canal.

Stan's prostate trouble had been corrected by surgery in Paris, but his diabetes impeded effective convalescence for a while, and on his return to Los Angeles, he went into a very strict regimen of diet and rest. Once when he called Babe to ask how he was, and Babe in turn asked after his health, Stan replied with the variation of a line from *Atoll K*. At one point in the film Ollie tells his pal to 'take a peep'. Stan then gasps out, 'I'm too pooped to peep.' In their phone call, Stan gave the line again, eliding the final 'p'. He had reason to be pooped. One of the selling points made to him about *Atoll K* was that it would take twelve weeks to make. It took twelve months – to the day.

Rest did the trick. Babe felt fine after some months. He had lost weight but gained it all back when he felt better. He fought, as had so many, the classic battle against fat, and like most people, lost. Stan had the opposite problem, needing to gain. Ida gave him nourishing soups and puddings, and finally he began to feel fit.

Back in England, Bernard Delfont had been waiting for Babe and Stan to recuperate, and when he knew from Shipman's report that they were in fairly good shape, he approached them about another British tour. Both Babe and Stan were pleased at the thought, and the money – which they now divided fifty-fifty – was fine. Stan set about writing a new sketch, this one based on their 1930 two-reeler, *Night Owls*. He set the sketch in 'a small town in the USA', retitling it in British idiom, *A Spot of Trouble*. The first of its two scenes is the waiting-room of a railway station where the boys attempt to share a small bench for sleeping purposes. Stan, inevitably disadvantaged by Ollie's bulk, tries desperately to gain some space. Their attempts to sleep are disrupted by a policeman, described by Stan in the programme as 'a small-town cop with a mind smaller than the town'. The boys are suborned by this blackguard to rob the police chief's house so the cop can arrest them, win the chief's regard thereby, and see that the boys are none the worse for it.

In the sketch's second scene, set in the chief's living-room, Stan and Ollie are considerably the worse for it. The chief, described in the programme as 'a fiery blustering type', turns out to be a sleepwalker until he is inadvertently aroused, this causing him to run amok, chasing the boys, then finally the cop around the room, at last giving Stan and Ollie the chance to escape. Slapstick dominates the sketch; dialogue is minimal. It is, all in all, pretty thin stuff.

A Spot of Trouble began its British tour on 25 February 1952 at the Embassy Theatre, Peterborough, doing two performances nightly, at 6:30 and 8:45. They played Glasgow, Newcastle, Sunderland, Hanley, Leeds, Nottingham, Shrewsbury, Edinburgh, Birmingham, Southampton, Liverpool, and went from there across the Irish Sea to Dublin, which Babe and Lucille found captivating. The following week they were playing the Grand Opera House in Belfast when Stan's diabetes acted up. He was sent to the hospital for treatment and observation, under medical instruction not to play for at least a week.

With this time off, Lucille and Babe returned to Dublin for some restful sight-seeing and to get him some new clothes. They were glad to get out of Belfast which was then plagued by labour strikes and noisy demonstrations. Moreover, their Belfast hotel was very, very cold. In Dublin Babe looked forward to getting some good Irish tweed. He had a beautiful tweed jacket measured for himself. Babe was always impeccably groomed and beautifully tailored. The only ready-made clothing he ever wore were undershirts. All else, from his boxer shorts to shirts to suits, was tailor-made, not only out of deference to his size but because of a natural fastidiousness. 'He always looked good. He had pride in looking good,' said Lucille.

When Stan was released from the Belfast hospital, the *Spot of Trouble* tour resumed at the Empire Theatre, Sheffield; and on to Brighton, Manchester, Rhyl, Bradford, Southend-on-sea, Coventry, Southport, Sutton, Bristol, Portsmouth, Dudley, Swansea, ending at New Theatre, Cardiff, the first week of October 1952.

By now Babe and Stan were finding touring, if not downright comfortable, at least agreeable in that they travelled only once a week, and they found the two nightly performances easy to do and rewarding emotionally. The applause was always tremendous, and terribly heartening. Crowds as always gathered nightly to see them enter and leave the theatre.

In one English city they went back to the hotel from the theatre in their costumes because they had to wear them next morning in a charity appearance as Stan and Ollie near the hotel. One woman in the crowd at the theatre, noticing their vagabond appearance, turned to her companion, sucked in her breath and said, 'Goodness! You'd think they could afford better clothes than that!'

Usually their hotel stays were pleasant because they were given adjoining suites with connecting sitting-room where, if required, they could hold joint interviews for the press. Dining out for them was only a problem when unthinking people approached their table mid-meal for autographs. Despite this unintentional rudeness, Babe was always polite, responding to the requests with, 'Would you wait until I've finished my meal, and then I'll be happy to sign it for you.' Stan was more inclined to be brusque about such matters, but usually he too smiled and asked the fans to wait until the meal was over. This kind of thing happened much more frequently in the States than in Britain, where respect for privacy was so deeply inbred.

Babe liked English food, feeling almost as strongly as Stan did about the virtues of fish and chips, a dish Stan regarded as ambrosial. Babe loved British beer but as a concession to his weight problem did not over-indulge. He enjoyed wine while not pretending to connoisseurship, happily allowing the sommelier to choose for him. He invariably liked his wine chilled, sometimes to the horror of the waiter. He had a tough time of it once in Italy when a waiter demurred strongly at Babe's request for ice. Babe, pushed too far, said, 'Goddamn it. I don't care what *you* do. I want some ice in my wine.' He got it.

He got no ice in England because none was available, for the most part, and there he got used to having his Scotch (bourbon being unavailable) without it. So accustomed did he become to iceless Scotch that on return to the States, he drank spirits without ice for the rest of his life. 'You can really *taste* it that way,' he said.

When he and Stan went home in 1952, they were made aware that something had changed. Shipman told them about it in detail. They were popular as never before. There was a new and potent force in American life – television – and Laurel and Hardy were everywhere, and bountifully, a part of it.

10

Last Bow

Babe, like Stan, was always a prodigious television viewer. He took a deep professional interest in every aspect of it, although he was not drawn to watching Laurel and Hardy. Unlike Stan who was inexpressibly pained by capricious television editing of their work – the most frequent offence being the removal of vital establishing shots – Babe just refused to watch. His reason was simple. He did not like to be reminded that he was fat. Occasionally he would see one of their films rich in production values like *Fra Diavolo* and *The Bohemian Girl*, just to enjoy those values.

Stan grew so infuriated with the slipshod, sometimes non-existent editing of their films on television, that he stopped watching their work almost completely. But he and Babe had a deeper reason to resent television. In major markets across the country, 'Laurel and Hardy Shows' were proliferating. Stations leasing the Roach product began to feature Laurel and Hardy, sometimes daily, in programmes ranging from fifteen minutes to an hour, all of them with a variety of commercials from beer to breath mints. It angered Babe and Stan to realize that their names – their totally legal entitlements – were being used to advertise these wares.

They followed closely a class action suit Roy Rogers had begun to get redress in the matter. Some of the films Rogers did not own were being used in the same fashion as Stan and Babe's – advertisers employing his name to merchandise products without remunerating him. The courts decided against him, and Ben Shipman told the boys there was nothing to be gained by their suing in like fashion.

Babe found the local *Laurel and Hardy Hour* especially repugnant because one of the products advertised was a brand of lunch meat he loathed. 'In effect,' he said, 'I am publicly recommending something I dislike intensely.' Yet another reason he and Stan resented their presence on TV was that they would be in competition with themselves if they went into television in new shows.

One bonus from these unwilling television appearances was recognition by the new generation. A cluster of youngsters began to hang around the Hardy front gate daily, hoping for a glimpse of him. When the group gathered, Babe went out, talked to them, signed autographs and in general enjoyed their company. When he and Lucille shopped at local markets, little kids would come up to him, tug at his sleeve, wonder–eyed, and ask him questions. One youngster said, 'Are you who I think you are?' Babe said gravely, 'I don't know. Who do you *think* I am?' 'I don't know,' said the child. 'But I've *seen* you!' Babe laughingly told him who he was and gave the boy an autograph. It surprised him that children so young knew him, and it made him realize the potency of television.

As the years of his happy domesticity went on, Babe left home less and less. What with his vigorous woodwork, golf had almost passed out of his schedule. Going to a movie was impossible because of the width of the average theatre seat. In all the years of their marriage, he and Lucille went out to see a movie only once. That was in 1941, to view *Sergeant York*, a film Babe loved not only for for its sterling acting but because it showed the South in an intelligent and searching light. The theatre where they saw it had loges and comfortable separate chairs. He installed excellent equipment to show films in The Laurel and Hardy Fun Factory: two 35mm projectors, together with a large projection booth and full screen. He would invite friends over for a double feature, frequently a Laurel and Hardy film and another rented for the evening. He did less of this as the years went on, but he always subscribed heart and soul to the slogan then current, 'Movies are your best entertainment'.

He and Stan had talked tentatively of Laurel and Hardy Feature Productions producing their own television series, but they wondered about format. Their age precluded any of the old knockabout-and-tumble comedies, and they had no doubt there was little in the world of 1953 that they were attuned to psychologically, or any other way. Why not, suggested Stan, try the world of Mother Goose and fairy tale, the world of eternal childhood, the enshrined stories so frequently done in the English pantomines? Babe, with his fond memories of Aunt Susie's cheerful readings of Mother Goose, and recalling their own *Babes in Toyland,* agreed. Stan began to ponder how Stan and Ollie would fit into that lovely world.

In the meantime Bernard Delfont was back, suggesting yet another British tour. The boys consented happily and Stan set about writing a new script. It took him two weeks. *Birds of a Feather** is typical exuberant Laurelian nonsense in which Stan and Ollie get jobs as whisky tasters – the principal task, Stan explains to his pal, being 'to keep tasting whisky until we get the proof'. When Ollie asks what proof, Stan says, 'Whether it's a single or a double.' Most of the action takes place in the mental ward of a hospital where Ollie is confined for jumping out of a top-floor window after tasting whisky all morning on a try-out basis. The boys qualified so well for the job that Ollie had three doubles to celebrate. As Stan explains it:

STAN   . . . then you said you felt as happy as a lark, and thought you'd like to fly around with the birds for a while.

OLLIE   Fly around with the birds?

STAN   Sure. Then you opened the window and out you went. I can see you now – flapping your arms just like a cuckoo.

OLLIE   Well, why didn't you *stop* me?

*The complete script is printed in my *Comedy World of Stan Laurel* (Robson Books, 1975).

STAN   Well, I was celebrating too – and I thought you could *do* it.

Stan has just brought Ollie a gift of two eggs ('I thought you'd like a hogneg'), placing them on his pal's night stand. Stan has also brought his friend an onion and jam sandwich as well as a sheaf of funereal lilies. An eccentric nurse, Rosi Parker, enters to advise Ollie that the famous surgeon, Dr Berserk, will operate on him, taking out his brains briefly for observation. Ollie has been diagnosed as thinking he is a bird. After she leaves, the script says 'a caricature of an undertaker, dead white face, wearing a high hat with black band, frock coat, white cotton gloves, looking the picture of death itself' enters with a tape to measure Ollie's dimensions, taking Stan's as well, before he exits 'very slowly'.

Ollie, thinking of how to flee the hospital, ties several sheets about himself, and sends Stan out for a barrister. Rosie enters and Ollie jumps back in bed. Stan returns with a *banister* which is (he explains) 'the best I could do when nobody was looking'. The extremely eccentric Dr Berserk enters, and Ollie convinces him that he is just a visitor and that Stan is the lunatic After examining Stan, the good doctor quite agrees, and Ollie almost gets away but Rosie identifies him as the patient. Dr Berserk proceeds to give Ollie the 'famous Dr Wombat's birdseed test' which will make the patient sing, thus allowing the doctor to tell what kind of bird the patient thinks he is – a canary or a buzzard. The doctor sees the eggs Stan brought, wants to know where they came from. Stan explains Ollie laid them. The doctor is thrilled, telling the nurse to keep them in a safe place. She puts them in Ollie's night stand and leaves.

In administering Dr Wombat's birdseed test, the doctor gives a cup of the seed to Stan, holds Ollie by the nose and chin, opens his mouth for him, and directs Stan to pour it down his throat. Stan, a literal soul, pours the birdseed down his own throat, and the doctor angrily orders Ollie to swallow his cupful of seed, which he does. The nurse enters to tell Dr Berserk that everything is prepared for him to operate on Ollie's cranium (Stan refers to it as his 'geranium'). The sketch ends:

> (*Doctor and nurse exit. Stan and Ollie sit for a minute. Stan gets up, starts gathering his belongings, puts sandwich in paper bag with the flowers. Starts toward door, turns to tell Ollie goodbye, but instead starts to chirp like a bird. Ollie tries to answer, and he starts chirping. Then they hold ad-lib chirping conversation until point where doctor and nurse enter. Both react big.*)
> DOCTOR (*to nurse*) Quick, get those eggs and rush them to the dissection room! (*Nurse opens cabinet, lets out a scream as two pigeons fly out, leaving some egg shells. Very loud chirping sounds. Pandemonium reigns.*)
> BLACKOUT

The Theatre of the Absurd (of which Stan heard mixed reports) might well have a minor triumph in *Birds of a Feather*. This is Ionesco out of Dan Leno, crossed with Beckett and impregnated by Grock.* The best in the Theatre of the Absurd states the essential in Laurel and Hardy and their peers: the winning, lasting charm of sincere foolishness. The world of clowndom.

In the full script all the Laurel touches are there: the malapropisms, the weird characters, the ludicrous names, the half-spelled pronunciation of a word ('potty: p, o, *otty*. Potty!'), and quintessential Stan and Ollie, with the former getting the latter into another nice mess.

*In 1977 Mel Gussow of the *New York Times* saw what he calls the 'quintessential performance' of *Waiting For Godot,* played in German by the Schiller Theatre. Samuel Beckett himself directed the production. 'Among their many accomplishments,' said Gussow, 'the German actors made one recognize that Estragon and Vladimir were not only opposites, they were also two halves of a single personality, the first rock-solid, the second spindly and ethereal. It also made one wonder if Beckett had not had Laurel and Hardy in mind when he wrote the play.' Personally, I have always believed that Beckett did.

Three British actors were hired through Delfont to play the supporting roles, and it was arranged for rehearsals to begin in Ireland in October 1953. The Hardys and Laurels left for Ireland on the pride of the American liner fleet, *SS America*. It was a rollicking trip, with Stan, who loved the sea, getting everyone out on deck for vigorous walks. As they pulled into Cork Harbour, just outside Cobh, the four of them were on deck, leaning over the rail, trying to see all they could.

Suddenly they noticed a motley fleet of sail boats, tenders, tugs and various other small craft approaching the *America*. The little boats were full of people, all standing, waving and shouting something. There were also people atop harbour buildings, waving, screaming loudly. Then, as the *America* got closer, they could hear what the people shouting: 'Laurel and Har-dy! Laurel and Har-dy! Laurel and Har-dy!'

Babe and Stan were astounded. They did not know their arrival had been announced in the Cork newspapers, and that the people in the harbour were part of a spontaneous move to greet them. By now most people saw them on the First Class deck. Babe and Stan waved, Lucille and Ida waved. The tugs and all the boats in the harbour blew their whistles. Then, most unexpectedly, from the tower of the dockside Cathedral of St Colman came the sound of rich, deep carillon bells playing the Laurel and Hardy theme, 'The Dance of the Cuckoos'.

Babe and Stan looked at each other, and wept unashamedly. Lucille and Ida held each other and cried too.

In Cork they were taken to lunch at City Hall, and a car was arranged to drive them part of the way to Dublin. They went first to nearby Blarney Castle, but the walk up the many steps in the Castle was too much for Babe, and he stayed below. Stan, Ida and Lucille walked up all the way, but Stan was the only one willing to be held by the guide and lowered over the parapet to kiss the Stone.

They took the train to Dublin, marvelling at the beautiful coutryside. At Dublin they checked into their hotel, and next day began rehearsals for *Birds of a Feather*. The three actors Delfont had hired were there, and the sketch was put together.

Lucille, as prompter, held the book, and Stan directed. They spent ten days in rehearsal, and then took a boat across the Irish Sea to Liverpool. From there they took a train to Northampton and at the New Theatre gave the première of the sketch.

The British audiences loved *Birds of a Feather*, and the tour was, except occasionally, 'packed out' in Bernard Delfont's phrase. He was paying them a goodly sum for the times, and hoped he would break even. This was the third time around 'on the halls', and he was not certain the boys would draw well. Delfont, now Lord Delfont, remembers them with great affection:

> They were both wonderful people. Absolutely marvellous. Stan, of course, had a great sense of comedy; he would always laugh at any small joke. He loved talking about comedy. Oliver Hardy, on the other hand, was a serious, thinking man. He was quite religious. He used to read the Bible every morning in bed. They were quite different in character, but they melded together as a couple. I was trying to make some profit out of the venture. I myself was quite surprised at their popularity at that time.

Delfont in fact made a considerable amount of money on the boys, and the boys were pleased to make a goodly amount themselves. Annuities Stan had invested in years before matured at last, and thereafter he had no financial worries. Babe was mostly free of his tax responsibilities but there was always the lurking threat of Myrtle's alimony lawsuits. On the tours Babe and Stan divided their income right down the middle, all profits going to their company, Shipman making the division.

From Northampton they went to Liverpool, Manchester and the Finsbury Park Empire Theatre, North London. One night at the Empire, Stan caught a severe chill, and knowing the potential trouble from that very English affliction, cancelled the performance just before it began. Babe went on stage that November night to announce the cancellation,

leaving a theatre of very disappointed people. Among them
was a nineteen-year old US Navy Petty Officer, and fervid
Laurel and Hardy fan, Leo Brooks. Leo continues the story:

A few days later I had to go to the American Embassy in
London, just down the street from the Naval Office, to
pick up some papers. I arrived at lunch-time so most people
there were gone. While waiting for their return, I sat down
on a couch and worked on my selection for that day's horse
races. Most of us in my office wagered a few bob on the
nags with our friendly betting shop down the street.

Then a rather portly, bespectacled gentleman sat down
beside me and inquired softly if there was anything 'worthwhile' running. I was almost speechless when I looked up
and realized that here next to me was the great Oliver
Hardy. He had come to the Embassy to pick up a letter.
I told him I had a tip, a long shot at 25–1, that couldn't
lose. Mr Hardy roared with laughter and said he had bet
on many horses like that in his life, and several of them
still hadn't come in. We talked for a few minutes about
his films, and I told him of my great disappointment at
not seeing him and Stan perform, but that I hoped to see
them before they left England. By now the Embassy staff
had returned from lunch, and Mr Hardy got his letter. As
he started to leave, he fished in his pocket and pulled out
a crumpled five pound note – a pound was worth about
$2.80 in those days – and asked me to put it on my 'sure
thing' for him. He winked and asked me to keep the wager
our little secret, as Mrs Hardy would not approve.

Shortly after, I stopped by the betting shop, bet his
money, added five pounds of my own, all on the long
short. The race was a complete joke. Our horse led from the
starting wire and won by over ten lengths. To my certain
knowledge the horse had never won before and never won
again. (A few years later my tipster friend was caught trying
to fix a race and went to jail. Draw your own conclusions.)

Laurel and Hardy meanwhile were touring the North
of England, and I was not able to catch up to *Birds of*

a Feather until it returned to Finsbury Park in February 1954. I watched the show, and like everyone else, had a glorious time. After the show, I waited at the stage entrance and when Babe Hardy came out, I handed him an envelope containing his £125 (about $350). He was caught by surprise as he looked at the envelope. When it dawned on him who I was – I had been in uniform at our first meeting – and *what* it was, he laughed delightedly and winked at me as he was whisked away to his cart. That was one of life's very special moments for me.

A few weeks after Stan's cancelled performance, the boys were at the Hippodrome Theatre in Birmingham, following a fortnight in Brixton and Newcastle. It was December 4, 1953 when this writer, then a graduate student in nearby Stratford-upon-Avon, met Babe and Stan backstage at the Hippodrome. There is no need to dilate the factors deriving from that meeting which led to my writing several books about them. What should be said here is that when it was first suggested to Babe and Stan that a book about them would be a worthy enterprise, they both drew back, and for the same reason.

So much had been written about their personal lives in the press, yellow and otherwise, that they were extremely sensitive about their past. When it was explained that the book would concern itself almost wholly with their careers and the content of their comedy, they were decidedly interested. They were both dubious about the marketability of such a book, but very cooperative.* During the tour of *Birds of a Feather*, I met them together and separately a number of times, and found my reverence for them as artists matched by my regard for them as men. There was, I saw, a sturdy sweetness about them both.

It was in my second interview with Babe that I said I was sure some of their films touched greatness. He had no need

---

*I cannot resist noting that *Mr Laurel and Mr Hardy* (Robson Books 1976) has been continuously in print for twenty-eight years.

to value the opinion of an unknown and statusless graduate student, but he came as close to blushing as a sophisticated sixty-one year old man could. 'Oh-h!' he said with embarrassment, and a friendly but dismissive wave of his hand. He went on to other things, but I sensed that he was pleased.

From Birmingham they went to Hull's Palace Theatre, and with some apprehension. Babe's circulation had been giving him difficulty, especially in the legs. They pained whenever he walked. Every time he sat down, Lucille saw to it that a chair was placed so he could get his feet off the ground, level with his seat.

Their last night in Hull, the theatre's stage manager, Ted Hunter, was astonished to see Babe climbing six flights of stairs backstage to ask the dancers in the show to sign his autograph book. Babe explained to Hunter, 'We always like the signatures of everyone that Stan and I have worked for.' Hunter was much struck by the word 'for'. He said, 'Mr Hardy, you shouldn't have climbed those stairs with your bad legs.' Babe said, 'But Stan and I wanted the young ladies' autographs.' 'They would gladly have called on you,' said Hunter, 'or one of my men could have asked them for you.' This surprised Babe, and he explained: 'Oh, no. I was asking the favour. So it was up to me to approach them.'

The next playing date was a long one, Nottingham, four weeks, a strenuous and happy stay – happy because Stan's sister lived there. The schedule was two shows a day, three shows a day in Christmas week, and three shows every Saturday. Playing with them at the Empire Theatre was a young ventriloquist named Harry Worth, who went on to bigger things as a comic in British show business. Sadly, he died in July 1989. Worth recalled Babe and Stan:

> They were very lovely people. They had time for you, and would talk to you, and I used to spend a lot of time particularly with Babe in his dressing-room. I used to sit and listen to him telling me about the old days . . . He'd sit there, rolling his own cigarettes with one hand. Stan was very busy writing letters, particularly to the children.

Wherever they came from, he answered each and every one by hand. Babe and Stan took an interest in *all* acts, and they took an interest in me because they liked my style. I'd introduce two or three minutes of patter before I brought in my dolls. It struck Stan and Babe as very funny, and Babe said, 'Now you develop that style. The ventriloquism is OK but comedy might to get you somewhere.' Eventually it turned out it did.

Babe was always interested in young performers. He shared this with Stan. When young performers asked for advice, Babe always gave it, qualifying it with, 'Now, don't take this for gospel, but I've found that . . .' His advice was summed up in the sentence, 'Entertain for the sake of entertaining.' Entertain because it is something people need, and in that way you will be a success no matter how much or how little money you make.

On Christmas Day at Nottingham, Babe, Lucille, Stan and Ida went over to The Bull, Stan's sister's pub, and had an old-fashioned holiday. The barmaid, Gert, prepared the dinner, and the boys played darts with Gert's children in the back room while dinner was cooking. This was the traditional turkey, and by the time it was consumed, it was pub time. The locals came thronging in while both Babe and Stan pulled a few pints for them.

During their Nottingham stay, there was a juvenile talent competition at the theatre and Babe and Stan supervised it. Youngsters, some as young as six, came up on stage to give their party piece, retiring to applause and a little prize. Joy Ingram today recalls being a contestant at the age of six: 'I can remember singing, and I can remember the clapping. I can remember dancing with Stan Laurel, and how white his face was, and how cold his hands were.'

The whiteness was make up, but the cold hands betokened the beginning of cardiac difficulties for Stan although his circulatory problems were as nothing compared to Babe's at that point. Notwithstanding, they soldiered on, taking the burden of extra shows and the publicity events local theatre managers asked of them. The tour went on to Portsmouth,

Chiswick, Finsbury Park (to make up for Stan's inability to perform in November), Brighton, Norwich, Sunderland, Glasgow, Wolverhampton, Sheffield, York, Grimsby, Leeds, Edinburgh, Carlisle, Bradford, Aston and Plymouth. It was at the Palace Theatre, Plymouth, that Babe became seriously ill.

First there was flu with laryngitis and high fever. This was a very inconvenient time to be sick because the Hardys, together with Stan, had been looking forward to a visit in Plymouth from tart-tongued Lady Astor, one of whose very few soft spots was her affection for Laurel and Hardy. They had to forgo that pleasure.

In examining Babe, the doctor listened long and carefully to his heart. He believed the flu had embarrassed the heart, and ordered immediate rest. Babe almost certainly had experienced a small heart attack. The tour had several months to go but it was cancelled. Lucille and Babe made their plans to go home in the way they had now discovered to be most rewarding, by freighter. The Laurels were returning on the *Queen Mary*, but the Hardys asked that they go with them on the freighter. 'I promise you, you'll like it,' said Lucille. She was right. They all went up to Hull and took the *SS Manchuria,* a Scandinavian ship, going home past the Azores and through tropical latitudes all the way across. It was a delightful trip home, certainly the best time they ever had together. The weather was fine, the food excellent, the company unmatchable.

On the three British tours, Babe and Stan had come to know each other as never before – and found they truly liked each other. All their social relationships in previous years had been conditioned by their hobbies. Babe had his golf, cards, race-track and Lakeside pals; Stan, outside of tuna fishing, hardly your everyday kind of hobby, found his avocation in his vocation – creating the films. There was little reason for them to be together except at work.

But the music hall tours brought them together constantly. 'Previously they got along so well,' said Lucille, 'because they never had a chance to get bored with each other. But on the tours, they were more normal with each other. They let their hair down, treated each other like one of the family, whereas before there was a certain amount of formality between them. They never really knew each other before. Now they were chummy.'

After night performances, the boys invariably shared a cold supper in the sitting-room between their suites. Then they could discuss how it had played, and anything else happening that day. The Hardys always breakfasted early, and Stan frequently joined them. Ida was strictly a night owl, sleeping until noon. She invariably did her house cleaning in the middle of the night.

Lucille was greatly pleased at the growing intimacy between Babe and Stan in these late years because she knew how much it meant to them both. Babe had found personal happiness at last with Lucille and now his professional life blossomed into a closer bond with his partner, one seasoned with warmth. Stan had exactly the same experience: a final happy marriage, and the seal of affection for Babe. In his last years, whenever Stan wrote or spoke of Babe he always called him 'my dear partner'.

When the Hardys returned to Los Angeles mid-1954, Lucille instituted almost draconian measures to make Babe rest and lose weight. For the most part she succeeded. His weight, in ill health or good, was always on his mind. Her most poignant memory of that time was his coming out of the shower, towel wrapped around him, looking at himself in a large mirror and saying to her, 'Do you love me?' 'Of course I love you!' she said. 'How can you love a big, fat old slob like me?' 'Don't you dare speak of my husband that way,' she said. She found it heart-rending because although it was said lightly, she knew he was serious. People meeting Babe were frequently taken aback by his 6 foot 2 inch height, saying things like, 'Why, I didn't realize you were so big.' This would hurt him because he thought they were referring to his weight. Stan was a thin 5 foot 9 inches, which always emphasized Babe's height and bulk.

Once when Babe spoke disparagingly of his appearance, Lucille sweetly but firmly scolded him, saying that outside of the heart factor involved, his weight was a matter of utter

indifference to her. 'I explained that his weight had nothing –
but nothing – whatever to do with the wonderful man I loved
so deeply. I explained to him, until he finally understood, that
in fact his very size had brought happinesss to people all over
the world – that his size brought the great gift of laughter to
people who loved him, many of whom were just like him,
with a weight problem so called.' Babe listened to her very
carefully. 'Above all,' said Lucille, 'I said it was his size that
gave him the opportunity to display that great talent of his
as an actor, that talent that brought so much joy to us all. It
was at that moment – I am certain – that he knew his life was
a success.'

So, in the sixty-second year of his existence, Oliver Norvell
Hardy's voyage of self-discovery ended. Through his petite
and indomitable wife, he came to understand that the outward appearance he so signally despised had nothing to do
with his human worth. At terribly long last, he was off the
treadmill of his life struggle – keeping risky balance between
his fear of being laughed at and his job of being laughed with.
The fear led him him to be an actor, the job made him an artist
and a man. He came now to realize that, through his artistry,
his size gave him something better than fame or money. His
unique, his *necessary* size, was the cause – almost the symbol
– of loving laughter to millions who cherished that great life
need.

One afternoon late in 1954, the phone rang and Lucille
answered it as usual. It was Ben Shipman, directing her to
find a phone out of Babe's earshot to call him back. When
she did, she learned that Ralph Edwards's tremendously
popular television programme, *This Is Your Life*, wanted
to do a programme on Babe and Stan. Lucille was eager
to cooperate and started to line up vital participating guests
from Babe's life. Babe's only surviving sibling, Lizzie, was
too ill to do the show. Instead, for Babe's half of the programme, Lucille was able to find his first childhood sweetheart, Alcia Miller Horne, and his old singing pal from
Jacksonville days, Margaret Arata O'Connor. Keeping all

this secret from Babe was difficult because he was home so much.

Lucille used subterfuge to obtain certain items from Babe's past. Shipman arranged a meeting of Laurel and Hardy Feature Productions at his office so Babe would be away from home in order for several photographs on his bedroom wall to be taken away by the Edwards' people, quickly copied and returned before he came home.

Ida was not let in on the plans until comparatively late in the game because her excitable temperament could well have revealed all. As it was, even after being let in on the secret, she forgot one of Edwards's instructions. He asked Lucille and Ida not to show their faces when the camera first caught the boys because they were to come in later as guests. Ida forgot this and at the moment Edwards's voice shocked Babe and Stan, she walked directly across the sight line of the camera,

The programme was a considerable surprise to Babe and Stan, and had its thrilling moments for them, although in retrospect Stan was not pleased. Always a stickler for thorough preparation, he found making their television début on an unrehearsed programme not very edifying. He said exactly twelve words during the show.

Babe, on the other hand, enjoyed not only seeing Alcia and Margaret but old Roach studio friends who appeared, former general manager Warren Jones and Leo McCarey. Stan, too, was touched by the presence of these two fellow workers, especially McCarey, whom he revered. But for the rest he found it chaotic and much ado about not very much.

The programme would have been well rounded out that evening if Hal Roach had come on as final guest. For reasons known only to himself, he refused Edwards's invitation to appear, and Hal Roach Jr was there instead to present a plaque designating the much-used pool on the Roach lot as 'Lake Laurel and Hardy. So called because these two world-famous comedians were first teamed here at the Hal Roach Studios and because they, more than any others, were in and out of these waters. *This Is Your Life.* December 1, 1954.' But a few days later when the boys went to the lot for a ceremony affixing the plaque, Hal Sr appeared, and all was cordiality. Pictures were taken of the three.

In one sense, it was appropriate that Hal Jr be on the programme because he wanted to bring Laurel and Hardy to television. Then in command of his father's studio, he was very aware of Babe and Stan's television-renewed popularity. After the show, he talked with Stan about the boys doing a series of hour-long, made-for-television shows, in colour, with Stan in complete control of his own scripts. Stan and Babe were enthusiastic. Remembering the earlier tentative plan for television he had discussed with Babe, Stan started to sketch out a series based on Mother Goose and similar legends to be called *Laurel and Hardy's Fabulous Fables*.

Hal Jr contracted for four of these with the boys. In high enthusiasm, Stan started to write, and had completed the scenario of the first show, *Babes in the Woods*, when in late April 1955 he suffered a stroke. It was not very debilitating but it left him with slightly slurred speech and a limp. Performing was out of the question until he got better. They were only ten days away from filming.

Babe forgot his old phobia about telephones and made sure to call Stan every three or four days. A few weeks after the stroke, Babe was invited to lunch at the Laurels'. As he settled himself on the couch, he said to Stan, 'Well, here's another nice mess you've gotten *yourself* into!' Stan spilled over with laughter.

Babe was not feeling awfully spry himself. Just a few days before the lunch, as the result of heat exhaustion, he suffered a little heart attack which required brief hospitalization. But he did not feel poorly. Six months after Stan's stroke, Babe had another heart attack, complicated by gall bladder trouble and a kidney infection. By Christmas 1955, he was feeling dreadful but absolutely refused to go to the hospital. Christmas was a very special time for the Hardys, and he could not imagine spending it there.

By this time in their lives Lucille came to realize their big home was too much for them to keep up, and she put it on the market. They moved to a smaller house they owned on

Woodman Avenue. For this house, Lucille rented a hospital bed, set it up in the living-room, and told him to get in it and stay there. From there he could watch television and see her putting up the Christmas tree. For his moments of difficult breathing – he also had a touch of asthma – she got a portable oxygen tank.

He improved very gradually, and his weight loss was now marked. He had been approached for interviews by a number of reporters but turned them all down. Stan and Ben, however, urged him to see one of them, Bob Thomas, an accurate reporter, and Babe did. Babe said, among other things, to Thomas:

Yes, I've lost 150 pounds ... I got pneumonia when we were touring England two years ago. My heart was jumping around a bit and I got asthma too. When I got back here I went to the hospital for a check-up, and the doctors said I should lose weight. My wife, who is a good task-master, kept me on a strict salt-free diet, with limited calories. No, I don't miss eating. I was never a tremendous eater. It was the drinking. I drank a lot of beer, and always there were guys around Lakeside Golf Club asking you to have a drink. I did it not because I liked the stuff but because it seemed friendly. I never did know how much I weighed because most scales don't go over 300. I know I was over 350. Now I'm down to 210.

Some time later Bob Thomas interviewed Babe and Stan together at the latter's home in Santa Monica, where a news photo was taken. Although he looks amply jolly in the picture, as indeed he felt at the time, the photograph had wide repercussions. Babe looked fine; he just didn't look like Babe Hardy. Expressions of shocked horror came from all sides, upsetting him dreadfully. Lucille, who was so close to him that she did not realize how very much he had altered, blamed herself. Thereafter Babe refused to leave home, and the only people he would see were the Laurels, Ben Shipman and old friends named the Callagans.

It is difficult to know if this mind set was conducive to triggering his final blow of ill health. On September 15, 1956, Babe had a massive heart attack that left him completely paralysed and unable to talk. He was taken directly to St Joseph's Hospital, and remained there a number of weeks in extremely grave condition. Lucille did not want this to be known, and the hospital cooperated. Unfortunately the ambulance drivers talked to the press, and the story duly appeared. Babe was not conscious of it. His stroke was so debilitating that he could not read.

After a month at St Joseph's, Lucille realized he was not likely to improve there, so she had him moved to her mother's house at 5421 Auckland, North Hollywood. Lucille's mother urged her to take the extra room she had available and fix it up like a hospital room. The room had its own bath and separate entrance. This was done. The hospital advised against it, suggesting that Babe be sent to the Motion Picture Home in Woodland Hills where he would have the advantage of superb medical care and excellent facilities.

Lucille said no. She and Babe had been so close for so many years that when he was lucid, as he was from time to time, she did not want him to think that she had deserted him. It was explained to her that he would need nurses around the clock, and she arranged for them. Babe could move his left arm and leg a bit, but his inner functions were all paralysed. He was unable to speak, despite enormous effort on his part to do so. When Lucille knew he was trying to say something, she would put her face next to his and say, 'I love you.' He would say the same, with his eyes.

She set up the bedroom with the same pictures on the wall just as they were in their previous home, and she felt sure he never knew he had been moved. When Babe opened his eyes, he could see a picture of himself and one of Lucille. When troubled, he would look at her picture and cry. The nurses knew the tears meant he wanted Lucille. They would get her. This was January 1957.

It was during this calamitous time that Myrtle sent out a process server to the house where her former husband lay, fighting for his physical and mental existence. When the server rang the bell, Lucille came to the door and on being told the contents of the paper to be served – another alimony claim – explained that yes, her husband was inside, totally incapacitated with a massive stroke. Appalled at the news and the circumstance in which he found himself, the man said, 'Please don't worry. I wouldn't dream of serving this, Mrs Hardy,' and went away quickly.

Lucille tried to interest Babe in television, but it became apparent he could not follow it. He was unable to think consecutively for very long, and that continuity of images on the screen never seemed to add up to anything for him. At times, seeing the frustration in his eyes, she sensed that he wished it was all over. When this happened, she would distract him with a kiss. That he understood.

Stan was dreadfully upset and worried at Babe's illness. Although recuperating himself, he asked Lucille to tell him when Babe's mind was clearing a bit, so he could visit. Periodically when she knew Babe was lucid, she would call Stan to say, 'If you hurry up, he will know you.' Stan would come at once.

At times Babe would strain so hard to talk with Stan that the tears rolled down his face when the words would not come. Stan would nod, pat his partner's hand and say, 'Yes, Babe. Yes.' The last time they were together, in the final irony of their lives, Babe and Stan could only communicate in pantomime. Stan remembered Babe at one point 'saying' with eyes and slight body movement, 'Look at me. Isn't this appalling?' Lucille and Ida, who had been in the room, withdrew, leaving the two friends alone to share what was to be their final visit. Stan wept as Ida drove him home.

The evening of August 6, 1957, Babe began to have a series of small strokes, convulsive in nature. His hands drew up in contractions, and when great spasms racked his body, Lucille got into his bed and held him tightly. She did this through the night. He died the morning of August 7.

When she knew he was gone, Lucille said aloud, 'Thank you, God, for taking him away from his suffering.'

*

When told of Babe's death, Stan lowered his head and could not speak for long minutes. His doctor did not allow him to go to the funeral. 'It's just as well,' he said. 'I might have done or said something funny to hide the hurt – and Babe would have understood. But I don't think others would have. I hope wherever he is, he realizes how much people loved him.'

Babe was cremated and his ashes interred in the Masonic section of the Garden of Valhalla Memorial Park in North Hollywood. The service was Masonic. Babe had mentioned his interment only once. After specifying cremation and the Masonic rite, he added, 'And I am willing to be buried anywhere but Forest Lawn.' He had had an unhappy experience there with the burial of his sister, Emily, though he never told Lucille what it was. His feelings on the matter were strong.

His will left everything to Lucille. Even after his death, Myrtle persisted in back alimony claims, forcing Lucille to go to court and defend Babe's estate. Myrtle lost. She drifted in and out of sanitariums and died, still an alcoholic but a rather sturdy one, at Palm Grove Convalescent Hospital, Garden Grove, California, on January 18, 1983. A feisty eighty-six, her fatal heart attack was caused by arteriosclerosis of long duration.

Lucille sought a new life for herself. She sold her property, and while living with her sister in Palm Springs, went to real estate school there. She settled again in North Hollywood, working for a realty company in Northridge. Three years later she met a retired business man, Ben Price, a widower living in her apartment building. Physically very small, like Lucille, he seemed Babe's opposite but was much like him in gentleness and humour. Lucille and Ben were married in November 1960, and moved to Studio City.

At that time she did not watch Laurel and Hardy films, convinced that she would be unable to bear the sight of Babe in all his charm and comic vigour. She had particularly loved his warm, sensitive, little-boy eyes, and now she dreaded the thought of seeing them again. Surely it would hurt too much.

But gently, gradually, Ben persuaded her to look at the Laurel and Hardy films then widely current on Los Angeles television. She found to her intense relief that the pain had gone, and she was able at last to watch her Babe with renewed love and enjoyment.

By 1970 the international Laurel and Hardy Appreciation Society, The Sons of the Desert, was flourishing in Los Angeles with its very active local chapter (or Tent) – the Way Out West Tent – operative. Lucille and Ben were, in effect, adopted by the Tent and became the top celebrity guests at their many meetings through the years. These meetings became the Prices' chief recreation. They had twenty-five years of very happy married life before he died in 1986. Lucille died of cancer the following year.

One of the comments Stan made to the press at the time of Babe's death was, 'That is the end of Laurel and Hardy.' No.

So committed was Stan to the unending comedic impulses of his mind and heart that he went on crafting Laurel and Hardy gags and routines for the rest of his days.* He knew the routines would never be used, but he did not care. Writing them became part of his retirement in addition to answering the undiminished flow of mail. Creatively, Laurel and Hardy did not die until Stan did, on February 23, 1965.

But of course they can never die. Laurel and Hardy exist to this day on film and television in almost all countries of the world. Cinema revivals and film society retrospectives continue everywhere. Videocassette marketing of their films is strong and growing stronger. In 1964 Stan said, 'Maybe people loved our pictures the way they do because we put so much love *in* them. I don't know.'

What is known is that where laughter lives among men and women, so – bounteously, warmly – do they.

*See pp. 145–171, *The Comedy World of Stan Laurel* (Robson Books, 1975).

The films of Oliver Hardy

(Title, release date (month, day, year), studio, length)

1914

Outwitting Dad (4/21/1914) – Lubin – 1 reel
A Brewery Town Romance (5/1914) – Lubin – 1 reel
A Lucky Strike (5/22/1914) – Lubin – 1 reel
A Female Cop (6/15/1914) – Lubin – 1 reel
Long May It Wave (6/15/1914) – Lubin – 1 reel
The Kidnapped Bride (6/29/1914) – Lubin – 1 reel
The Rise of the Johnsons (7/27/1914) – Lubin – 1 reel
He Wanted Work (8/10/1914) – Lubin – 1 reel
They Bought a Boat (8/10/1914) – Lubin – 1 reel
Making Auntie Welcome (8/17/1914) – Lubin – 1 reel
Back to the Farm (8/18/1914) – Lubin – 1 reel
A Fool There Was (8/31/1914) – Lubin – 1 reel
The Green Alarm (8/31/1914) – Lubin – 1 reel
Never Too Old (8/31/1914) – Lubin 1 reel
Pins are Lucky (9/14/1914) – Lubin – 1 reel
When the Ham Turned (10/10/1914) – Lubin – 1 reel
The Smuggler's Daughter (10/17/1914) – Lubin – 1 reel
The Soubrette and the Simp (10/18/1914) – Lubin – 1 reel
Kidnapping the Kid (10/31/1914) – Lubin – 1 reel
The Honor of the Force (11/7/1914) – Lubin – 1 reel
The Daddy of Them All (11/14/1914) – Lubin – 1 reel
She Was the Other (11/14/1914) – Lubin – 1 reel
The Servant Girl's Legacy (11/28/1914) – Lubin – 1 reel
Dobs at the Shore (12/5/1914) – Lubin – 1 reel
The Fresh Air Cure (12/5/1914) – Lubin – 1 reel

1915

What He Forgot (1/2/1915) – Lubin – 1 reel
Spaghetti and Lottery (1/15/1915) – Lubin – 1 reel
Cupid's Target (1/19/1915) – Lubin – 1 reel
Gus and the Anarchists (1/19/1915) – Lubin – 1 reel
Shoddy the Tailor (1/23/1915) – Lubin – 1 reel
Charlie's Aunt (3/5/1915) – Lubin – 1 reel
Artists and Models (3/11/1915) – Lubin – 1 reel
The Tramps (3/15/1915) – Lubin – 1 reel
Prize Babe (3/20/1915) – Lubin – 1 reel
An Expensive Visit (3/23/1915) – Lubin – 1 reel
Cleaning Time (4/13/1915) – Lubin – 1 reel
Mixed Flats (4/20/1915) – Lubin – 1 reel
Safety Worst (5/1/1915) – Lubin – 1 reel
The Twin Sister (5/8/1915) – Lubin – 1 reel
Baby (5/10/1915) – Lubin – 1 reel
Who Stole the Doggies? (5/15/1915) – Lubin – 1 reel
The New Butler (5/20/1915) – Lubin – 1 reel
Matilda's Legacy (5/25/1915) – Lubin – 1 reel
Her Choice (6/29/1915) – Lubin – 1 reel
The Cannibal King (7/6/1915) – Lubin – 1 reel
What a Cinch (7/13/1915) – Lubin – 1 reel
Avenging Bill (8/13/1915) – Lubin – 1 reel
The Dead Letter (8/17/1915) Lubin – 1 reel
The Haunted Hat (8/31/1915) – Lubin – 1 reel
Babe's School Days (9/14/1915) – Lubin – 1 reel
Three Rings and a Goat (10/11/1915) – Pathé – 1 reel
A Bungalow Bungle (10/14/1915) – Pathé – 1 reel
Ethel's Romeos (10/17/1915) – Casino – 1 reel
A Rheumatic Joint (10/18/1915) – Pathé – 1 reel
Fatty's Fatal Fun (10/23/1915) – Pathé American – 1 reel
Clothes Make the Man (1915) – Edison – 1 reel
The Simp and the Sophomores (1915) – Edison – 1 reel
A Janitor's Joyful Job (1915) – Novelty – 1 reel
Something in Her Eye (1915) – Novelty – 1 reel
Ups and Downs (12/31/1915) – Vim – 1 reel

1916

The Way Out (1/7/1916) – Vim – 1 reel
Chickens (1/14/1916) – Vim – 1 reel
Frenzied Finance (1/21/1916) – Vim – 1 reel
A Special Delivery (1/27/1916) – Vim – 1 reel
Busted Hearts (1/28/1916) – Vim – 1 reel
A Sticky Affair (2/13/1916) – Vim – 1 reel
Bungles' Rainy Day (2/10/1916) – Vim – 1 reel
The Tryout (2/10/1916) – Vim – 1 reel
One Too Many (2/17/1916) – Vim – 1 reel
Bungles Enforces the Law (2/24/1916) – Vim – 1 reel
The Serenade (3/2/1916) – Vim – 1 reel
Bungles' Elopement (3/10/1916) – Vim – 1 reel
Nerve and Gasoline (3/16/1916) – Vim – 1 reel
Bungles Lands a Job (3/23/1916) – Vim – 1 reel
Their Vacation (3/30/1916) – Vim – 1 reel
Mamma's Boy (4/6/1916) – Vim – 1 reel
A Battle Royal (4/13/1916) – Vim – 1 reel
All For a Girl (4/20/1916) – Vim – 1 reel
Hired and Fired (4/21/1916) – Vim – 1 reel
What's Sauce For the Goose (4/27/1916) Vim – 1 reel
The Brave One (5/4/1916) – Vim – 1 reel
The Water Cure (5/11/1916) – Vim 1 reel
Thirty Days (5/18/1916) – Vim – 1 reel
Baby Doll (5/25/1916) – Vim – 1 reel
The Schemers (6/1/1916) – Vim – 1 reel
The Sea Dogs (6/8/1916) – Vim – 1 reel
Hungry Hearts (6/15/1916) – Vim – 1 reel
Edison Bugg's Invention (6/22/1916) – Vim – 1 reel
Never Again (6/24/1916) – Vim – 1 reel
Better Halves (6/29/1916) – Vim – 1 reel
A Day at School (7/6/1916) – Vim – 1 reel
A Terrible Tragedy (7/8/1916) – Vim – 1 reel
Spaghetti (7/13/1916) – Vim – 1 reel
Aunt Bill (7/20/1916) – Vim – 1 reel
The Heroes (7/27/1916) – Vim – 1 reel

It Happened in Pikersville (7/29/1916) – Vim – 1 reel
Human Hounds (8/3/1916) – Vim – 1 reel
Dreamy Knights (8/10/1916) – Vim – 1 reel
Life Savers (8/17/1916) – Vim – 1 reel
Their Honeymoon (8/24/1916) – Vim – 1 reel
An Aerial Joyride (8/31/1916) Vim – 1 reel
Side-Tracked (9/7/1916) – Vim – 1 reel
Stranded (9/14/1916) – Vim – 1 reel
Love and Duty (9/21/1916) – Vim – 1 reel
Artistic Atmosphere (9/27/1916) – Vim – 1 reel
The Reformers (9/28/1916) – Vim – 1 reel
Royal Blood (10/5/1916) – Vim – 1 reel
The Candy Trail (10/10/1916) – Vim – 1 reel
A Precious Parcel (10/12/1916) – Vim – 1 reel
A Maid to Order (10/26/1916) – Vim – 1 reel
Twin Flats (11/2/1916) – Vim – 1 reel
A Warm Reception (11/9/1916) – Vim – 1 reel
Pipe Dreams (11/23/1916) – Vim – 1 reel
Mother's Child (11/26/1916) – Vim – 1 reel
The Prize Winners (11/30/1916) – Vim – 1 reel
Ambitious Ethel (12/4/1916) – Vim – 1 reel
The Guilty One (12/7/1916) – Vim – 1 reel
He Winked and Won (12/20/1916) – Vim – 1 reel
Fat and Fickle (12/28/1916) – Vim – 1 reel

1917

Boycotted Baby (1/4/1917) – Vim – 1 reel
Wanted – A Bad Man (1/21/1917) – Vim – 1 reel
The Other Girl (2/1/1917) – Vim – 1 reel
The Love Bugs (3/1/1917) – Vim – 1 reel
Back Stage (5/15/1917) – King Bee – 2 reels
The Hero (6/1/1917) – King Bee – 2 reels
Dough Nuts (6/15/1917) – King Bee – 2 reels
Cupid's Rival (7/1/1917) King Bee – 2 reels
The Villain (7/15/1917) – King Bee – 2 reels
The Millionaire (8/1/1917) – King Bee – 2 reels
A Mix-up in Hearts (8/8/1917) – King Bee – 2 reels

The Genius (8/22/1917) – King Bee – 2 reels
The Goat (8/15/1917) – King Bee – 2 reels
The Stranger (8/29/1917) – King Bee – 2 reels
The Fly Cop (9/1/1917) – King Bee – 2 reels
The Modiste (9/8/1917) – King Bee – 2 reels
The Star Boarder (9/15/1917) – King Bee – 2 reels
The Chief Cook (10/1/1917) – King Bee – 2 reels
The Candy Kid (10/15/1917) – King Bee – 2 reels
The Station Master (10/22/1917) – King Bee – 2 reels
The Hobo (11/1/1917) – King Bee – 2 reels
The Pest (11/15/1917) – King Bee – 2 reels
The Prospector (11/29/1917) – King Bee – 2 reels
A Day's Vacation (1917) – King Bee – 2 reels
Little Nell (1917) – King Bee – 2 reels

1918

The Bandmaster (1/1/1918) – King Bee – 2 reels
The Artist (1/15/1918) – King Bee – 2 reels
The Barber (1/22/1918) – King Bee – 2 reels
King Solomon (1/24/1918) – King Bee – 2 reels
The Orderly (1/30/1918) – King Bee – 2 reels
The Slave (1/8/1918) – King Bee – 2 reels
His Day Out (2/1/1918) – King Bee – 2 reels
The Rogue (3/1/1918) – King Bee – 2 reels
The Scholar (4/1/1918) – King Bee – 2 reels
The Messenger (4/15/1918) – King Bee – 2 reels
The Handyman (5/1/1918) – King Bee – 2 reels
Bright and Early (6/1/1918) – King Bee – 2 reels
The Straight and Narrow (6/16/1918) – King Bee – 2 reels
Playmates (7/1/1918) – King Bee – 2 reels
The Freeloader (1918) – King Bee – 2 reels
Globe Hotel (1918) – King Bee – 2 reels
All Is Fair (1918) – Novelty Film Co. – 2 reels
The Lucky Dog (Filmed 9/1918 for G. M. Anderson; released 1922 by Metro Sun-Lite Comedy Series) – With Stan Laurel – 2 reels

1919

Freckled Fish (1/22/1919) – L-KO – 2 reels
Hop the Bellhop (1/29/1919) – L-KO – 2 reels
Lions and Ladies (2/26/1919) – L-KO – 2 reels
Hello Trouble (1919) – L-KO – 2 reels
Painless Love (1919) – L-KO – 2 reels
Mules and Mortgages (4/14/1919) – Vitagraph – 2 reels
Tootsies and Tamales (5/13/1919) – Vitagraph – 2 reels
Healthy and Happy (5/31/1919) – Vitagraph – 2 reels
Flips and Flops (6/28/1919) – Vitagraph – 2 reels
Yaps and Yokels (8/12/1919) – Vitagraph – 2 reels
Mates and Models (9/6/1919) – Vitagraph – 2 reels
Squabs and Squabbles (9/27/1919) – Vitagraph – 2 reels
Bungs and Bunglers (10/31/1919) – Vitagraph – 2 reels
Switches and Sweeties (11/28/1919) – Vitagraph – 2 reels
The Applicant (1919) – Vitagraph – 2 reels

1920

Dames and Dentists (1/7/1920) – Vitagraph – 2 reels
Maids and Muslin (2/16/1920) – Vitagraph – 2 reels
Squeaks and Squawks (3/12/1920) – Vitagraph – 2 reels
Fists and Fodder (4/10/1920) – Vitagraph – 2 reels
Pals and Pugs (4/23/1920) – Vitagraph – 2 reels
He Laughs Last (5/27/1920) – Vitagraph – 2 reels
Springtime (7/20/1920) – Vitagraph – 2 reels
The Decorator (8/26/1920) – Vitagraph – 2 reels
His Jonah Day (9/26/1920) – Vitagraph – 2 reels
The Back Yard (10/2/1920) – Vitagraph – 2 reels

1921

The Nuisance (1/10/1921) – Vitagraph – 2 reels
The Blizzard (2/14/1921) – Vitagraph – 2 reels
The Tourist (4/29/1921) – Vitagraph – 2 reels

The Fall Guy (7/1921) – Vitagraph – 2 reels
The Bellhop (9/1921) Vitagraph – 2 reels
The Trouble Hunter (1921) – Vitagraph – 2 reels
The Stagehand (1921) – Vitagraph – 2 reels
The Bakery (1921) – Vitagraph – 2 reels

1922

The Sawmill (1/1/1922) – Vitagraph – 2 reels
The Show (3/1922) – Vitagraph – 2 reels
Golf (8/5/1922) – Vitagraph – 2 reels
Fortune's Mask (8/18/1922) – Vitagraph – 6 reels
The Little Wildcat (11/12/1922) Vitagraph – 6 reels
The Counter Jumpers (12/9/1922) Vitagraph – 2 reels
A Pair of Kings (1922) – Vitagraph – 2 reels
The Sleuth (1922) – Vitagraph – 2 reels

1923

One Stolen Night (1/22/1923) – Vitagraph – 2 reels
The Barnyard (1923) – Vitagraph – 2 reels
No Wedding Bells (1923) – Vitagraph – 2 reels
The Gown Shop (1923) – Vitagraph – 2 reels
Horseshoes (1923) – Vitagraph – 2 reels

1924

A Perfect Lady (2/24/1924) Roach-Pathé – 2 reels
The King of Wild Horses (4/13/1924) – Roach-Pathé – 5 reels
The Girl in the Limousine (7/25/1924) – Chadwick-First National – 6 reels
Her Boy Friend (9/28/1924) – Chadwick-First National – 2 reels
Kid Speed (11/16/1924) Chadwick-First National – 2 reels
The Four Wheeled Terror (re-titling of *Kid Speed*)

All Wet (11/23/1924) – Roach–Pathé – 2 reels

1925

Hop To It (5/19/1925) – Arrow – 2 reels
The Wizard of Oz (6/27/1925) – Chadwick – 7 reels
Isn't Life Terrible? (7/5/1925) – Roach-Pathé – 2 reels
Yes, Yes, Nanette (7/12/1925) – Roach-Pathé – 2 reels
Should Sailors Marry? (11/8/1925) Roach-Pathé – 1 reel
The Perfect Clown (11/16/1925) – Chadwick – 6 reels
Enough to Do (1925) – Roach-Pathé – 1 reel
Stick Around (5/8/1925) – Arrow – 2 reels
The Paper Hanger's Helper (Retitled 1 reel version of *Stick Around*)
Hey, Taxi! (1925) – Arrow – 2 reels
Wandering Papas (1925) – Roach-Pathé – 1 reel

1926

Stop, Look and Listen (1/1/1926) – Adams-Pathé – 6 reels
A Bankrupt Honeymoon (2/7/1926) – Fox – 2 reels
Madame Mystery (4/18/1926) – Roach-Pathé – 2 reels
Say It With Babies (5/16/1926) – Roach-Pathé – 2 reels
Long Fliv the King (6/13/1926) – Roach-Pathé – 2 reels
The Gentle Cyclone (6/27/1926) – Fox – 2 reels
Thundering Fleas (7/4/1926) – Roach-Pathé – 2 reels
A Sea Dog's Tail (7/11/1926) – Sennett-Pathé – 2 reels
Along Came Auntie (7/25/1926) – Roach-Pathé – 2 reels
Crazy Like a Fox (8/22/1926) – Roach-Pathé – 2 reels
Bromo and Juliet (9/19/1926) – Roach-Pathé – 2 reels
Be Your Age (11/14/1926) – Roach-Pathé – 2 reels
The Nickel Hopper (12/5/1926) – Roach-Pathé – 2 reels
45 Minutes From Hollywood (12/1926) – Roach-Pathé – 2 reels – With Stan Laurel
His One Ambition (1926) – Roach-Pathé – 2 reels

1927

Should Men Walk Home? (1/20/1927) – Roach-Pathé – 2 reels

Why Girls Say No (2/20/1927) – Roach-Pathé – 2 reels

Duck Soup (3/13/1927) – Roach-Pathé – 2 reels – With Stan Laurel

Slipping Wives (4/3/1927) – Roach-Pathé – 2 reels – With Stan Laurel

The Honorable Mr Buggs (4/24/1927) – Roach-Pathé – 2 reels

No Man's Law (5/1/1927) – Roach-Pathé – 7 reels

Crazy To Act (5/15/1927) – Sennett-Pathé – 2 reels

Love 'Em and Weep (6/12/1927) – Roach-Pathé – 2 reels – With Stan Laurel

Fluttering Hearts (6/19/1927) – Roach-Pathé – 2 reels

Why Girls Love Sailors (7/17/1927) – Roach-Pathé – 2 reels – With Stan Laurel

The Lighter That Failed (10/1/1927) – Roach-Pathé – 2 reels

Baby Brother (6/1927) – Roach-Pathé – 2 reels

With Love and Hisses (8/28/1927) – Roach-Pathé – 2 reels – With Stan Laurel

Sugar Daddies (9/10/1927) – Roach-MGM – 2 reels – With Stan Laurel

Sailors, Beware (9/25/1927) – Roach-Pathé – 2 reels – With Stan Laurel

The Second Hundred Years (10/8/1927) – Roach-MGM – 2 reels – With Stan Laurel

Call of the Cuckoos (10/12/1927) – Roach-MGM – 2 reels – With Stan Laurel

Love 'Em and Feed 'Em (10/17/1927) – Roach-MGM – 2 reels

Hats Off (11/5/1927) – Roach-MGM – 2 reels – With Stan Laurel

Do Detectives Think? (11/20/1927) – Roach-Pathé – 2 reels – With Stan Laurel

Putting Pants on Philip (12/3/1927) – Roach-MGM – 2 reels – With Stan Laurel. The 'first' Laurel and Hardy team film, according to Laurel.
Assistant Wives (12/4/1927) – Roach-MGM – 2 reels
The Battle of the Century (12/31/1927) – Roach-MGM – With Stan Laurel

1928

(The following films are all with Stan Laurel except where indicated)
Leave 'Em Laughing (1/28/1928) – Roach-MGM – 2 reels
Flying Elephants (2/12/1928) – Roach-Pathé – 2 reels
The Finishing Touch (2/25/1928) – Roach-MGM – 2 reels
Galloping Ghosts (3/1/1928) – Roach-MGM – 2 reels – Hardy alone
From Soup to Nuts (3/24/1928) – Roach-MGM – 2 reels
Barnum and Ringling Inc. (4/7/1928) – Roach-MGM – 2 reels – Hardy alone
You're Darn Tootin' (4/21/1928) – Roach-MGM – 2 reels
Their Purple Moment (5/19/1928) – Roach-MGM – 2 reels
Should Married Men Go Home? (9/8/1928) – Roach-MGM – 2 reels
Early To Bed (10/6/1928) – Roach-MGM – 2 reels
Two Tars (11/3/1928) – Roach-MGM – 2 reels
Habeas Corpus (12/1/1928) – Roach-MGM – 2 reels
We Faw Down (12/29/1928) – Roach-MGM – 2 reels

1929

Liberty (1/26/1929) – Roach-MGM – 2 reels
Wrong Again (2/23/1919) – Roach-MGM – 2 reels
That's My Wife (3/23/1929) – Roach-MGM – 2 reels
Big Business (4/20/1929) – Roach-MGM – 2 reels

Unaccustomed As We are (5/4/1929) – 2 reels – Their first sound film. Except where noted, the following are sound films.

Double Whoopee (5/18/1929) – Roach-MGM – 2 reels – Silent

Berth Marks (6/1/1929) – Roach-MGM – 2 reels

Men O' War (6/29/1929) – Roach-MGM – 2 reels

Perfect Day (8/10/1929) – Roach-MGM – 2 reels

They Go Boom (9/21/1929) – Roach-MGM – 2 reels

Bacon Grabbers (10/19/1929) – Roach-MGM – 2 reels – Silent

The Hoose-Gow (11/16/1929) – Roach-MGM – 2 reels

The Hollywood Revue of 1929 (11/23/1929) – MGM – 12 reels

Angora Love (12/14/1929) – Roach-MGM – 2 reels – Silent

1930

Night Owls (1/4/30) – Roach-MGM – 2 reels

The Rogue Song (1/17/1930) – MGM – 11 reels – Technicolor

Blotto (2/8/1930) – Roach-MGM – 3 reels.

Brats (3/22/1930) – Roach-MGM – 2 reels

Below Zero (4/26/1930) – Roach-MGM – 2 reels

Hog Wild (5/31/1930) – Roach-MGM – 2 reels

The Laurel–Hardy Murder Case (9/6/1930) – Roach-MGM – 3 reels.

Another Fine Mess (11/29/1930) – Roach-MGM – 3 reels.

1931

Be Big (2/7/1931) – Roach-MGM – 3 reels

Chickens Come Home (2/21/1931) – Roach-MGM – 3 reels.

The Stolen Jools (4/1931) – National Variety Artists charity short – Cameo appearance – 2 reels

Laughing Gravy (4/4/1931) – Roach-MGM – 2 reels
Our Wife (5/16/1931) Roach-MGM – 2 reels
Pardon Us (8/15/1931) – Roach-MGM – 6 reels – First feature film
Come Clean (9/19/1931) – Roach-MGM 2 reels
One Good Turn (10/31/1931) – Roach-MGM – 2 reels
Beau Hunks (12/12/1931) – Roach-MGM – 4 reels.
On the Loose (12/26/1931) – Roach-MGM – 2 reels – Cameo appearance

1932

Helpmates (1/23/1932) – Roach-MGM – 2 reels
Any Old Port (3/5/1932) – Roach-MGM – 2 reels
The Music Box (4/16/1932) – Roach-MGM – 3 reels
The Chimp (5/21/1932) – Roach-MGM – 3 reels
County Hospital (6/25/1932) – Roach-MGM – 2 reels
'Scram!' (9/12/1932) – Roach-MGM – 2 reels
Pack Up Your Troubles (9/17/1932) – Roach-MGM – 7 reels
Their First Mistake (11/22/1932) – Roach-MGM – 2 reels
Towed in a Hole (12/31/1932) – Roach-MGM – 2 reels

1933

Twice Two (2/25/1933) – Roach-MGM – 2 reels
Me and My Pal (4/22/1933) – Roach-MGM – – 2 reels
The Devil's Brother (*Fra Diavolo*) (5/5/1933) – Roach-MGM – 9 reels
The Midnight Patrol (8/3/1933) – Roach-MGM – 2 reels
Busy Bodies (10/7/1933) – Roach-MGM – 2 reels
Wild Poses (10/28/1933) – Roach-MGM – 2 reels – Cameo appearance
Dirty Work (11/25/1933) – Roach-MGM – 2 reels
Sons of the Desert (12/29/1933) – Roach-MGM – 7 reels

1934

Oliver the Eighth (2/1934) – Roach-MGM – 3 reels
Hollywood Party (6/1/1934) – MGM – 7 reels
Going Bye Bye! (6/23/1934) – Roach-MGM – 2 reels
Them Thar Hills (7/21/1934) – Roach-MGM – 2 reels
Babes in Toyland (11/30/1934) – Roach-MGM – 8 reels
The Live Ghost (12/8/1934) – Roach-MGM – 2 reels

1935

Tit for Tat (1/5/1935) – Roach-MGM – 2 reels – Their
only sequel, continuing the events in *Them Thar Hills*, made
half a year earlier.
The Fixer-Uppers (2/9/1935) – Roach-MGM – 2 reels
Thicker Than Water (8/1935) – Roach-MGM – 2 reels
Bonnie Scotland (8/23/1935) – Roach-MGM– – 7 reels

1936

The Bohemian Girl (2/14/1936) – Roach-MGM – 7 reels
On the Wrong Trek (6/1936) – Roach-MGM – 2 reels –
Cameo appearance
Our Relations (10/30/1936) – Roach-MGM – 7 reels

1937

Way Out West (4/16/1937) – Roach-MGM – 6 reels
Pick A Star (5/21/1937) – Roach-MGM – 7 reels

1938

Swiss Miss (5/20/1938) – Roach-MGM – 7 reels
Block-Heads (8/19/1938) – Roach-MGM – 6 reels

1939

Zenobia (4/21/39) – Roach-UA – 8 reels – Hardy alone
The Flying Deuces (10/20/1939) – Boris Morros Productions – 7 reels

1940

A Chump at Oxford (4 reel version, 2/16/1940; 6 reel version, early 1941) – Roach
Saps at Sea (5/5/1940) – Roach – 6 reels

1941

Great Guns (10/10/1941) – 20th Century-Fox – 7 reels

1942

A-Haunting We Will Go (8/7/1942) – 20th Century-Fox – 7 reels

1943

A Tree in a Test Tube (early 1943) – US Dept of Agriculture – 1 reel – Technicolor
Air Raid Wardens (4/4/1943) – MGM – 7 reels
Jitterbugs (6/11/1943) – 20th Century-Fox – 7 reels
The Dancing Masters (11/19/1943) – 20th Century-Fox – 6 reels

1944

The Big Noise (9/1944) – 20th Century-Fox – 7 reels

1945

Nothing But Trouble (3/1945) – MGM – 7 reels
The Bullfighters (5/18/1945) – 20th Century-Fox – 7 reels

1949

The Fighting Kentuckian (9/18/1949) – Republic Pictures – 10 reels – Hardy alone

1950

Riding High (4/10/1950) – Paramount Pictures – 10 reels – Hardy alone

1950–1951

Atoll K (In France, 1951; in Great Britain, 1953; in US, 1954) – Fortezza Film and Les Films Sirius – 10 reels – Released in England as *Escapade*, then as *Robinson Crusoe Land*; and in the US as *Utopia*.)

INDEX